New Perspectives on Intercultural Language Research and Teaching

Illustrated by an empirical study of English as a Foreign Language reading in Argentina, this book argues for a different approach to the theoretical rationales and methodological designs typically used to investigate cultural understanding in reading, in particular foreign language reading. It presents an alternative approach which is more authentic in its methods, more educational in its purposes, and more supportive of international understanding as an aim of language teaching in general and English language teaching in particular.

Melina Porto is Professor of English Language at Universidad Nacional de La Plata, Argentina and Researcher at Consejo Nacional de Investigaciones Científicas y Técnicas (CONICET), Argentina.

Michael Byram is Professor Emeritus at University of Durham, UK, Guest Professor at University of Luxembourg, and Visiting Professor at University of Sussex, UK.

Routledge Research in Education

For a full list of titles in this series, please visit www.routledge.com

167 **Women Education Scholars and their Children's Schooling**
 Edited by Kimberly A. Scott and Allison Henward

168 **The Improvised Curriculum**
 Negotiating Risky Literacies in Cautious Schools
 Michael Corbett, Ann Vibert, Mary Green with Jennifer Rowe

169 **Empowering Black Youth of Promise**
 Education and Socialization in the Village-minded Black Church
 Sandra L. Barnes and Anne Streaty Wimberly

170 **The Charter School Solution**
 Distinguishing Fact from Rhetoric
 Edited by Tara L. Affolter and Jamel K. Donnor

171 **Transforming Education in the Gulf Region**
 Emerging Learning technologies and Innovative Pedagogy for the 21st Century
 Edited by Khalid Alshahrani and Mohamed Ally

172 **UNESCO Without Borders**
 Educational campaigns for international understanding
 Edited by Aigul Kulnazarova and Christian Ydesen

173 **Research for Educational Change**
 Transforming researchers' insights into improvement in mathematics teaching and learning
 Edited by Jill Adler and Anna Sfard

174 **The Development of the Mechanics' Institute Movement in Britain and Beyond**
 'A practical education in reach of the humblest means'
 Martyn Walker

175 **New Perspectives on Intercultural Language Research and Teaching**
 Exploring Learners' Understandings of Texts from Other Cultures
 Melina Porto and Michael Byram

New Perspectives on Intercultural Language Research and Teaching
Exploring Learners' Understandings of Texts from Other Cultures

Melina Porto and Michael Byram

NEW YORK AND LONDON

First published 2017
by Routledge
711 Third Avenue, New York, NY 10017

and by Routledge
2 Park Square, Milton Park, Abingdon, Oxon, OX14 4RN

First issued in paperback 2018

Routledge is an imprint of the Taylor & Francis Group, an informa business

© 2017 Taylor & Francis

The right of Melina Porto and Michael Byram to be identified as authors of this work has been asserted by them in accordance with sections 77 and 78 of the Copyright, Designs and Patents Act 1988.

All rights reserved. No part of this book may be reprinted or reproduced or utilised in any form or by any electronic, mechanical, or other means, now known or hereafter invented, including photocopying and recording, or in any information storage or retrieval system, without permission in writing from the publishers.

Trademark notice: Product or corporate names may be trademarks or registered trademarks, and are used only for identification and explanation without intent to infringe.

Library of Congress Cataloging-in-Publication Data
Names: Porto, Melina, author. | Byram, Michael, author.
Title: New perspectives on intercultural language research and teaching : exploring learners' understandings of texts from other cultures / By Melina Porto and Michael Byram.
Description: New York : Routledge, [2016] | Series: Routledge Research in Education ; 175
Identifiers: LCCN 2016008563 | ISBN 9781138672406
Subjects: LCSH: Multilingualism and literature—Cross-cultural studies. | Intercultural communication in education—Cross-cultural studies. | Reading comprehension—Study and teaching—Cross-cutural studies. | Interaction analysis in education—Cross-cultural studies. | Multilingualism—Cross-cultural studies. | Sociolinguists.
Classification: LCC P115.25 .P67 2016 | DDC 418/.4071—dc23
LC record available at http://lccn.loc.gov/2016008563

ISBN 13: 978-1-138-60017-1 (pbk)
ISBN 13: 978-1-138-67240-6 (hbk)

Typeset in Sabon
by Apex CoVantage, LLC

Contents

List of Figures and Table vii
Foreword ix
Acknowledgements xiii
Introduction xv

1 Reading and Cultural Understanding 1
2 A Model of Cultural Understanding of Texts 19
3 Using the *Model of Cultural Understanding* in Text Selection and Analysis 35
4 Analysing Comprehension of Texts in Readers' First Language 52
5 Developing New Instruments for Research and Teaching 80
6 The Reading Response Task and Foreign Language Texts 93
7 The Visual Representation Task and Foreign Language Texts 117
8 Using the *Model of Cultural Understanding* in Self-Assessment 138
9 Conclusions 155

Appendix: Literary extracts used in this book 163
Index 169

Figures and Table

Figures

2.1	Scarlet Rose, visual representation, *Cat's Eye*	27
4.1	Tacuara, visual representation, *Mi planta de naranja-lima*	61
4.2	Beryl, visual representation, *Mi planta de naranja-lima*	65
4.3	Scarlet Rose, visual representation, *Mi planta de naranja-lima*	72
7.1	Tess, visual representation, *Cat's Eye*	118
7.2	Enrique Alejandro, visual representation, *Desert Wife*	128

Table

2.1	Model of Cultural Understanding	21

Foreword

The purpose of this book is to propose a theoretically informed pedagogic approach to reading. A key issue here is the way written texts, particularly of a literary kind, give rise to variable interpretations, and thinking about an appropriate preface to the book brings to mind the preface to another book. This is one which Doris Lessing wrote for a reprint of her novel *The Golden Notebook* ten years after it was first published. In it she expresses surprise at the very different ways in which her novel has been understood "why one person sees one pattern and nothing at all of another pattern"—in spite of the fact that it is "the same book" (Lessing, 1972: xix–xx). But although the book as written text is the same for all readers it clearly is not read as a novel in the same way: whatever the author may have intended by the text, people will tend to read their own different meanings into it so as to bring them in line with their own preconceptions. But this can of course lead to a narrowing of understanding, a lack of the openness to other possible meanings which it is the purpose of education to promote. This present book has the educational purpose of developing a model of cultural understanding to offset this tendency for readers to interpret texts only on their own terms and to guide students to adjust their interpretation, focusing particularly on the cultural factors that regulate the different ways that literary texts can be understood.

As I have argued elsewhere (Widdowson, 2004) Doris Lessing's observation about her book can be explained by invoking a distinction between text and discourse. *The Golden Notebook* is a text, a compilation of words and sentences that stays the same, but different readers derive different discourses from it—discourses that may well be very different from the discourse that the author intended to textualize. And the same applies to any text, large or small, literary or not. All texts are indexical in that the language is used only to direct attention to some reality external to language, a reality that the text producer assumes to be sufficiently familiar for the recipient to recognise. In the normal communication process texts are always motivated by a discourse purpose and are indexically designed to impart information, make a point, express an opinion or whatever in such a way as to engage and influence the recipient. A text is the linguistic trace of discourse intentions and only has meaning to the extent that it can be indexically interpreted. It therefore makes no sense to ask what a text means for a text in itself means nothing. The question is what its producer might have meant by a text, and what a text might mean to its recipient, that is to say, what discourse did the producer intend by a particular text, and what discourse might the recipient derive from it. It is this problematic relationship between discourse intention and interpretation that, in my reading of the text, underlies the process of cultural understanding that is explored in this book.

This problematic nature of this relationship becomes particularly apparent when there is what we might call contextual displacement—when texts are interpreted by recipients for whom they were not originally designed, when the text producer's intentions are not ratified because there is a disparity between the reality that the producer intends to indexically invoke and that which is experienced by the recipient. It is here, of course, that we encounter the cross-cultural dissonances that are discussed in detail in this book, occasions when these realities are seen as schematically specific to particular cultures.

The concept of schema is crucial here. The authors note that the tendency has generally been to see schemata as an individual's cognitive representations of reality. The focus in this book, however, is on the sociocultural differences in these representations, and not as preconceived static constructs that are imposed on texts and determine how they are understood but as adaptive and emergent conceptualizations that shift and vary as a function of the process of interpretation itself. In this view, culture itself becomes negotiable and contextually variable, not a stable property but as performance—a view consistent with current philosophical and sociolinguistic thinking about performativity and the dynamic indeterminacy of discourse.

This book then explores reading comprehension as a discourse process, how meanings are derived from texts emergently on line and how far this might involve a continual schematic adaptation of cultural preconceptions. It is this performative orientation that makes the book distinctive. As its authors point out, the conventional approach to the study of reading comprehension is by means of recall protocols which presuppose that what has been understood corresponds with what has been remembered. The obvious difficulty with this approach is that it does not take into account what might have been understood at the time of reading but subsequently forgotten. This difficulty is resolved by focusing on immediate understanding as a performative on line process, as is proposed in this book. But this raises a crucial issue which is less easily resolved. It can be plausibly argued that what memory edits out of immediate understanding is what subsequently ceases to be significant. This editing however, is also a feature of on line understanding. All communication, written or spoken, is regulated by purpose and readers will quite naturally attend selectively to textual features, take in what they deem to be of interest or relevance and disregard the rest, even if they understand it. The schemata that readers bring to their interpretation of text are, as the authors point out, continually adapted in the reading process itself, and such adaptation will necessarily involve this kind of discriminatory editing.

So one can think of the reading process as operating on two levels. At one level, it follows the linearity of text and understanding is of superficial sequential kind. But reading as the normal communicative activity of deriving discourse from text involves moving into a different and differential level of understanding where significance is selectively assigned according to the reader's schematic knowledge and purpose in engaging with the text in the first place. We thus arrive at the rather paradoxical conclusion that effective reading may depend on deciding on what parts of a text **not** to pay attention to. A major failing of traditional reading comprehension exercises is that since students are typically not primed with a purpose they have no basis for discriminating what is significant and so their understanding is confined at a superficial level.

As the authors of this book point out, recall protocols can be criticised because of their assignment of significance in dissociation from the actual reading process. But the reading process itself is also a matter of assigning significance and the question is how this is done on line rather than after the event, and the extent to which this can be incorporated into the proposed model of cultural understanding and operationalized in pedagogic activities. These are the kinds of intriguing questions that are raised by the performative approach to reading taken in this book. Another question relates not to the purpose of reading as a determining factor in how discourse is derived from text, but to the effect of the process. The aim of this book is not only to develop an ability to understand written texts which have been displaced from the linguacultural contexts which were presupposed in their design, but also, more importantly from an educational point of view, to develop an understanding of how cultures relate to each other, an awareness, and tolerance, of cultural difference. And here, one might argue, what matters is not only, perhaps not so much, the process of interpretation itself, but how lasting an effect it has on deep seated cultural attitudes and values that are resistant to change and survive the tactical schematic adaptations of on line interpretation. One might suggest, indeed, that recall protocols, to the extent that they capture the longer term effects of reading, do provide insights which need to be taken into account in the study of how written texts are understood.

What is important about this book is that it exemplifies and encourages a critical reconsideration of established assumptions—not only about reading but about communication in general. In this respect it too can be seen as the expression of schematic adaptation, the reformation in the disciplinary culture of language study usually referred to as paradigm shift. As such the book is informed by the temper of the times. With the unprecedented rapidity of demographic change and the ever shifting spread of networks of global interaction, we no longer live in a world of stable boundaries and enclosed communities. This naturally calls for a rethinking about such concepts as community and culture and about the very nature of communication itself. It is this kind of rethinking that this book promotes and in this respect is both topical and timely.

Henry G. Widdowson
Emeritus Professor, University of London
Honorary Professor, University of Vienna
3 May 2016, Vienna

References

Lessing, D. (1972) Preface to *The Golden Notebook* (pp. xix–xx). London: HarperCollins.

Widdowson, H.G. (2004) *Text, Context, Pretext. Critical Issues in Discourse Analysis*. Malden and Oxford: Blackwell Publishing.

Acknowledgements

An overview of the research project on which this book draws can be found in:

Porto, M. (2014) Extending reading research with a focus on cultural understanding and research on intercultural communication: An empirical investigation in Argentina. *Intercultural Education* 25, 518–539.

It benefited from the insights of members of the research group H511 carried out at Universidad Nacional de La Plata during 2008–2011. We are grateful to Silvana Barboni, Verónica Di Bin, Gabriela Iacoboni, Silvana Fernández, Ana Cendoya and Mariela Riva.

Part of Chapter 1 is based on:

Porto, M. (2014) The role and status of English in Spanish-speaking Argentina and its education system: nationalism or imperialism? Sage Open. DOI: 10.1177/ 2158244013514059

Porto, M. (2013) Cultures and identities in ELT classrooms: Global considerations in the local context of Argentina. In Barboni, S. and Porto, M. (eds) Language Education from a South American Perspective: What does Latin America have to say? (pp.45–85). La Plata: Dirección General de Cultura y Educación de la Provincia de Buenos Aires.

Porto, M., López-Barrios, M. and Montemayor-Borsinger, A. (2016) Research on English language teaching and learning in Argentina (2007–2013). *Language Teaching* 49, 356–389.

Chapter 2 is based on the following article:

Porto, M. (2013) A model for describing, analysing and investigating cultural understanding in EFL reading settings. *The Language Learning Journal* 41, 284–296. Special Issue on Teaching and Learning Intercultural Communication in the Second/Foreign Language Classroom. Editors: Michael Byram, Prue Holmes and Nicola Savides.

Part of Chapter 2 is based on:

Porto, M. (2013) Cultures and identities in ELT classrooms: Global considerations in the local context of Argentina. In Barboni, S. and Porto, M. (eds) *Language*

Education from a South American Perspective: What does Latin America have to say? (pp.45–85). La Plata: Dirección General de Cultura y Educación de la Provincia de Buenos Aires.

Part of Chapter 3 is based on:

Porto, M. (2009) La otredad, la diferencia, y la extrañeza en *Desert Wife* de Hilda Faunce: elementos de opacidad textual. In Montezanti, M. (ed) *I came upon it in a dream . . . Ensayos sobre cultura y literatura anglosajonas. Tomo 2* (pp.181–187). La Plata: UNLP.

Porto, M. (2009) Perspectivas culturales en *Cat's Eye*: un entramado de culturas. In Montezanti, M. (ed) *I came upon it in a dream . . . Ensayos sobre cultura y literatura anglosajonas. Tomo 2* (pp.173–179). La Plata: UNLP.

Part of Chapter 4 is based on:

Porto, M. (2013) Social identifications and culturally located identities: Developing cultural understanding through literature. In Houghton, S. and Rivers, D. (eds.) *Social Identities and Multiple Selves in Foreign Language Education* (pp.103–120). London: Bloomsbury Academic.

Part of Chapters 5, 6 and 7 are based on:

Porto, M. (2013) The visual representation: An instrument for research and instruction on the cultural dimension of foreign language education. In Houghton, S., Furumura, Y., Lebedko, M. and Li, S. (eds) *Critical Cultural Awareness: Managing Stereotypes through Intercultural (Language) Education* (pp.221–248). Newcastle upon Tyne, UK: Cambridge Scholars Publishing.

Chapter 5 has benefited from the contributions of our colleague Dr. Silvana Barboni, to whom we are sincerely grateful.

Part of Chapter 6 is based on:

Porto, M. (2013) Pensamiento crítico, reflexión, conciencia cultural crítica: Características de la interculturalidad en la lectura en lengua extranjera. In Renart, L. and Banegas, D. (eds.) *Roots and Routes in Language Education. Bi/Multi/Plurilingualism, interculturality and identity.* Selected papers from the 38th FAAPI Conference (e-book) (pp.86–97).

We are grateful to three anonymous reviewers for their careful reading of the text and their suggestions for improvements. We would also like to thank Henry Widdowson not only for his stimulating foreword but also for his encouragement and support for the PhD on which this book is based.

Introduction
An Experiment in Reading

Let us begin with an experiment. Please read the following text once and then, without looking again, try to recall it in writing as accurately as you can.

> **Kayatuq—the Red Fox**
>
> A boy living alone at the mouth of a river occasionally feeds fish to a red fox. On one occasion he captures the fox and pounds his face, which develops into the face of a man and tells the boy of a couple who have an unmarried daughter. They set out to find the couple, and on the way approach a village. The fox scares the people away by stories of an approaching enemy party, and the fox and boy take over one of the best houses. The fox causes a change in the weather, which freezes to death all of the villagers caught out in the open. The red fox then lures the daughter of the couple back to the village with a promise that she will marry the two sons of a rich man. The girl and her parents believe that only a very rich man could send a red fox with a marriage proposal. The daughter becomes aware of the deception when she arrives at the village and marries the boy. Thereafter, the red fox makes occasional visits to the parents, assuring them that she has much more wealth than they. 'And since that time the red foxes know how to make tricks against people and fool them.'[1]

Now compare your text and the original. Probably you will notice differences, not only in the language you used but also in the content you recalled. It is likely for instance that at different points in the story you introduced information from your own cultural background, that you distorted some culturally alien details that you did not understand well or that you omitted some information altogether, when this information was too different, strange or obscure for you. If you were to recall the text again in a week's time, the differences would be more profound. Why does the boy live alone? Why does he feed a fox? Is the detail that the fox is red important? Why does the boy follow the fox in its acts? How does the family fit in? Is the daughter happy? Are her parents better off in the end? These questions, among many others, reveal the points at which possible intrusions, distortions and omissions are likely to be observed. Schema theorists and researchers concerned with the cultural dimension of reading comprehension say that these qualitative differences between a text and its recall reveal the schemata that readers draw upon in attempting to comprehend the text. They study and quantify these differences. They divide the text into idea units, and then check how many idea units are recalled by readers in their own texts. The more idea units present in a recall, the more a reader is said to have comprehended the text in question.

This book takes a different stance. It proposes a new view of how people comprehend the cultural content of texts. We will argue that when you are asked to recall a text as accurately as possible, the focus is in fact not on comprehension but on memory. The text that you produced about the red fox is a *product* of recall that takes place *after* reading. By contrast, this book analyses cultural understanding as a fluid *process* on a continuum of cultural familiarity and unfamiliarity. Rather than quantifying idea units as a means of analysing how people of different cultural backgrounds understand texts, we develop a notion of text comprehension which is based on layers of understanding and accounts for the whole process of comprehension, i.e. *during* and *after* reading.

The purpose of this book is thus to focus on the cultural dimension of reading within an analysis of how reading—both in general and in a foreign language in particular—has been hitherto conceived, and to suggest a new and better approach. It has both research and pedagogical perspectives, and is based on an empirical study of reading in English as a Foreign Language (EFL) in Argentina. The approach is more authentic in its methods of investigating reading, more educational in its purposes, and more supportive of international understanding as an aim of language teaching in general and English language teaching (ELT) in particular.

Since the book illustrates this approach with data from an Argentinean context, it also involves the notion of 'periphery' of ELT and introduces the Argentine case as a valid and significant perspective from where to add to what is known in the 'centre', thus challenging the periphery/centre contrast. Furthermore, because the book is about readers reading a text in their first language, Spanish, as well as texts in a foreign language, English, it crosses the boundaries so frequently observed between those involved in first language (L1) and foreign language (FL) reading. This is therefore not just an ELT book; it speaks as much to the researcher and teacher of reading in any L1 and/or in a foreign language context.

The Project

Dissatisfied with the dichotomies and simplicities of laboratory-based reading research with inauthentic texts, the research on which this book is based took a different position. The first element is the importance of a classroom context, in this case it is a university setting. There were 10 participants, future teachers and/or translators of English. They were in their second year of undergraduate studies at Universidad Nacional de La Plata, a prestigious, access-for-all state university. They were aged 18–22 and had good competence in English, at about C1 level in the *Common European Framework of Reference* (Council of Europe, 2001). They were all volunteers willing to spend time reading three short text extracts and performing a number of tasks. They worked over a period of three weeks with one text per week in the academic year 2009–10.

The second element was the focus on authentic texts. In this case, the three extracts were literary, but the approach taken throughout the book can be developed and applied to other kinds of text, including visual texts. The chosen extracts describe Christmas celebrations in different settings, and thus present the content schema of 'Christmas' with variations in the form of different celebrations. The content is presented through different perspectives, for instance those of insiders or outsiders—and some hybrid perspectives—in the different settings. This is consistent with Sharifian, Rochecouste and Malcolm's (2004) concept of a continuum of varying degrees of familiarity with cultural schemata. The first text, written in Spanish, presents a cultural reality relatively familiar to the participants, with an insider perspective, a narrator who participates in the celebration and is located in the Brazilian setting (from *Mi planta de naranja-lima*, Vasconcelos, 1971: 39–43).[2] The second text, written in English, portrays a cultural reality different from that of the participants': a Canadian context, with an insider perspective (from *Cat's Eye*, Atwood, 1998: 137–140). The third text, also in English, presents a distant cultural reality as it describes a Christmas celebration in a Native American context with an outsider perspective, a narrator who participates in the celebration but is not a member of the group (from *Desert Wife*, Faunce, 1961: 173–181).

Rather than the emphasis on recall in previous research, we sought tasks which would better represent the reading process. The participants responded to each text in their native language, Spanish, in a reading response task and a visual representation, which we describe in later chapters. The native language in instructions and task completion has been used by others (Chang, 2006; Yu, 2008) because it guarantees a better measure of comprehension in the second language (L2) than the use of the L2 itself (Martínez-Roldán and Sayer, 2006; Yu, 2008).

In addition to the two comprehension tasks, we used a questionnaire to collect biographical information and two questionnaires to learn more about participants' reading in Spanish and in English. There was also a 'prior knowledge' task which sought to establish what they already knew about the cultural context and contents of the texts they were about to read, and this helped us establish knowledge of the participants' position before they began the comprehension tasks. For instance, the biographical questionnaire included questions about religion (because of the important religious content in the three texts) and more generally about the participants' experiences and contacts with other cultures (through trips abroad and within their country, the Internet, contact with foreigners, etc.). The questions about reading aimed at gathering information about the participants' interest in reading, their reading habits, their reading preferences as regards genres, the time spent on reading outside formal education, their difficulties experienced during reading, their attitudes towards reading, the availability of reading material at home, and the use of libraries. This gave us insight into how the participants conceived of reading and what values and assumptions they associated with it.

The 'prior knowledge' task, which the participants completed before seeing each text, aimed at identifying their prior knowledge about a Christmas celebration in each context and their attitudes toward it. This prior knowledge is fundamental as it constitutes the point of entrance to any text.

In each text, the participants underlined the difficult or confusing parts and wrote a brief explanation of such difficulties in note form in the text itself. They then wrote an immediate reflection log ('retrospective self-observation') referring to cultural aspects of the text and the comprehension difficulties they had found. Then came the reading response task and the visual representation task (described in Chapters 5, 6 and 7). An individual semi-structured interview (Corbin and Strauss, 2014; Kvale, 1996; Mertens, 2015) was conducted, one week after the reading of each text, to encourage participants to comment upon their modes of response, in particular on specific issues arising from their reading response and visual representation tasks. Through specific questions, the participants reflected upon the thinking behind their writing in these tasks, particularly on issues which emerged from our preliminary analyses. During the interviews, the texts were available to the participants, a procedure which contrasts with other studies in which the texts were withdrawn after the reading and before the writing of the recall.

The underlined texts, the reflection logs and the interviews allowed us to explore the *process* of reading, how these readers approached the cultural content of the texts *during* the reading itself, instead of using a recall task which emphasises the product of reading, or what happens *after* someone finishes reading a text.

The Texts

In previous research, the texts used to investigate cultural understanding were short and experimentally modified. Hammadou (1991), Rice (1980) and Steffensen, Joag-Dev and Anderson (1979) resort to texts of 250–500 words, and Sharifian et al. (2004) vary between one paragraph and transcribed oral conversations of between ten and forty lines. Allington and Swann (2009: 224) refer to these kinds of texts as "bibliographically idiosyncratic texts (or 'textoids')". Mecartty (2001) is one of the few who adopts a one-page text. By contrast, our research takes unmodified texts which are considerably longer (between one and three pages long) and which allow us to investigate cultural understanding in a natural reading context, or "ordinary reading" in a natural setting (Allington and Swann, 2009: 224), in our case the classroom.

One limitation here is that, at the college level in Argentina, literary texts tend to be associated with fixed interpretations that 'the reader' should arrive at. The problem with this notion of 'the reader' as Allington and Swann (2009: 220) remark is that it ignores

> the conditions of literature's material production and consumption, because the reader in whose encounters those critics [literary critics] locate meaning has no 'specific cultural situation'—and indeed, no particular identity.

In the analysis in later chapters, we shall bring this 'specific cultural situation' to the fore by integrating the social and individual dimensions of reading, and we shall also give voice to the periphery by taking note of

> not only the politically and socially dominant [interpretation] in a state or power bloc, but also the shifting and overlapping dominance of micro cultures on regional, local, personal and even textual levels.
> (Jeffries, 2001: 341)

A New Approach to Analysing Cultural Comprehension

The general approach can be adapted and adopted to many kinds of text, but the advantages of literature and in particular of narrative for the development of an understanding of otherness also led us to decide for this kind of text. Narrative genre is close to our daily experiences in contextually specific situations (Graesser, Singer, and Trabasso, 1994). Both narratives and daily experiences involve people performing actions to achieve their aims, the existence of obstacles to these objectives, emotional reactions to events, strong motivations and powerful feelings (Bruner, 1986). In addition, literary texts allow readers to bring to the surface the feelings and thoughts that guide the values and beliefs of their lifestyles and encourage awareness of them (Pang, Colvin, Tran, Barba, 1998). As Bruner (2002) explains, stories transform individual experience into collective experience and allow the reading of the minds of others by facilitating access to the intentions and mental states of characters. Finally, literature provides an "imaginative leap that will enable learners to imagine cultures different from their own" (Kramsch, 1995: 85) and can therefore "be used to develop an understanding of otherness" (cf. Bredella, 2000, 2003; Burwitz Melzer, 2001: 29; Matos, 2005).

xx *Introduction*

Recall studies analyse data which indicate comprehension both quantitatively and qualitatively. In quantitative analysis the text is first divided into idea units, which are then identified and counted in the recalls. The more idea units present in a recall, the more a reader is said to have comprehended the text in question. It is important to clarify briefly here that in this book we propose instead a notion of comprehension based on six layers of understanding represented in a *Model of Cultural Understanding*. This model, discussed in detail in Chapter 2, draws on work by Alred, Byram and Fleming (2006), Byram and Morgan (1994) and Kramsch (1993, 1998), and is consistent with Sharifian et al. (2004) in the sense that the comprehension of the cultural content of (literary narrative) texts during EFL reading is not an all-or-nothing affair, but rather a question of increasing degrees of complexity and detail.

The first step in analysis is to assign either stage 0 or level 1 to each reading response task and visual representation task. This first step is critical because it involves noting a reader's perception, or lack of perception, of cultural elements of a text on the basis of their own cultural context. The perception of the different, exciting and attractive elements of a given cultural content is possible through the identification of key vocabulary and this works as a bridge to stages 2, 3, 4, and 5 in the model. The second step might have been to allocate readers' responses to one of stages 2, 3, 4, 5, but, as we shall show in a later chapter, this is not possible because readers move back and forth between the stages at all times in all the tasks they produce.[3]

Overview

The results of the project are drawn on throughout this book. We hope it will be read by pre-service and in-service FL and L1 teachers who want to understand the theoretical nature of reading and its cultural dimension, and who are interested in acquiring a repertoire of tools to address it in the classroom. This is the pedagogical purpose of the book. We also hope it will be read by those interested in analysing and developing a richer understanding of reading in both foreign and first language education. This is the research dimension.

After this introduction, Chapter 1 explores reading and cultural understanding in a historical perspective, with a focus on matters of theory. This involves a discussion of the product-process dichotomy in reading comprehension, introduced briefly above. It also analyses conceptualisations of culture, identity and schema, and concludes that schema-based research which is laboratory-based—for example in the study where the red fox text was used—is in many respects inadequate. In contrast, taking a dynamic conception of culture, the chapter introduces a sociocultural perspective on schemata which acquires a particular importance in this book and is related to the question of the 'periphery'.

Chapter 2 introduces the *Model of Cultural Understanding* mentioned already that embodies a conceptualisation of comprehension as layers of understanding. One purpose of this chapter is to explain and describe such layers in terms of six levels in the model and to describe how the model has been used in this study. In order to do so, a first example of data created in the process of comprehension is provided from one of the participants in the research project. Other examples will follow in later chapters.

Chapter 3 illustrates the use of the model to analyse texts learners might wish to read, in a cultural perspective. Taking the fragments from *Mi planta de naranja-lima, Cat's Eye* and *Desert Wife*, the chapter provides an analysis of these in terms of the levels in the model. The analysis shows the ways in which a text can be seen to illustrate the different levels in the model, and the kind of reflection and critical perspective that can be expected from student readers.

Chapter 4 illustrates how the approach can be used with texts in the readers' first language. The process is illustrated with the case of Victoria, a student of English in Argentina who reads and responds to a text in Spanish from a context, Brazil, which is relatively familiar to her as an Argentinean. Analysing Victoria's case demonstrates the effectiveness of the approach in detail and shows that the divide often found between work on comprehension of texts in the first language and in foreign languages can be overcome.

Chapter 5 focuses on the instruments which were developed as alternatives to recall tasks and similar activities. It explains the problems of recall tasks in detail and describes how the alternative tasks were adapted from existing theory to provide a more authentic approach for use both in research and in teaching. As indicated above, participants in the project were asked to provide a range of information about their prior knowledge of the themes of the text extracts they read and then to engage with two main tasks, the 'reading response' and the 'visual representation'.

Chapter 6 analyses the reading response task and how participants carried it out in detail, demonstrating its power as a means of capturing their understanding of texts both during and after their reading. The combination of the reading response with an individual interview a week after the reading was particularly rich in insights into the complexity of their interpretations during and after the reading process itself.

Chapter 7 focuses on the second main task, the production of a visual representation of the reading and participants' interpretations and understandings. Again the follow-up interview proves to be crucial in indicating how the task itself demonstrates choices readers make in their interpretations whilst they remain conscious of other options and variations.

Chapter 8 demonstrates the use of the *Model of Cultural Understanding* for self-assessment. The suggestion is that students can create a profile of their reading as a form of self-assessment by reference to the model. The chapter illustrates with the cases of Tess and Victoria.

Finally, Chapter 9 presents the conclusions of the investigation as well as its implications for teaching and research. The theoretical contribution lies in the conceptualisations of culture, identity and schema, encapsulated

xxii *Introduction*

in the *Model of Cultural Understanding*. The model then also captures the complexity, fluidity, criticality and reflexivity of cultural understanding in this Argentinean setting. The methodological discussion, for both research and teaching, presents the reading response and visual representation tasks which overcome the weaknesses of previous research that relied so much on 'recall'. The pedagogic value of the reading response and the visual representation tasks is also highlighted as they encourage readers to transform a text in multiple and varied ways. The model can thus be used, as the book shows, in selecting teaching materials, in materials design and development, and in assessment.

Notes

1. Quoted in Rice (1980:169).
2. The fragment is, in fact, a translation from Portuguese. Vasconcelos, J.M. de (1968) *Meu Pé de Laranja Lima*. São Paulo: Edicoes Melhoramentos.
3. A full account of the project can be seen in Melina Porto (2011) PhD thesis entitled "An exploratory study of cultural understanding in English as a Foreign Language (EFL) reading in Argentina" Universidad Nacional de La Plata. http://www.memoria.fahce.unlp.edu.ar/tesis/te.425/te.425_en.pdf and http://www.memoria.fahce.unlp.edu.ar/tesis/te.425/te.425_es.pdf.

References

Allington, D. and Swann, J. (2009) Researching literary reading as social practice. *Language and Literature* 18, 219–230.

Alred, G., Byram, M. and Fleming, M. (2006) *Education for Intercultural Citizenship: Concepts and Comparisons*. Clevedon: Multilingual Matters.

Atwood, M. (1998) *Cat's Eye*. Bantam: Anchor Books.

Bredella, L. (2000) Literary texts. In Byram, M. (ed) *Routledge Encyclopedia of Language Teaching and Learning* (pp. 375–382). London: Routledge.

Bredella, L. (2003) For a flexible model of intercultural understanding. In Alred, G., Byram, M., and Fleming, M. (eds) *Intercultural Experience and Education* (pp. 31–49). Clevedon: Multilingual Matters.

Bruner, J. (1986) *Actual Minds, Possible Worlds*. Cambridge, MA: Harvard University Press.

Bruner, J. (2002) *Making Stories*. Cambridge, MA: Harvard University Press.

Burwitz Melzer, E. (2001) Teaching intercultural communicative competence through literature. In Byram, M., Nichols, A., and Stevens, D. (eds) *Developing Intercultural Competence in Practice* (pp. 29–43). Clevedon: Multilingual Matters.

Byram, M. and Morgan, C. (1994) *Teaching-and-Learning Language-and-Culture*. Clevedon: Multilingual Matters.

Chang, Y. (2006) On the use of the immediate recall task as a measure of second language reading comprehension. *Language Testing* 23(4), 520–543.

Corbin, J. and Strauss, A. (2014) *Basics of Qualitative Research: Techniques and Procedures for Developing Grounded Theory. Fourth Edition*. Thousand Oaks, CA: Sage.

Council of Europe. (2001) *Common European Framework of Reference for Languages: Learning, Teaching, Assessment*. Strasbourg: Council of Europe.

Faunce, H. (1961) *Desert Wife*. Lincoln: University of Nebraska Press.
Graesser, A. C., Singer, M. and Trabasso, T. (1994) Constructing inferences during narrative text comprehension. *Psychological Review* 101(3), 371–395.
Hammadou, J. (1991) Interrelationships among prior knowledge, inference, and language proficiency in foreign language reading. *The Modern Language Journal* 75(1), 27–38.
Jeffries, L. (2001) Schema affirmation and White Asparagus: Cultural multilingualism among readers of texts. *Language and Literature* 10(4), 325–343.
Kramsch, C. (1993) *Context and Culture in Language Teaching*. Oxford: Oxford University Press.
Kramsch, C. (1995) The cultural component of language teaching. *Language, Culture, and Curriculum* 8, 83–92.
Kramsch, C. (1998) *Language and Culture*. Oxford: Oxford University Press.
Kvale, S. (1996) *Interviews*. London: Sage Publications.
Martínez-Roldán, C. and Sayer, P. (2006) Reading through linguistic borderlands: Latino students' transactions with narrative texts. *Journal of Early Childhood Literacy* 6(3), 293–322.
Matos, A. G. (2005) Literary texts: A passage to intercultural reading in foreign language education. *Language and Intercultural Communication* 5, 57–71.
Mecartty, F. (2001) The effects of modality, information type and language experience on recall by foreign language learners of Spanish. *Hispania* 84(2), 265–278.
Mertens, D. (2015) *Research and Evaluation in Education and Psychology: Integrating Diversity with Quantitative, Qualitative and Mixed Methods. Fourth Edition.* Los Angeles, LA: Sage.
Pang, V. O., Colvin, C., Tran, M., and Barba, R. (1998) Beyond chopsticks and dragons: Selecting Asian American literature for children. In Opitz, M. (ed) *Literacy Instruction for Culturally and Linguistically Diverse Students: A Collection of Articles and Commentaries* (pp. 204–212). Newark, DE: International Reading Association Inc.
Rice, E. (1980) On cultural schemata. *American Ethnologist* 7(1), 152–171.
Sharifian, F., Rochecouste, J. and Malcolm, G. (2004) 'But it was all a bit confusing . . .': Comprehending Aboriginal English texts. *Language, Culture and Curriculum* 17, 203–228.
Steffensen, M., Joag-Dev, C. and Anderson, R. (1979) A cross-cultural perspective on reading comprehension. *Reading Research Quarterly* XV, 10–29.
Vasconcelos, J. M. de (1971) *Mi planta de naranja-lima*. Translated by H. Jofre Barroso. Buenos Aires: El Ateneo.
Yu, G. (2008) Reading to summarize in English and Chinese: A tale of two languages? *Language Testing* 25(4), 521–551.

1 Reading and Cultural Understanding

Conceptualising Reading, Identity, Culture and Schema

Reading in any language, whether L1 or a foreign language, is complex. People read for different purposes in particular contexts and circumstances, and respond in individually significant ways to different texts. They unconsciously draw on their cultural and linguistic backgrounds as well as their past experiences, beliefs and emotions. They use their imagination. So what a reader gets from a text is always personal and specific, and in some aspects unique. Language itself also contributes to this process because of the complexity of meanings, which change over time but also have shifting connotations. At one and the same time, language is "a carrier and [a] shaper of individual and group identities" (Guiora, 2005: 185) that affects how people read. Who the reader is in terms of ethnicity, nationality, gender, social class, religion, etc. contributes to his/her understanding of a text. Writers from different disciplines have pointed out that it is hard to get from a text (or a situation, an experience) more than what one is willing or able to know (Archer, 1997; Derrida, 1994; Gadamer, 1992; Moreiras, 1991). There is a limit to what is understood because people tend to disregard what they do not understand. This means that no interpretation can be other than provisional. Let us call this a sociocultural view of reading.

A sociocultural view of reading takes into account the individual and the social. Individuals see themselves in particular ways as a result of a reading experience, and each reading experience plays a role in their identifications and positionings in their own society (McCarthey and Moje, 2002; Tsui, 2007). Identifications are multiple, hybrid, complex, fluid and contradictory (de Nooy, 2006; Genetsch, 2007; Norton, 2000; Norton and Toohey, 2011; Rosaldo, 1993), and this means it is always possible, in any reading experience, to enact simultaneously more than one identification depending on the relationships, interactions and identifications in the life of an individual that are foregrounded. This continuous construction of cultural identifications relates to the concept of 'performativity', particularly associated with the work of the philosopher Judith Butler. Identifications are seen as "rehearsals" in "temporary identifications" (Butler, 1997: 266) and all individuals can construct their identities differently at different points in time. Identity is not an essence.

The social dimension of a sociocultural perspective involves a conceptualisation of 'culture'. However, the concept is usually too vague and complex (Byram and Grundy, 2002; Kramsch, 1995). From an anthropological standpoint, culture refers to the ways in which people conceive their lives and attribute importance to human experience by selecting and organising it. Culture is everywhere and mediates all human behaviour (Rosaldo, 1993). Our actions, thoughts and feelings are culturally determined and are influenced by our biography, the social situation and the historical context (Rosaldo, 1993).

The individual and the social interact. Individuals build their own stories, but on the basis of conditions which are not of their choice and which exceed their control. The complexity of cultural understanding lies in the fact that social life is simultaneously inherited and in permanent movement. The individual and the idiosyncratic mingle with, and cannot be separated from, the social. Such a dynamic conception of culture emphasises processes rather than facts, distances itself from monolithic and static perspectives, and highlights the concept of social construction.

Several other concepts from cultural anthropology (Rosaldo, 1993) are useful for the purposes of this book. One is that each culture is so unique that it is impossible to evaluate one as in some sense 'better' than another, because, it is argued, no culture is superior or inferior, richer or poorer, bigger or smaller than any other. The concept of 'cultural visibility' is also important and refers to the notion that certain human phenomena may appear to be more susceptible of cultural analysis than others. This is related to the idea of 'difference'. 'Difference' helps to make cultures visible to external observers, for instance those who read a text from another cultural background. At the same time, 'differences' are problematic because they are relative to and determined by the cultural practices of observers. We see what is 'different' from what we know in our own culture and tend to overlook everything else. As Genetsch (2007: x) puts it:

> difference is a category which can be filled differently (. . .) difference is no intrinsic quality or an objective factor in a social relationship but the definition of such a relationship. The decision to regard someone as different is always a positioning or an interpretation.

Finally, in theoretical approaches to understanding there is the crucial notion of 'schema'. As an abstract knowledge structure that represents generic concepts stored in memory (Anderson and Pearson, 1984; Rumelhart and Ortony, 1977) schemata have been given different names such as 'frame' (Minsky, 1975), 'script' (Schank and Abelson, 1977), 'plan' (Schank, 1975, 1982) and 'macrostructure' (Kintsch and van Dijk, 1978). Historically, the notion of schema referring to the structure of human knowledge as represented in memory can be traced to Plato, Aristotle and Kant in philosophy, and Bartlett and Piaget in psychology (McVee, Dunsmore and Gavelek, 2005). In a sociocultural perspective on schemata (ibid.) the contributions of Kant and Bartlett are particularly relevant because they stress the developmental, social and cultural dimensions of schemata, not only what happens within individuals' minds. Kant (1929) refers to schemata as mediating structures which link an individual's mental structures with the external world. Bartlett (1932) prefers the term 'pattern' and also highlights the functional role of schemata as adaptations between individuals and the environment. The underlying idea is that "schemas were necessary to explain the constitutive role of culturally organized experience in individual sense making" (McVee et al., 2005: 535). This view of schemata will allow us to inspect the functioning of schemata in experience with literary texts and reveals the nature of reading in a particular sociocultural context, in this case from Argentina.

Diverging Views of Reading, Identity, Culture and Schema

The sociocultural view of reading is at odds with the position taken by studies such as the one that used the 'Kayatuq—the red fox' text in our Introduction. The use of a recall task as an instrument for investigating reading implies a view of reading in which text interpretation is fixed, predetermined and standardised. Because a reader is thought to have comprehended a text when there is sufficient agreement between his or her recall and the text itself, there is no room for personal readings; for the enactment of specific, simultaneous (and perhaps conflicting) identifications; for the consideration of 'difference' as a positioning; and culture as dynamic and evolving. There is no room either for acknowledging the fact that what is visible for one reader can be invisible for another, even within the same social and cultural group, because of their unique and idiosyncratic perspectives. By contrast, whatever is different from the 'Kayatuq—the red fox' text in a recall is seen as deviant, culturally distorted and lacking in understanding. Schemata are seen as static and as phenomena that occur exclusively in a reader's head:

> Schemas, as traditionally conceived in relation to reading, were limited to in-the-head categories, in part because they were removed from materiality connected to cultural context and processes.
> (McVee et al., 2005: 546)

In this view, an individual reader either has the schema needed to interpret a text, or not. The dichotomy is between available versus unavailable schemata, present versus absent schemata.

Despite the contributions of Kant, Bartlett and others mentioned above, the sociocultural perspective on schemata has become lost in contemporary conceptions. The reason for this can be traced to work by cognitive scientists in the 1970s in artificial intelligence (Minsky, 1975; Schank and Abelson,

1977) which involved the exploration of knowledge construction using computers in the laboratory. Other scholars applied and developed this work in the analysis of reading in the late 1970s and during the 1980s, producing a vast amount of research that contributed to foregrounding the cognitive paradigm of schema theory (Anderson, 1977; Anderson and Pearson, 1984; Bransford and Johnson, 1972, 1973; Rumelhart, 1975, 1980). On the other hand, the marginalisation of the sociocultural in favour of the cognitive and the individual does not mean that the social and cultural dimensions were not explored at all. Anderson (2004, study undertaken in 1984), Harris, Lee, Hensley and Schoen (1988), Lipson (1983), Pritchard (1990), Reynolds, Taylor, Steffensen, Shirey and Anderson (1982), Steffensen, Joag-Dev and Anderson (1979) and others investigated the influence of cultural background and background knowledge, acknowledging the power of social and cultural factors in reading comprehension. However, as McVee et al. (2005) point out, in these studies cultural variations were taken as an independent variable in reading rather than as a constitutive and integral component of schemata in their own right. These empirical investigations portrayed an impoverished and limited conception of culture, in dissonance with the complex views that were emerging from the fields of anthropology, cultural psychology and educational anthropology in the 1980s.

In later chapters, we shall recover the social and the cultural dimensions of schemata and show that cultural schemata are not a static characteristic of an individual's cognition, not an in-the-head phenomenon, but rather are shared by members of a cultural group, are constantly being negotiated and renegotiated through time and generations, and are instantiated in cultural artefacts such as reflective narratives, drawings and interviews. Before doing so, however, we shall analyse more closely the characteristics of those studies which introduced a sociocultural approach so that the characteristics of our approach become more evident by contrast and comparison.

Culture as an Independent Variable

Some studies which investigate the role of cultural background in text comprehension and use cultural differences as an independent variable focus on texts read in English as mother tongue, second language or foreign language. Others explore texts in other second and foreign languages such as Hebrew (Abu-Rabia, 1996, 1998), Spanish (Martínez-Roldán and Sayer, 2006), Italian (Hammadou, 1991) and French (Hammadou, 1991).

The studies that focus on English as a second/foreign language (ESL) have shown that ESL readers have a better understanding and recall of texts for which they have a relevant culturally-specific content schema (Chihara, Sakurai and Oller, 1989; Malik, 1990; Sasaki, 2000; Van Hell, Bosman, Wiggers and Stoit, 2003).

There are two types of study here. One is referred to as cross-cultural research because informants belong to two different cultures and societies.

The most influential one in this group is Steffensen et al. (1979), which stimulated other investigations (Carrell, 1983a, b; Halasz, 1988; Noda, 1980; Pritchard, 1990). Overall, these investigations found strong support for the crucial role of culture-specific schemata in reading comprehension. The second type is called subcultural research because informants belong to two or more subcultures in one culture and society. The exemplar study here is Reynolds et al. (1982). Instead of having participants from two cultures and societies respond to two matched texts (one from their own and one from a different culture), in this study participants came from two different social groups and responded to the same text. While Reynolds et al. (1982), together with other studies using similar designs (Hooper-Weil, 1989; Lipson, 1983; Spears-Bunton, 1992), found a positive influence of culture on reading comprehension (readers understand more when the cultural background presupposed by a text is familiar to them), other studies had mixed results; they showed that culture was a powerful factor but not unequivocally positive (Altieri, 1995; Baker, 1990; Beach, 1994; Busch, 1994; Jordan and Purves, 1993).

Three studies can be analysed in more detail as representative of this general approach and will also serve to clarify the research design of the project on which this book is based.

In their pioneering research to investigate the influence of culture on reading comprehension, Steffensen et al. (1979) presented letters about Indian and American weddings, with a narrative component and written in English, to 19 adult Indian and 20 adult American subjects all of whom lived in the United States. A pre-test questionnaire asked for information about the subjects' existing knowledge of the different weddings. The participants then had to read and recall the texts and in this case they were asked to produce *verbatim* recall because they were told to "maintain the same order and use the same words," to "write down every bit" they could remember, and if they could not remember the exact words, to write down the sentence "as close to the original as possible" (ibid.: 16). The researchers analysed the recalls in terms of the degree of influence they showed from the participants' own culture. They specifically observed the modifications that the participants introduced in their recalls, overt errors such as elaborations of cultural content, distortions and significant omissions, and quantified the changes. The results showed that participants recalled more textual information and generated more culturally appropriate elaborations of the "native passage", and that they produced more cultural distortions of the "foreign passage" (which required more reading time) (ibid.: 10). In the subsequent literature (Carrell, 1983a, b; Chihara et al., 1989; Halasz, 1988; Hooper-Weil, 1989; Lipson, 1983; Malik, 1990; Noda, 1980; Pritchard, 1990; Sasaki, 2000; Spears-Bunton, 1992; Van Hell et al., 2003), these results were interpreted as indicative of the power of content schemata in reading comprehension.

The researchers claim that theirs is a cross-cultural study with a 'complete' design, i.e. both Indian and American subjects read two letters, each describing one wedding (Indian or American). However, although the Indian subjects were natives of India, they resided in the United States, and we observe here the simplifications concerning the notions of culture and identity discussed above; no contextual or background information is provided to allow further conclusions. For instance, nothing is said about the language and the cultural practices in the home, the school and the community, and the interrelationship between native language/heritage culture and second language/foreign culture in those settings. The categories 'Indian' and 'American' are isolated and compartmentalised as if individuals could be described as being only 'Indian' or only 'American' in an essentialist way. The notion of identity is reduced to just one aspect of an individual's identifications in isolation, in this case ethnicity.

Similarly, Lipson (1983) compartmentalised the fluid notion of identifications by exploring the influence of religious affiliation on reading comprehension. The explicit aim of the study was again to investigate the impact of culturally specific prior knowledge, in this case the religious. The participants were 32 American children, between 10 and 12 years old, with Catholic and Jewish backgrounds and practices. The author used three expository passages, one categorised as 'culturally neutral', one entitled *Bar Mitzvah*, and the other *First Communion*. From the perspective on culture presented earlier in this chapter, we can question the possibility that a 'culturally neutral' passage can actually exist. Again, the participants were asked to recall the texts and the researcher analysed and quantified how accurate the recalls were. The results indicated that the children recalled more propositions, with fewer errors, from the culturally familiar passage. Accuracy decreased and distortions increased in the comprehension of the culturally unfamiliar passage. It is useful to note that Lipson (1983: 456) considered that these readers produced "constructivist errors of omission, elaboration, and distortion" and this is something to which we return when we object to the use of recall within a constructivist view of reading.

The third study is by Rice (1980), who carried out an experiment with 60 English-speaking participants at the University of California to investigate the role of rhetorical schemata, namely a 'story schema', and found that participants used three strategies to deal with the missing or unclear structural aspects of the experimental texts in order to accommodate them to a story schema. They imported information to fill the gap, they completely deleted an episode if it was incomplete, or they elided or condensed two or more episodes. This approach to the identification of intrusions (imported information), omissions and distortions is a common methodology in all these studies.

In another experiment, Rice (1980) had 70 participants from the same university who read and recalled two versions of three Eskimo stories. One version was the complete, original Eskimo story, and the other was an 'Americanised' version, modified to suit a familiar story schema, respecting the length and content of the original. 'Kayatuq—the red fox', the text we met at the beginning of this book, is an adaptation prepared by Rice in which the original Eskimo story was rewritten in order to fit the hypothesised American story schema. After reading the texts, the participants recalled them immediately and again after a one-week interval. Rice argued that as the interval between reading and recall increased, the readers relied more heavily on their schemata for particular content. Again, the participants were instructed to recall the passage from memory as accurately as possible. Results showed that when the content of the texts did not meet the participants' cultural norms, confusion arose, to the point that the extremely foreign material became unintelligible. Heavy stereotyping and distortions to fit cultural expectations occurred. Rice concluded that "the study has demonstrated that a theory of comprehension based on assimilation to, or by, cultural schemata can account for the stereotypical or characteristic form of cultural interpretations of meaningful materials" (1980: 168).

Theoretically Rice acknowledged the cultural component of schemata and explained that a schema is related to both structural and processing aspects of knowledge, operates in perception, memory and recall, and is "a theory of the comprehension *process*" (Rice, 1980: 155, our emphasis). Furthermore, she distinguished three types of schemata on a continuum: universal at one end, such as Piaget's cognitive schemata; idiosyncratic, highly variable according to each individual's experience at the other end; and culturally derived schemata in the middle of the continuum, which are associated with what anthropologists call 'world view.' This notion of a continuum contrasts with the usual dichotomy of available versus unavailable schemata. However, despite her acknowledgement of complexity, Rice nonetheless used a simplified and artificially modified text and investigated comprehension using a recall task, the weaknesses of which will be reviewed below.

Overall, the studies by Lipson (1983), Rice (1980) and Steffensen et al. (1979), together with others such as Abu-Rabia (1996, 1998), Garth-McCullough (2008), Hammadou (1991), Hollingsworth and Reutzel (1990), Martínez-Roldán and Sayer (2006) and Sharifian, Rochecouste and Malcolm (2004) have found strong support for the crucial role of culture-specific schemata in reading comprehension, but the contradiction between process and continuum on the one hand and product and recall on the other remains problematic, and needs further analysis.

Product-Process Dichotomy in Reading Comprehension

Although these studies were pioneering in the field of reading, they are also problematic because the researchers claim that they investigate the comprehension process while we observe that they in fact focus on the product of comprehension. The methodological decisions in these studies emphasise memory and product; the use of a recall task as a research instrument implies that the ability to reproduce the content of a text is a reliable indicator of comprehension. The recall required is usually *verbatim* or as close as possible to the original, and comprehension is assumed to have occurred when a text is recalled as accurately as possible. This means that the researchers observe the match, in terms of idea units (content or textual information) between a text and its recall. The closer the match, the more comprehension there is. The researchers also quantify the deviations from the original text in a recall whether in the form of errors, omissions, intrusions, distortions or other. The fewer errors, omissions, intrusions and distortions observed, the more a reader is said to have comprehended a text.

Furthermore, in the theoretical conceptions of culture, identity and schema in these investigations, static and essentialist views dominate. The cultural dimension is isolated as one unique aspect of a reader's individuality, such as religion, nationality or ethnicity. Secondly, the fact that text comprehension is determined by examining whether a reader's recall is consistent or inconsistent with the schema presupposed by a text brings about a static conceptualisation of schemata: either a reader has the schema needed to understand a text, or not.

In contrast, we shall propose a notion of comprehension based on layers of understanding which distances itself from the focus on how much is remembered from a text. We shall adopt a notion of understanding framed within a constructivist view of learning, and reading in particular, where there is modification of what is already present rather than the acquisition of new knowledge on a *tabula rasa*.

Classroom-Based Research and the Focus on the Local in the 'Periphery'

The sociocultural view of reading we take here is consistent with calls from theorists such as Canagarajah (2002) to pay attention to the importance of the individual and the local in classroom-based research (Canagarajah, 1995, 2006; Vavrus, 2002). Tasks, activities and materials should function as mediators of the transactions of any group of students engaged with them (McVee et al., 2005) so that a "sense of the classroom" develops (Canagarajah, 1995: 592). This means it is necessary to understand schemata as sociocultural and historical constructions that appear through transactions with others in real and specific contexts, and that are mediated by cultural activities, materials and artefacts. This requires methodologies which seek '*understanding* of the experience of people involved in education' (Byram, 2008: 91, his emphasis), and the necessary focus on the local contrasts with the 'truth of objectivism':

> The truth of objectivism—absolute, universal, and timeless—has lost its monopoly status. It now competes, on more nearly equal terms, with the truths of case studies that are embedded in local contexts, shaped by local interests, and coloured by local perceptions.
>
> (Rosaldo, 1993: 21)

The research and argument presented here thus deals with "domains of folk experience" (Widdowson, 2006: 96) by describing how literacy in English is lived in a 'peripheral' country such as Argentina.

As a consequence, the notion of 'periphery' acquires importance. The Argentinean setting is thus both local in the sense discussed above but also 'peripheral', not least because of its geographical location, and one important aspect of this book is to address the need to "engage with the reality of language as experienced by users and learners" (Widdowson, 2000: 23) within culturally specific contexts. Although Canagarajah and Said (2009, 2011) argue that terminology distinctions such as 'centre' and 'periphery' and 'inner and outer circles' are reductive and no longer appropriate due to the effects of globalisation, we agree with Canagarajah (personal communication 2012), that, despite drawbacks, terms such as 'centre' and 'periphery', when used critically and contextually, have the potential to highlight unavoidable power inequality relationships that other distinctions deliberately hide (also 'Southern theories', Connell, 2007). A critical and contextual use of the terms acknowledges complex influences and distances us from stereotyped assumptions that people in the periphery are always passive, ignorant and poor, and that people in the centre are always powerful and evil. One way in which these assumptions can be overcome is by observing transcultural flows (Appadurai, 1996) and translanguaging practices in local contexts (Canagarajah, 2011), or in other words by looking at the issues from a bottom-up approach (Hornberger and McCarty, 2012). A bottom-up view involves exploring how the people in either context, periphery or centre, but particularly in the periphery, live their everyday experiences in connection with their use of languages and their cultural influences. Canagarajah (personal communication, 2012) explains that community-based or classroom-based research in specific local settings is empowering for the people involved because it allows them to see themselves as individuals with agency within particular power structures. Elsewhere, he argues that

> it is important to find out how linguistic hegemony is carried out, lived, and experienced in the day-to-day life of the people and communities in the periphery.
>
> (1995: 592)

In this sense, one aim of this book is to give voice to a local community in Latin America, in the city of La Plata in Argentina, in order to discover how a group of college students experience reading in English in a setting where English is a foreign language. In later chapters we shall show that these readers were far from dependent and passive and in fact engaged in different forms of critical cultural awareness. We shall argue that the complex and subtle ways in which cultural understanding took place in this community provide insights that might well be useful for the 'centre'.

The Argentinean 'Periphery'

The notion of periphery acquires importance because the research on which this book is based investigates reading in English as a foreign language (EFL) in a country in which Spanish has been the national and official language since the declaration of independence from Spain in 1816. The brief historical account that follows reveals the significance of the association of EFL with a discourse of imperialism.

The Spanish domination in the region between the 16th and the 19th centuries had an effect on the configuration of the current population of the country through the different immigration flows that took place in those times. The 2010 census (INDEC, 2010) shows that the majority of the population (over 85%) is of European origin with a *mestizo* minority (mixed European and Indian origin) of 8%. The immigrants brought their languages with them (Bolivian Quechua, Catalán, German, Guaraní, Italian, Japanese, Korean, Levantine Arabic, South Mandarín, Welsh and others) (Lewis, 2009), and these languages coexisted with 16 or more living indigenous languages (Censabella, 1999; Gordon, 2005).

Towards the end of the 19th century, the Argentinean state fulfilled a crucial role in the unification and homogenisation of the population through education, especially language education (López Armengol and Persoglia, 2009). This process of homogenisation began with the enactment of Law 1420 in 1884, whose aim was to form and create the Argentinean citizen. It did so through primary school education (universal, obligatory, nonreligious and free) and the obligatory military service system. In the first half of the 19th century, Sarmiento, a key historical figure in education, put into motion the imposition of the central culture and language and the elimination of difference (linguistic, social, cultural) represented by the *gaucho* and the several Indian languages alive in those times (Puiggrós, 1990). The aim of education was to reproduce the dominant culture in the younger generations—a culture that mirrored Europe, particularly France.

This paradigm of homogenisation continued to dominate the thought of politicians, pedagogues and intellectuals during the 20th century (Puiggrós, 1990). The military governments adopted a repressive and overt intent to dominate the thinking and behaviour of the masses in the 1970s. The system of education toward the end of the 1980s also realised this drive toward conformity (regarding school routines, methods, accepted versions of disciplinary content, adult-youth relationships, etc.) (Puiggrós, 1990). Education was seen as a driving unifying force (Rivas, 2005).

It is against this background that we need to place the teaching of English. However, although experiences of English Language Teaching (ELT) in other areas of the world are well documented (Bruthiaux, 2002; Clemente, 2007; Matsuda, 2003; McKay and Warshauer Freedman, 1990; McKay and Weinstein-Shr, 1993; Nunan, 2003; Tsui, 2007; Vavrus, 2002), Latin American countries tend to be underrepresented, and this book is in part an attempt to remedy this situation.

In Argentina, the teaching of English in schools began almost exclusively in the private sector through subtractive models based on a monoglossic conception of language learning (Porto, 2012). Many traditional bilingual schools grew in the 19th century to provide education for the children of the British settlers of those times (Banfi and Day, 2005; Tocalli-Beller, 2007). This British influence was very important in the country throughout the 19th century. Even though the Spanish and Italian immigrants outgrew the Irish, Scottish, Welsh and English immigrants in number, the latter shaped the identity of the nation through their business penetration in the railway and in farming, among other areas (Maersk Nielsen, 2003). In the 20th century, private institutions spread this model of an English-Spanish bilingual curriculum, targeted mainly at high-income sectors in the main cities. The cultural influence of the British is present nowadays through cultural associations devoted to the teaching of English and the promotion of British culture such as the British Council and the Asociación Argentina de Cultura Inglesa (Argentine Association of British Culture); through theatre and cultural activities in English; and through sports such as football, rugby, tennis, yachting, polo and golf (Maersk Nielsen, 2003). The names of famous clubs in these sports reflect their British origin (Newell's Old Boys, Boca Juniors, River Plate, Buenos Aires Lawn Tennis Club, Yacht Club Argentino, among many others) (Maersk Nielsen, 2003).

In the public sector, English was first introduced into the curriculum for secondary school in the 1960s, and with the Federal Law of Education passed in 1993, English became a compulsory subject in the primary and secondary school curriculum. This affected the status of other foreign languages that used to be taught in high school in the 1980s, such as French (Zappa-Hollman, 2007). However, the impact of an education in languages was restricted to a limited population simply because secondary school was not compulsory until 2006. At the same time, the National Law of Education (2006) prescribed the teaching of English as a Foreign Language in primary school and extended its obligatory teaching throughout secondary school.

English is thus a dominant and prestigious foreign language in the country (Maersk Nielsen, 2003; Rajagopalan, 2010; Tocalli-Beller, 2007). Rajagopalan (2010) speaks of the nativisation of English in Latin America (through borrowings that later become accepted terms in Spanish) and mentions the perceived need of English as something vital among Argentineans. The prestige associated with English stems in part from the penetration of the English language and culture in the 19th century referred to above but at present, even though English is not an official language, it is predominant in business with foreign countries and in tourism.

According to Maersk Nielsen (2003), the use of English in Argentina fulfils several functions. One is the 'interpersonal', achieved through the prevalence of English in advertising, consumer goods (brand names of clothes, cars, perfumes, music, food and many other areas), businesses, etc. English is strongly associated with auras of prestige, modernity and sophistication. Another is the 'instrumental' function, whereby English is used as a medium of instruction in some schools, in teacher training colleges, in EFL professional development courses, in international conferences in different disciplines and so on. The third, 'regulative' function refers to the fact that sworn translators of English are necessary to translate all the business and commercial contracts with foreign companies, which, by law, must be written in the official language, Spanish. Finally, the 'innovative' function refers to the frequent borrowings from English, which are then nativised, for instance in sports, computing, shopping and advertising, among many other areas. These functions are related to a process of Americanisation observable through television and films for instance, and Argentina can be thought of as a country in which English is additive rather than subtractive, becoming an additional language rather than replacing existing language(s) (Phillipson, 2008b).

There exists, however, a discourse of imperialism in Argentina, associated with this spread of English. The point is not new and follows the argument which has been made for other countries, namely that ELT is a form of ideological and cultural colonisation (Holly, 1990; Valdes, 1990) whereby the norms and values associated with English in specific sociocultural contexts are transmitted and imposed through a hegemonic relationship. One consequence, so the argument runs for other countries, is that local languages and cultures are "totally submerged" (Alptekin and Alptekin, 1984: 15) and constitute a threat to the national identity. Phillipson and Skutnabb-Kangas (1996: 436) referred to "the infectious spread of English within a wider language policy framework" and saw English as 'triumphant' as a result of processes of Americanisation, Europeanisation and McDonaldisation (Phillipson and Skutnabb-Kangas, 1996: 440). Phillipson (2001: 191) warned that "these developments embody and entail hegemonising processes that tend to render the use of English 'natural' and 'normal', and to marginalise other languages".

Some local politicians and political scientists have adopted this general rhetoric of imperialism to highlight the profoundly evil impact of English on many Latin American countries and their inhabitants (Borón, 2009; Borón and Vlahusic, 2009). Borón (2009), a political scientist, argues that in Argentina this evil influence has led to the crisis of a model of civilisation which has resulted in social unrest, violence, xenophobia and racism, among other diabolic forces. The labelling of English as "lingua frankensteinia" (Phillipson, 2008a: 250) is replicated in the local context, with deep implications at the economic, financial, political, ideological and military levels. Because Argentina has an ambivalent love-hate relationship with the US, (Rajagopalan, 2010), Borón (2009) and Borón and Vlahusic (2009) emphasise this tension and tend to highlight the hegemonic role that the US plays in economic, financial, political, ideological and military terms. They state that Americanisation, Europeanisation and McDonaldisation are symptoms that represent the visible tip of a broader imperialist penetration through

> mechanisms of domination, and the multiplication of its [the United States'] devices of manipulation and ideological and political control.
> (Borón, 2005: 271; our translation from Spanish)

Furthermore, one key historical event which has contributed to this ingrained negative view of the English language, as well as the predominance of the discourse of imperialism in some sectors of Argentinean society, is the Malvinas/Falklands War (*Guerra de las Malvinas*) fought in 1982 between Argentina and the United Kingdom over the Falkland Islands, South Georgia and the South Sandwich Islands. The dispute regarding their sovereignty dates back to the 19th century, is still unresolved and evokes a strong and pervasive sentiment of nationalism among the population. Similar intricate connections among politics, historical events and their commemorations, nationhood, the media and language use have been pointed out by scholars in other countries such as Canada (Mock, 2012), Chile (Tjaden, 2012), China (Kuever, 2012), Ireland and England (Scully, 2012), Malaysia (Chung, 2012) and México (Hoyo, 2012). In this complex context in which the notions of periphery and imperialism interact, our research reveals how a group of college students experience English in La Plata by exploring cultural understanding in EFL reading, using literary texts.

References

Abu-Rabia, S. (1996) Are we tolerant enough to read each other's culture? Evidence from three different social contexts. *Educational Psychology* 16(4), 379–388.

Abu-Rabia, S. (1998) Social and cognitive factors influencing the reading comprehension of Arab students learning Hebrew as a second language in Israel. *Journal of Research in Reading* 21(3), 201–212.

Alptekin, C. and Alptekin, M. (1984) The question of culture: EFL teaching in non-English speaking countries. *ELT Journal* 38(1), 14–20.

Altieri, J. (1995) Multicultural literature and multiethnic readers: Examining aesthetic involvement and preferences for text. *Reading Psychology* 16, 43–70.

Anderson, R. C. (1977) The notion of schemata and the education enterprise: General discussion of the conference. In Anderson, R., Spiro, R., and Montague, W. (eds) *Schooling and the Acquisition of Knowledge* (pp. 415–431). Hillsdale, NJ: Erlbaum.

Anderson, R. C. (2004) Role of the Reader's Schema in comprehension, learning, and memory. In Ruddell, R. and Unrau, N. (eds) *Theoretical Models and Processes of Reading. Fifth Edition* (pp. 594–606). Newark, DE: International Reading Association Inc.

Anderson, R. C. and Pearson, P. (1984) A schema theoretic view of basic processes in reading comprehension. In Pearson, P., Barr, R., Kamil, M., and Mosenthal, P. (eds) *Handbook of Reading Research* (pp. 255–292). New York: Longman.

Appadurai, A. (1996) *Modernity at Large: Cultural Dimensions of Globalization.* Minneapolis: University of Minnesota Press.

Archer, M. (1997) *Cultura y teoría social.* Buenos Aires: Nueva Visión.

Baker, J. Jr. (1990) An ethnographic study of cultural influences on the responses on college freshmen to contemporary Appalachian short stories (Doctoral dissertation, Virginia Polytechnic Institute). *Dissertation Abstracts International*, 51, 1534A.

Banfi, C. and Day, R. (2005) The evolution of Bilingual Schools in Argentina. In de Mejía, A. (ed) *Bilingual Education in South America* (pp. 65–78). Clevendon: Multilingual Matters.

Bartlett, F. (1932) *Remembering.* Cambridge, England: The University Press.
Beach, R. (1994) Students' resistance to engagement with multicultural literature. In Rogers, T. and Soter, A. (eds) *Reading across Cultures: Teaching Literature in a Diverse Society* (pp. 69–94). New York: Teachers College Press, Columbia University.
Borón, A. (2005) Un imperio en llamas. *Observatorio social de América Latina*, VI/18, 271–287. Buenos Aires: CLACSO.
Borón, A. (2009) *De la guerra infinita a la crisis infinita.* Original article published on March 13th, 2009. Translated by S. Machetera, C. Campbell, L. Carroll, and M. Talens. Available in Tlaxcala http://www.tlaxcala.es/pp.asp?reference=7302&lg=en. Last accessed 6 May 2014.
Borón, A. and Vlahusic, A. (2009) *El lado oscuro del imperio: La violación de los derechos humanos por los Estados Unidos.* Buenos Aires: Ediciones Luxemburg.
Bransford, J. and Johnson, M. (1972) Contextual pre-requisites for understanding: Some investigations of comprehension and recall. *Journal of Verbal Learning and Verbal Behavior* 11, 717–726.
Bransford, J. and Johnson, M. (1973) Considerations of some problems of comprehension. In Chase, W. (ed) *Visual Information Processing* (pp. 383–438). New York: Academic Press.
Bruthiaux, P. (2002) Hold your courses: Language education, language choice, and economic development. *TESOL Quarterly* 36, 275–296.
Busch, K. (1994) Black Elk speaks: College students respond: Reader response to multicultural literature (Doctoral dissertation, University of Minnesota). *Dissertation Abstracts International*, 481A.
Butler, J. (1997) Merely cultural. *Social Text* 52/53, 265–277.
Byram, M. (2008) *From Foreign Language Education to Education for Intercultural Citizenship.* Clevedon: Multilingual Matters.
Byram, M. and Grundy, P. (2002) Introduction: Context and culture in language teaching and learning. *Language, Culture, and Curriculum* 15, 193–195.
Canagarajah, A. S. (1995) Review. *Language in Society* 24, 590–594.
Canagarajah, A. S. (2002) Globalization, methods and practice in Periphery classrooms. In Block, D. and Cameron, D. (eds) *Globalization and Language Teaching* (pp. 134–150). London: Routledge.
Canagarajah, A. S. (2006) TESOL at forty: What are the issues? *TESOL Quarterly* 40, 9–34.
Canagarajah, A. S. (2011) Translanguaging in the classroom: Emerging issues for research and pedagogy. *Applied Linguistics Review* 2, 1–28.
Canagarajah, A. S. (2012) Personal communication.
Canagarajah, A. S. and Said, S. (2009) English language teaching in the outer and expanding circles. In Maybin, J. and Swann, J. (eds) *Routledge Companion to English Language Studies* (pp. 157–170). New York and Abingdon: Routledge.
Canagarajah, A. S. and Said, S. (2011) Linguistic imperialism. In Simpson, J. (ed) *The Routledge Handbook of Applied Linguistics* (pp. 388–400). Abingdon, UK: Routledge.
Carrell, P. (1983a) Three components of background knowledge in reading comprehension. *Language Learning* 33, 183–207.
Carrell, P. (1983b) Background knowledge in second language comprehension. *Language Learning and Communication* 2, 25–34.
Censabella, M. (1999) *Las lenguas indígenas de la Argentina: Una mirada actual.* Buenos Aires: Eudeba.

Chihara, T., Sakurai, T. and Oller, J. (1989) Background and culture as factors in EFL reading comprehension. *Language Testing* 6(2), 143–149.

Chung, S. S.-Y. (2012) An occasion for collective engagement: Shifting political hegemonies in early Malay Epic Dramas. *Studies in Ethnicity and Nationalism* 12, 136–154.

Clemente, A. (2007) English as cultural capital in the Oaxacan Community of Mexico. *TESOL Quarterly* 41, 421–425.

Connell, R. (2007) *Southern Theory: The Global Dynamics of Knowledge in Social Science*. Cambridge: Polity.

de Nooy, J. (2006) Border patrol in the borderless world: Negotiating intercultural internet discussion. *Language, Society and Culture* 19, 1–8.

Derrida, J. (1994) *Márgenes de la Filosofía: Segunda edición*. Translated by C. González Marín. Madrid: Ediciones Cátedra.

Gadamer, H. G. (1992) *Verdad y Método II*. Translated by Manuel Olasagasti. Salamanca: Ediciones Sígueme.

Garth-McCullough, R. (2008) Untapped cultural support: The influence of culturally bound prior knowledge on comprehension performance. *Reading Horizons* 49(1), 1–30.

Genetsch, M. (2007) *The Texture of Identity*. Toronto: TSAR Publications.

Gordon, R. G., Jr. (ed) (2005) *Ethnologue: Languages of the world. Fifteenth Edition*. Dallas, TX: SIL International. Available at http://www.ethnologue.com. Last accessed 6 May 2014.

Guiora, A. (2005) The language sciences—The challenges ahead. A farewell address. *Language Learning* 55(2), 183–189.

Halasz, L. (1988) Affective-structural effect and the characters' perception in reception of short stories. *Poetics* 17, 417–438.

Hammadou, J. (1991) Interrelationships among prior knowledge, inference, and language proficiency in foreign language reading. *The Modern Language Journal* 75(1), 27–38.

Harris, R., Lee, D., Hensley, D. and Schoen, L. (1988) The effect of cultural script knowledge on memory for stories over time. *Discourse Processes* 11, 413–431.

Hollingsworth, P. and Reutzel, R. (1990) Prior knowledge, content-related attitude, reading comprehension: Testing Matthewson's Affective model of reading. *Journal of Educational research* 83(4), 194–199.

Holly, D. (1990) The unspoken curriculum, or how language teaching carries cultural and ideological messages. In Harrison, B. (ed) *Culture and the Language Classroom. ELT Documents 132* (pp. 11–19). London: Modern English Publications and The British Council.

Hooper-Weil, S. (1989) Literature and culture: An analysis of the effects of cultural background on Puerto Rican and American reader response to selected short stories (Doctoral dissertation, New York University). *Dissertation Abstracts International*, 397A.

Hornberger, N. and McCarty, T. (2012) Globalization from the bottom up: Indigenous language planning and policy across time, space, and place. *International Multilingual Research Journal* 6(1), 1–7.

Hoyo, H. (2012) Fresh views on the old past: The postage stamps of the Mexican Bicentennial. *Studies in Ethnicity and Nationalism* 12, 19–44.

INDEC (2010) *Censo Nacional de Población, Hogares y Vivienda 2010*. Buenos Aires: Ministerio de Economía.

Jordan, S. and Purves, A. (1993) Issues in the responses of students to culturally diverse texts: A preliminary study (New York: National research Center on Literature Teaching and Learning). *ERIC Document Reproduction Service*, No. ED 361 701.

Kant, I. (1929) *Critique of Pure Reason*. New York: St. Martin's Press (Original work published in 1781).

Kintsch, W. and van Dijk, T. (1978) Toward a model of text comprehension and production. *Psychological Review* 85, 363–394.

Kramsch, C. (1995) The cultural component of language teaching. *Language, Culture, and Curriculum* 8, 83–92.

Kuever, E. (2012) Performance, spectacle, and visual poetry in the sixtieth anniversary national day parade in the People's Republic of China. *Studies in Ethnicity and Nationalism* 12, 6–18.

Lewis, M. P. (ed) (2009) *Ethnologue: Languages of the World. Sixteenth Edition*. Dallas, TX: SIL International. Available at http://www.ethnologue.com/. Last accessed 6 May 2014.

Lipson, M. (1983) The influence of religious affiliation on children's memory for text information. *Reading Research Quarterly* XVIII, 448–457.

López Armengol, M. and Persoglia, L. (2009) El sistema universitario Argentino. In Olaskoaga Larrauri, J. (coordinator). *Hacia una educación superior de calidad. Un análisis desde la perspectiva del profesorado en Argentina, Chile, España y México* (pp. 19–42). La Plata: Edulp.

Maersk Nielsen, P. (2003) English in Argentina: A sociolinguistic profile. *World Englishes* 22, 199–209.

Malik, A. (1990) A psycholinguistic analysis of the reading behavior of EFL-proficient readers using culturally familiar and culturally nonfamiliar expository texts. *American Educational Research Journal* 27(1), 205–223.

Martínez-Roldán, C. and Sayer, P. (2006) Reading through linguistic borderlands: Latino students' transactions with narrative texts. *Journal of Early Childhood Literacy* 6(3), 293–322.

Matsuda, A. (2003) Incorporating world Englishes in teaching English as an international language. *TESOL Quarterly* 37, 719–729.

McCarthey, S. and Moje, E. (2002) Conversations: Identity matters. *Reading Research Quarterly* 37, 228–238.

McKay, S. and Warshauer Freedman, S. (1990) Language minority education in Great Britain: A challenge to current US Policy. *TESOL Quarterly* 24, 385–405.

McKay, S. and Weinstein-Shr, G. (1993) English literacy in the US: National policies, Personal consequences. *TESOL Quarterly* 27, 399–419.

McVee, M., Dunsmore, K. and Gavelek, J. (2005) Schema theory revisited. *Review of Educational Research* 75(4), 531–566.

Minsky, M. (1975) A framework for representing knowledge. In Winston, P. (ed) *The Psychology of Computer Vision* (pp. 211–277). New York: McGraw-Hill.

Mock, S. J. (2012) 'Whose game they're playing': Nation and emotion in Canadian TV advertising during the 2010 Winter Olympics. *Studies in Ethnicity and Nationalism* 12, 206–226.

Moreiras, A. (1991) *Interpretación y diferencia*. Madrid: Visor.

Noda, L. (1980) Literature and culture: Japanese and American reader responses to modern Japanese stories (Doctoral dissertation, New York University). *Dissertation Abstracts International*, 41, 4894A.

Norton, B. (2000) *Identity and Language Learning: Gender, Ethnicity and Educational Change*. London: Longman and Pearson Education.

Norton, B. and Toohey, K. (2011) Identity, language learning, and social change. *Language Teaching* 44, 412–446.

Nunan, D. (2003) The impact of English as a global language on educational policies and practices in the Asia-Pacific region. *TESOL Quarterly* 37, 589–613.

Phillipson, R. (2001) English for globalisation or for the world's people? *International Review of Education* 47, 185–200.

Phillipson, R. (2008a) Lengua franca or lingua frankensteinia? English in European integration and globalization. *World Englishes* 27, 250–267.

Phillipson, R. (2008b) Response. *World Englishes* 27, 282–284.

Phillipson, R. and Skutnabb-Kangas, T. (1996) English only worldwide or language ecology. *TESOL Quarterly* 30, 429–452.

Porto, M. (2012) Academic perspectives from Argentina. In Byram, M. and Parmenter, L. (eds) *The Common European Framework of Reference: The Globalisation of Language Education Policy* (pp. 129–138). Bristol: Multilingual Matters.

Pritchard, R. (1990) The effects of cultural schemata on reading process strategies. *Reading Research Quarterly* 25, 273–295.

Puiggrós, A. (1990) *Imaginación y crisis en la educación latinoamericana*. México, DF: Consejo Nacional para la Cultura y las Artes.

Rajagopalan, K. (2010) The English language, globalization and Latin America: Possible lessons from the 'Outer circle'. In Saxena, M. and Omoniyi, T. (eds) *Contending with Globalization in World Englishes* (pp. 175–195). Clevedon: Multilingual Matters.

Reynolds, R., Taylor, M., Steffensen, M., Shirey, L. and Anderson, R. (1982) Cultural schemata and reading comprehension. *Reading Research Quarterly* 17, 353–366.

Rice, E. (1980) On cultural schemata. *American Ethnologist* 7(1), 152–171.

Rivas, A. (2005). Tiempos de inversión educativa: Comentarios a la propuesta de Ley de Financiamiento Educativo. *[Times of Investment on Education. Commentary Based on the Proposal for a Law for the Financing of Education]*. Políticas públicas. Análisis No15. Buenos Aires: Fundación CIPPEC. www.cippec.org

Rosaldo, R. (1993) *Culture and Truth: The Remaking of Social Analysis*. Boston: Beacon Press.

Rumelhart, D. E. (1975) Notes on a schema for stories. In Bobrow, D. and Collins, A. (eds) *Representation and Understanding: Studies in Cognitive Science* (pp. 211–235). New York: Academic Press.

Rumelhart, D. E. (1980) Schemata: The building blocks of cognition. In Spiro, R., Bruce, B., and Brewer, W. (eds) *Theoretical Issues in Reading Comprehension* (pp. 35–58). Hillsdale, NJ: Erlbaum.

Rumelhart, D. E. and Ortony, A. (1977) The representation of knowledge in memory. In Anderson, R., Spiro, R., and Montague, W. (eds) *Schooling and the Acquisition of Knowledge* (pp. 99–135). Hillsdale, NJ: Erlbaum.

Sasaki, M. (2000) Effects of cultural schemata on students' test-taking processes for cloze tests: A multiple data source approach. *Language Testing* 17(1), 85–114.

Schank, R. (1975) The structure of episodes in memory. In Bobrow, D. and Collins, A. (eds) *Representation and Understanding: Studies in Cognitive Science* (pp. 237–272). New York: Academic Press.

Schank, R. (1982) *Dynamic Memory*. Cambridge, England: Cambridge University Press.

Schank, R. and Abelson, R. (1977) *Scripts, Plans, Goals, and Understanding*. Hillsdale, NJ: Erlbaum.

Scully, M. (2012) Whose day is it anyway? St. Patrick's day as a contested performance of national and diasporic Irishness. *Studies in Ethnicity and Nationalism* 12, 118–135.

Sharifian, F., Rochecouste, J. and Malcolm, G. (2004) 'But it was all a bit confusing...': Comprehending Aboriginal English texts. *Language, Culture and Curriculum* 17, 203–228.

Spears-Bunton, L. A. (1992) Cultural consciousness and response to literary texts among African-American and European-American juniors (Doctoral dissertation, University of Kentucky). *Dissertation Abstracts International*, 2719A.

Steffensen, M., Joag-Dev, C. and Anderson, R. (1979) A cross-cultural perspective on reading comprehension. *Reading Research Quarterly* XV, 10–29.

Tjaden, J. D. (2012) The (re-)construction of 'national identity' through selective memory and Mass Ritual Discourse: The Chilean Centenary, 1910. *Studies in Ethnicity and Nationalism* 12, 45–63.

Tocalli-Beller, A. (2007) ELT and bilingual education in Argentina. In Cummins, J. and Davison, C. (eds) *International Handbook of English Language Teaching: Part I* (pp. 107–122). Springer.

Tsui, A. (2007) Complexities of identity formation: A narrative inquiry of an EFL teacher. *TESOL Quarterly* 41, 657–680.

Valdes, J. (1990) The inevitability of teaching and learning culture in a foreign language course. In Harrison, B. (ed) *Culture and the Language Classroom: ELT Documents 132* (pp. 20–30). London: Modern English Publications and The British Council.

Van Hell, J., Bosman, A., Wiggers, I. and Stoit, J. (2003) Children's cultural background knowledge and story telling performance. *International Journal of Bilingualism* 7(3), 283–303.

Vavrus, F. (2002) Postcoloniality and English: Exploring language policy and the politics of development in Tanzania. *TESOL Quarterly* 36, 373–397.

Widdowson, H. G. (2000) On the limitations of linguistics applied. *Applied Linguistics* 21(1), 3–25.

Widdowson, H. G. (2006) Applied linguistics and interdisciplinarity. *International Journal of Applied Linguistics* 16, 93–96.

Zappa-Hollman, S. (2007) EFL in Argentina's schools: Teachers' perspectives on policy changes and instruction. *TESOL Quarterly* 41, 618–625.

2 A Model of Cultural Understanding of Texts

Models of Understanding Other Cultures

The model that we developed was needed for classroom settings. Most existing models of cultural understanding in the research literature have also arisen from specific conditions and are intended to cater for particular and local needs, often focusing on interaction and communication in naturalistic settings. Like others, our model rests on a view of culture as dynamic and heterogeneous, and of language and culture as inseparable. Although it draws elements from several of these existing models, and is consistent with widespread agreement in the literature regarding cultural understanding (Deardorff, 2009), it has a specific focus on reading.

Two models have been fundamental in its conceptualisation. One is Kramsch's (1993: 210, 1998), defined as "a four-step approach to crosscultural understanding," and although Kramsch has more recently developed a model of 'symbolic competence' (Kramsch and Whiteside, 2008), this earlier work is particularly relevant to developing a model of reading texts. Central to it is the conception of context "as a social construct, the product of linguistic choices made by two or more individuals interacting through language" (Kramsch, 1993: 46). Just as culture is viewed as dynamic and relational (involving an individual interacting with others), context is too (Kramsch, 2003, 2007). A key role is consequently attributed to language: "language expresses cultural reality (. . .) language embodies cultural reality (. . .) language symbolizes cultural reality" (Kramsch, 1998: 3).

Our model takes up this notion of culture and context and reflects the centrality of language since cultural understanding is investigated through reading. Kramsch also emphasises the role of perceptions in her model and argues that cultural understanding is a process centred not so much on the discovery of the factual and objective characteristics of another culture but rather on the exploration of how other cultures relate to one's own. Perceptions include those that individuals have of themselves, of their own cultures, of others, and of others' cultures. Because of the difficulties of perceptions (for instance, perceptions may end up being caught in misperceptions),

Kramsch (1993: 210) proposes the notion of a "third perspective that would enable learners to take both an insider's and an outsider's view on C1 [one's own culture] and C2 [another culture]".

This focus on perceptions and the relational is present in our model in the shifts of perspective that each level captures and in the focus on one's own as well as other cultures. Our characterisation of cultural understanding as fluid and procedural is also consistent with the notion of a third perspective.

The second influence is a Model of Intercultural Competence (Byram, 1997, 2009), conceived for foreign language education contexts. It consists of five *savoirs* or dimensions of knowledge, skills and attitudes: *savoir être* (attitudes of curiosity and inquisitiveness), *savoirs* (knowledge of different aspects of life in a certain society, such as work, education, traditions, etc., and knowledge of processes of social interaction), *savoir comprendre* (the skill of interpreting and relating those *savoirs* of one's own and another culture), *savoir apprendre/savoir faire* (the skills of discovery and interaction), and *savoir s'engager* (critical cultural awareness). Several of these aspects are also foregrounded in our model, namely the relational aspect and perspective-taking (Byram, 2009), the emphasis on processes rather than facts (for example observing, describing, analysing, relating, interpreting), and a recognition of the importance of empathy, adaptability, flexibility, sensitivity and criticality, among other characteristics of intercultural competence as stated in Byram (2012).

A New Model of Cultural Understanding

The model we have developed is a six-level model which describes, in the first instance, the ways in which EFL learners in this Argentine context approached cultural issues during reading and emphasises the centrality of cultural understanding as a fluid process in a continuum of cultural familiarity and unfamiliarity. It attempts to capture the double angle of vision (us-them) achieved through readers' imaginations, attributing importance to both the capacity of movement in and out of different perceptions, and the significant role of imagination in cultural understanding. Following Kramsch (1993), this *double* vision needs to be stretched to reach *multiple* perspectives, and in fact the model can be thought of as a vehicle for the creation of a third space in cultural understanding, a space that foregrounds the fluid, the relative and the unstable. Exploring *multiple* perspectives thus posits culture as "negotiation" (Genetsch, 2007: 26).

The model is represented schematically by the following Table 2.1, although the dynamic interaction and the interrelationship among all levels is an important factor that the table cannot capture.

The use of the terminology 'culture C1/C2' does not imply an essentialised or reductive concept. We adopt a dynamic concept of culture rather than one which implies a static, monolithic and homogeneous entity usually associated

Table 2.1 Model of Cultural Understanding

Level 0. Erratic perception or omission of cultural aspects.
Level 1. Perception/identification of cultural differences. Access to levels 2, 3, 4 and 5.
Level 2. Identification of own values and ideas. Identification of the cultural assumptions behind one's own culture (insider perspective).
Level 3. Perception of the cultural C2 from one's own frame of reference (C1) (outsider perspective). Stereotyped views of the cultural C2.
Level 4. Perception of the cultural C2 from the frame of reference of members of culture C2 (insider perspective).
Level 5. Perception of the cultural C1 from the perspective of the cultural C2 (outsider perspective).

---

with geographical and national boundaries. However, despite the impossibility of describing a culture as a homogenous construct, the term "culture" is in general used in the singular in the literature (for instance Bennett, 1998: 2; Byram, 2001: 98; Byrnes, 2008: 108; Garner, 2008: 117; Kramsch, 1995: 85; Scarano, 2002: 159; Trujillo Sáez, 2005: 25). The research literature also uses other terms that are equally problematic for the same reason such as "cultural content" (Abu-Rabia, 1998: 203; Smith-Maddox, 1998: 312), "cultural meaning" (Byrnes, 2008: 108), "cultural significance" (Steffensen, Joag-Dev and Anderson, 1979: 12), "cultural difference" (Deveney, 2007: 311; Kramsch, Cain and Murphy-Lejeune, 1996: 100; Rollin, 2006: 58), "cultural type" (Deveney, 2007: 313), "cultural pattern" (Cordier, 1946: 362) and "elements or features of a cultural schema" (Sharifian, Rochecouste and Malcolm, 2004: 206). García Canclini (2006) proposes to refer to *the cultural* rather than *culture* in order to capture its fluid and dynamic nature and whenever possible we adopt this shift from the noun *culture* to the adjective *cultural*.

Thus we mean by 'the cultural' the shared beliefs, values and behaviours of a social group large or small, with determined or fuzzy boundaries. The beliefs, values and behaviours of a group can embrace diversity within what is shared synchronically, and inevitably change diachronically. At a given point in time however, the diversity will include some phenomena which all members of the group recognise as crucial even if they do not participate in them all. We take a synchronic perspective in the use of this model in this book, although the diachronic approach could also be considered by taking historical texts either from the readers' own or an unfamiliar cultural group.

We turn now to a more detailed explanation of each level.

Level 0. Erratic Perception or Omission of Cultural Aspects

At this level readers may fail to perceive cultural matters, which leads to their omission, or they may perceive them erratically, either accepting or rejecting them.

There is an underlying theoretical tension here between a notion of blindness to difference which posits universal values on the one hand and the recognition and appreciation of difference in its own right on the other (Genetsch, 2007). The indeterminacy of meaning is also fundamental. Any interpretation is provisional because whoever interprets is prepared to know certain things and not others (Rosaldo, 1993) and the notion that there exists a horizon beyond which something always remains incomprehensible, underlies this first level.

Secondly, the concept from cultural anthropology that each culture is so distinctive that it is virtually impossible to compare one to another in a truly deep way (Rosaldo, 1993) is also relevant, and we agree with Rosaldo that no culture is superior or inferior, richer or poorer, bigger or smaller than any other. However, since theoretically the investigation of cultural understanding *is* feasible despite limitations, the notion of cultural visibility means that some aspects of another culture may become noticeable more than others. In spite of the fact that all ways of perceiving and organising reality are culture-specific, there are always visible and invisible elements in all cultures (Rosaldo, 1993). In practical terms, this means that certain human phenomena may appear to be more susceptible of cultural analysis than others. From this perspective, at this level in the model, there is an attempt to capture the visible elements of a certain culture. At the same time, the notion that there is a horizon beyond which comprehension is not possible points to the inherent difficulty, at this level in the model, of capturing or understanding the whole of 'the cultural' of any social group.

Level 1. Perception/Identification of Cultural Differences. Access to Levels 2, 3, 4 and 5

This level involves the perception of cultural differences, with identification of the different, exciting, attractive, etc. elements of a given culture. The perception of cultural differences through comparison, confrontation and contrast works as a bridge for the other stages in the model (levels 2, 3, 4 and 5), and is accessed through the identification of key vocabulary.

The connection between key vocabulary and culture is close (Byram, 2011; Goddard and Wierzbicka, 1994; Kramsch, 2007; Lehrer, 1974; Salzmann, 1993; Sapir, 1963; Whorf, 1956; Wierzbicka, 1986, 1992). The link constitutes one rationale for the distinction between levels 0–1 because

> some key words are particularly heavily connoted and reveal shared meanings of another society (. . .) The acquisition of these words and their connotations is not simply a cognitive process but one which can threaten the affective attachment to the world one knows.
>
> (Alred and Byram, 2002: 342)

In addition, the role of vocabulary in the perception, storing, recall and comprehension of information is crucial (Carmichael, Hogan and Walter, 1932; Clarke, Losoff, Dickenson McCracken and Rood, 1984; Loftus, 1979).

Furthermore, Atkinson (1999: 641) points out the "basic human urge to categorize those in some ways different from oneself as radically, irreducibly other." Similarly, Byram (1997, 2001), Byram, Gribkova and Starkey (2002), Palfreyman (2005), and others agree with Ridgeway (2006: 12) that

> to define self and others in order to act, actors first must develop a way of categorizing the other on the basis of comparison and contrast—that is, as different from or similar to known, socially predictable objects such as the self.

Categorisations are often linked directly to vocabulary items, and the distinction between levels 0 and 1 in our model thus reflects how readers demarcate their selves in this way.

The focus on difference in this level is useful because it contributes to making cultures particularly visible to external observers. At the same time, it is problematic because such differences are not absolute but relative to the cultural practices of the observers themselves and therefore contestable. The decision to regard someone as different is always "a positioning or an interpretation" (Genetsch, 2007: x). In other words, part of the difficulty in cultural understanding is that the Other can be "represented in ways that could suggest difference as well as sameness, depending on who did the defining and for what purposes" (Genetsch, 2007: 16). Ultimately, the perception or understanding of the Other is always problematic, being both difficult in practice and contestable in theory.

Level 2. Identification of Own Values and Ideas. Identification of the Cultural Assumptions Within One's Own Culture (Insider Perspective)

Comprehending the cultural C1 from an insider perspective means analysing one's behaviours, values, ideas, etc. in the light of one's cultural norms. Given its familiarity, observing one's cultural reality is not easy. Access to this level requires guidance (for instance the teacher's) as in general, access is accompanied by ethnocentric positions and a lack of cultural sensitivity.

The discovery of alternative perspectives in the interpretation of familiar and unfamiliar phenomena within one's cultural practices as well as disposition to question the values and assumptions within those practices is important (*savoir s'engager* in Byram's 1997 model). Reflecting on one's culture reveals one's attitudes toward it, and may ultimately change those attitudes. In this process, one distances oneself from the familiar, and this distance makes the familiar look different, strange, unfamiliar (*savoir comprendre* in Byram's model). In this process, the identification of the others' stereotypes about one's culture leads to awareness of oneself and one's cultural reality. This level is important because self-understanding appears to be inevitably linked to understanding otherness (Byram and Morgan, 1994).

Theoretically, this level rejects the possibility of establishing pure or authentic identities (one's own as well as those of others). When an identity is defined through a process of abstracting features (language, traditions, some stereotypical behaviour), there is a tendency to separate related practices from the history of mixing in which they were formed and to prescriptively present their use as absolute. On the contrary, this level represents heterodox ways of speaking a language, enacting cultural performances or interpreting traditions. In this view, "identity is not an essence but a positioning" (Genetsch, 2007: 15). In other words, at this level individuals critically ask themselves who they are, who that Other is against whom their own identity is sketched and how that otherness, i.e. difference, is evaluated.

Level 3. Perception of the Cultural C2 from One's Own Frame of Reference (C1) (Outsider Perspective)

This level involves comprehending the cultural C2 from an outsider perspective and requires becoming aware of how the behaviours, values and ideas of others are interpreted from the perspective of one's own cultural frame of reference (an observer perspective).

The notion of stereotype is relevant here because the ideological construction of otherness is produced when what is different (in racial, cultural, historical or other terms) is perceived as rigid, static, degenerate and inordinate (Bhabha, 1994). Initially, the identification of stereotypes constitutes one way of classifying the cultural C2 in manageable categories (Allport, 1954); it is the first step toward the appreciation of the unknown, and makes access to levels 4 and 5 possible.

However, the mere accumulation of stereotypes helps comprehend another culture only superficially and often prejudicially (Allport, 1954). Stereotyped visions are distinct from cultural understanding, which depends on attitudes of curiosity, openness and willingness to suspend disbelief and value judgments with regard to other people's beliefs and behaviours (Byram, 1997; Byram and Morgan, 1994) (*savoir être* and *savoir comprendre* in Byram's model). There must also exist willingness to approach the unfamiliar, recognising the importance of understanding the manifestations of a different culture in the context in which they are framed, but at this level, the approach is stereotyped.

Level 4. Perception of the Cultural C2 From the Frame of Reference of Members of Culture C2 (Insider Perspective)

This stage involves the comprehension of the cultural C2 from an insider perspective. How the members of another culture behave and what values they have are interpreted in the light of their own cultural norms.

Awareness about how others behave according to their own cultural norms is partly gained through information about the private and social world of the Other (*savoirs* in Byram's model). The perceptions that the members of another culture have of themselves make the access to their cultural codes possible, even though those perceptions influence the selection of content and the perspective adopted by outsiders.

Different areas can be analysed, in particular those directly related to the experiences of the members of a given cultural group. There exists the capacity to describe the phenomena of contemporary life in this group's culture and explain the connotations and semantic fields of key words revealing cultural schemata—always from an insider perspective. However, this level amounts to more than information in these areas, because it adds layers of description and interpretation with the aim of leading to the identification of the value systems, social norms and expectations of the members of culture C2.

Another way of describing this is in terms of 'positionality', i.e. readiness to perceive, grasp, know, apprehend, etc. some things and not others. In common parlance, we refer in English to 'putting ourselves in someone else's shoes', and in other languages, e.g., French, 'putting ourselves in someone else's skin'. Andreotti and de Souza (2008: 27) take the shoe metaphor to suggest that we cannot put ourselves in someone else's shoes unless we take off our own, but that it is impossible to do this and "forget all of our experience, language and concepts". The skin metaphor—with the English version of 'getting under the skin' of someone else—is even more radical in its implications that one can shake off one's cultural positioning.

Level 5. Perception of the Cultural C1 From the Perspective of the Cultural C2 (Outsider Perspective)

This level means apprehending the cultural C1 from an outsider perspective. It involves awareness of how one's own behaviour, values and ideas are seen through the eyes of the members of other cultural groups.

The capacity to recognise and articulate the difficulties found in the process of perceiving the cultural from inside (level 4) is present here. Also, there is the capacity to accept that one's cultural perspectives and one's values and expectations influence one's visions. The decentralisation in relation to one's cultural norms promotes awareness about their cultural relativity. One is able to explore one's reactions to one's own behaviours as well as the behaviours of others. It is possible to place oneself in the shoes of the Other through imagination. This level matches Kramsch's "third perspective" (Kramsch, 1993: 210), which permits the adoption of insider, outsider and hybrid perspectives in the apprehension of C1 and C2.

A critical and reflexive attitude is present (fundamental elements in Byram's *savoir s'engager*). Facts are not accepted without critical analysis of their validity. One is able to go beyond the descriptive, appreciating diversity and exploring different, alternative interpretations in the representation of another culture.

What is specific about one's own culture is used to explain aspects of the other culture. One can critically observe one's culture and one's society, evaluating them from the perspective of C2, which guarantees the critical distancing and the decentralisation of one's beliefs. Seeing one's cultural norms through the eyes of an outsider facilitates the understanding of how an outsider might react to these norms. This level is crucial since there cannot possibly be negotiation of shared meanings or understanding of the Other's world if the relationship between one's views and those of others is not captured. The validity of the cultural C2 is acknowledged and appreciated in its own terms.

Using the Model to Analyse Comprehension of Texts in a Foreign Language

As explained in the Introduction, there were texts in Spanish and in English in the research project, and we shall first show how the model works in the analysis of readers' comprehension of one of the texts in English, the selection from *Cat's Eye* (Atwood, 1998: 137–140). This text describes the Christmas celebration of a Canadian family and presents a different cultural reality from that of the participants. In the text, there is an insider perspective, a narrator, Elaine, who participates in the celebration described and belongs to the Canadian setting. Mr. Banerji, a student from India, is a guest in the celebration, invited by the father, a professor of biology. Elaine is a child, the professor's daughter. Readers notice tension since they perceive the visitor feels awkward in a context where he does not understand the cultural meaning of the celebration and can only fully interact in conversation when he and his professor, the father of the family, use scientific language.

Let us now analyse a visual representation (cf. Chapter 7, this volume) by one of the participants, Scarlet Rose, a pseudonym like all names given to participants.

Excerpt 1

Figure 2.1 Scarlet Rose, visual representation, *Cat's Eye*

English Translation of Excerpt 1

1. Look at him . . . brown . . . long arms . . . he doesn't even know what Christmas is.
2. Alone . . . he's scared of us.
3. How not to be scared? I could be in the place of that turkey next Christmas.

The first scene illustrates comprehension at level 1 in the model through the comparison and contrast between Elaine's and Banerji's cultures. Scarlet Rose identifies cultural differences explicitly, and these are portrayed visually by the magnifying glass. She mentions some of Banerji's features which she perceives as exotic or attractive, and identification of the exotic, the attractive and the different is a characteristic of level 1. The features are Banerji's brown skin ("marrón"), his long arms ("brazos largos") and the fact that he does not celebrate Christmas ("ni siquiera sabe qué es la Navidad", "he doesn't even know what Christmas is"). This is Scarlet Rose's interpretation in which she draws explicitly from the text.

At the same time, this first scene illustrates level 3 in the model, which involves the perception of another cultural reality different from one's own norms (i.e., Elaine's in this case), revealed linguistically by "even" ("ni siquiera"), which is in the original. How can it be possible that Banerji doesn't celebrate Christmas? This shows that the starting point of cultural understanding was what was familiar to the participants (level 2 in the model), in this case that Christmas is a universal celebration. Scarlet Rose's use of "even" ("ni siquiera") is an evaluative comment which reflects her position as she presents her interpretation of the text through the visual representation. The position of external observer that characterises level 3 in the model is revealed linguistically by "mírenlo" ("look at him") in the first scene, and by the location of the characters at the dinner table in the second scene. The family and Banerji are physically distant, which may be seen as representing the confrontation *we/he*.

The second scene also illustrates level 1 in the model through the explicit identification of the cultural features that attracted Scarlet Rose's attention, such as the abundance of food and the central location of the turkey. There are several culturally appropriate details in the portrayal of the typical Christmas food and drink: for example, the enormous turkey, the glasses. In addition, the fact that Elaine's father is wearing glasses, a suit and a tie can be seen as representing level 3 in the model since there is an implied and stereotyped association between being a professor and this specific outfit (at least in an Argentinean's view). Here there is a switch toward level 4 in that Elaine's position is represented as her placing herself on Banerji's side in an attempt to understand how he feels at that moment: "he is afraid of us" ("nos tiene miedo"), also in the original text. Worth remarking is the importance of affect in cultural understanding: Banerji is "*afraid* of us" ("nos tiene *miedo*").

Then the last scene has indications of level 4 with traces of level 5. Banerji perceives Elaine's culture (C1) from his own outsider perspective (C2). At the same time, Scarlet Rose's final question "¿cómo no les voy a tener miedo si yo puedo ocupar el lugar de ese pavo la próxima Navidad?" ("how am I not to be scared if I can take this turkey's place next Christmas?") reveals her abilities to decentre, think critically and reflect, which are characteristic of the most complex levels of cultural understanding in this model (*savoir s'engager* in Byram's model). Simultaneously, this question again shows the importance of affect and emotions in cultural understanding through the reference to "being scared" ("tener miedo"). Clearly the confrontation with the values and ideas present in the perspectives of others (members of different groups as are Elaine and Banerji) in *Cat's Eye* favoured a process of decentring or critical distancing from Scarlet Rose's own perspectives. Involved in this process is a recognition of the importance of empathy, perspective-taking and adaptability, stressing not only the individual or personal dimension of cultural understanding but also the relational facet.

The example shows that Scarlet Rose moved back and forth among levels in the model at various points during the reading process since indicators of almost all levels can be identified in this task. In other words, the process of cultural understanding in this setting was fluid and cannot be said to be composed of independent and discrete elements, processes or stages. The process of data analysis, illustrated briefly here, also reveals that cultural understanding was consequently complex because of this impossibility to use one level or levels in isolation to describe cultural understanding.

Emotions and Imagination

The recognition of the importance of emotion in cultural understanding is a significant finding of our research. It traversed all data types (reading response, visual representation, interview)—not only the visual representation illustrated above. For instance, in the follow-up interview, Scarlet Rose explains further what she meant by the question in her visual representation "¿cómo no les voy a tener miedo si yo puedo ocupar el lugar de ese pavo la próxima Navidad?" ("How am I not to be scared if I can take this turkey's place next Christmas?"). We highlight in bold key terms related to emotions. The focus in this interview extract is on Barnerji.

Excerpt 2

SR.: Y esto . . . no es que lo van a comer la próxima Navidad, es para . . . para hacer énfasis en esto de . . . de que **se siente excluido y miserable** y . . . que **no puede entender** . . . Bueno, lo del pavo que dijimos antes, bueno, un poco marcado en esto, y **el sentimiento de aislado** . . .

(Scarlet Rose, interview, *Cat's Eye*)

English Translation of Excerpt 2

SR.: And this . . . it isn't that they are going to eat him next Christmas; it's to place emphasis on the fact that **he feels excluded and miserable** and . . . that **he cannot understand** . . . Well, the turkey thing we mentioned before. Well, it's to point out this a little and **the feeling of isolation** . . .

A little later in the interview (Excerpt 3) Scarlet Rose reveals her ability to decentre and shuttle among different positions and perspectives, in this case by placing herself on Elaine's side in an attempt to understand how she might be feeling.

Excerpt 3

SR.: Ella [Elaine] dice que **está igual de . . . de isolated que el indio**.
(Scarlet Rose, interview, Cat's Eye)

English Translation of Excerpt 3

SR.: She [Elaine] says she's **as isolated as the Indian boy**.

In the process of decentring, Scarlet Rose makes a conscious and explicit effort to focus on how the characters might be feeling under the circumstances. Her reading response task described below (Excerpt 4) is interesting because she intertwines the character's feelings as she perceived them (in bold), as well as her own position toward the celebration described (in italics):

Excerpt 4

El texto refleja cómo una familia norteamericana celebra la Navidad *en una situación inusual, no tradicional*: invitando a un estudiante indio a la *típica gran* cena navideña. Este *no es un texto cualquiera* ya que *no describe simplemente cómo pasan la Navidad en los Estados Unidos*: el tema central es el contraste entre dos culturas muy diferentes (Oriente/Occidente).

    La cultura norteamericana refleja, en el texto, *el estereotipo de una blanca Navidad con abundante comida (¡y el clásico pavo!)*. **Desde el punto de vista emocional,** se nota que a la familia norteamericana **le importa pasar las fiestas felices** ('. . . as long as they make people happy') **y se sienten incómodos** con los silencios producidos por el enfrentamiento de las culturas. El contraste principal (que puede notarse mejor al final del fragmento) es el del mundo capitalista (EEUU) y el mundo 'naturalista' (India), por llamarlo de algún modo. Mientras que al padre le **preocupan** más los gastos del experimento reciente hecho con un pavo, el estudiante indio se concentra en el hecho de que al hombre **no le importa** 'jugar con la naturaleza', que **no la respeta**. Como el narrador

dice, el padre norteamericano **se preocupa por** cuidarse a sí mismo, no al medio ambiente ('Wild things (. . .) look out for themselves').
(Scarlet Rose, reading response task, *Cat's Eye*)

English Translation of Excerpt 4

The text shows how an American family celebrates Christmas *in an unusual nontraditional situation*: by inviting an Indian student to *the typical big* Christmas dinner. *This text isn't like any other; it doesn't simply describe how Christmas is celebrated in the US*: the central theme is the contrast between two very different cultures (Orient/Occident).

The American culture shows, in the text, *the stereotype of a white Christmas, with plenty of food (and the classic turkey!)*. **From the emotional point of view,** one can see that they **really care about celebrating the holidays happily** ('. . . as long as they make people happy') **and that they feel uncomfortable with** the silence produced by the clash of cultures. The main contrast (best seen at the end of the fragment) is that of the capitalistic (US) and 'naturalistic' world (India), just to give it a name. While the father is **concerned about** the expenditures of the recent experiment done on a turkey, the Indian student focuses on the fact that the man **doesn't care about** 'playing with nature', that *he doesn't respect it*. As the narrator says, the American dad **worries about** taking care of himself, not about the environment ('Wild things . . . look out for themselves').

These examples show that cultural understanding in the Argentinean context was linked as much to what the prompt texts had to offer, as to what Scarlet Rose—and other readers in the data as we show in other chapters—brought with them, regarding the Christmas schema in particular, but also regarding all the interconnections that this schema triggered in other dimensions, including the emotional. Cultural understanding was also enhanced by the revisiting of textual content that the research instruments allowed for (in this case the visual representation, the reading response task and the interview). This revisiting took place through the skills of self-understanding, perspective-taking, empathy, decentring, reflection and critical analysis that characterise cultural understanding.

Using the Model in Teaching

We have so far emphasised that the *Model of Cultural Understanding* can be used to investigate and analyse cultural understanding in language education contexts. This chapter has illustrated how the model departs from the static notion of 'available versus unavailable' schemata frequently found in the reading research reviewed in Chapter 1. Furthermore, the illustration with the case of Scarlet Rose has revealed the centrality of criticality and reflexivity in cultural understanding. Confrontation with the values and ideas present in the perspectives of members of other cultural groups in the prompt texts favoured a process of decentring or critical distancing from her and other participants' perspectives.

Cultural understanding involves putting oneself in someone else's shoes, and this requires imagination (Byram and Morgan, 1994). The visual representation in particular offers a forum for its manifestation and we shall say more about this in Chapter 7. For the moment, Scarlet Rose's example shows the power and simplicity of visual imagery in capturing the cultural in reading, and we shall argue in Chapter 7 that this mode of response could become an appropriate tool for developing the imaginative and emotional dimension of cultural understanding through reading. Overall, it is clear that *image* and *emotion* schemata are important within the cultural dimension of reading.

The model can also be used in teaching, in materials selection, design and development, and in assessment. Teachers can use the model to select, design and develop reading materials for specific contexts by analysing a certain text in terms of the levels of the model. By 'text' we mean anything that can be 'read' and 'interpreted' in a variety of semiotic systems and mediums, including print, nonprint, visual, digital, multimodal (Hagood and Skinner, 2012; Handsfield, Dean and Cielocha, 2009). In the following chapter, we show how this can be done by illustrating with the fragments from *Mi planta de naranja-lima*, *Cat's Eye* and *Desert Wife*.

The model can also be used in self-assessment. We shall suggest in Chapter 8 that the focus be on the skills of cultural understanding rather than on the achievement of levels in the model. These are the skills of observing, discovering, describing, analysing, comparing and contrasting, relating, interpreting, perspective-taking, decentring, critical thinking and reflexivity. We have shown that the participants in our research moved back and forth among the six levels in the model and displayed a range of skills of cultural understanding in their interpretations of text. This means that it would be misleading to associate cultural understanding predominantly with the highest levels in the model (levels 4 and 5) because each level involves specific skills and all are important. The key is the extent to which a reader is able to show evidence of a range of these skills in text interpretation. We will suggest in Chapter 8 how students can create a profile of their reading as a form of self-assessment by reference to the model.

References

Abu-Rabia, S. (1998) Social and cognitive factors influencing the reading comprehension of Arab students learning Hebrew as a second language in Israel. *Journal of Research in Reading* 21(3), 201–212.

Allport, G. (1954) *The Nature of Prejudice*. Cambridge, MA: Addison-Wesley.

Alred, G. and Byram, M. (2002) Becoming an intercultural mediator: A longitudinal study of residence abroad. *Journal of Multilingual and Multicultural Development* 23, 339–352.

Andreotti, V. and de Souza, L. M. T. M. (2008) Translating theory into practice and walking minefields: Lessons from the project 'Through Other Eyes'. *International Journal of Development Education and Global Learning*, 10(1), 23–36.

Atkinson, D. (1999) TESOL and culture. *TESOL Quarterly* 33, 625–654.
Atwood, M. (1998) *Cat's Eye*. Bantam: Anchor Books.
Bennett, M. J. (1998) Intercultural communication: A current perspective. In Bennett, M.J. (ed) *Basic Concepts of Intercultural Communication: Selected Readings* (pp. 1–34). Yarmouth, ME: Intercultural Press.
Bhabha, H. K. (1994) *The Location of Culture*. London: Routledge.
Byram, M. (1997) *Teaching and Assessing Intercultural Communicative Competence*. Clevedon: Multilingual Matters.
Byram, M. (2001) Language teaching as a political action. In Bax, M. and Zwart, J. (eds) *Reflections on Language and Language Learning: In Honour of Arthur van Essen* (pp. 91–104). Amsterdam, The Netherlands and Philadelphia, PA: John Benjamins Publishing Company.
Byram, M. (2009) Intercultural competence in foreign languages: The intercultural speaker and the pedagogy of foreign language education. In Deardorff, D. (ed) *The SAGE Handbook of Intercultural Competence* (pp. 321–332). Thousand Oaks, CA: Sage Publications, Inc.
Byram, M. (2011) Researching the didactics of intercultural competence. In Blanchet, P. and Chardenet, P. (eds) *Guide de recherche en didactique des langues: Une approche contextualisée* (pp. 253–260). Paris: Editions AUF/EAC.
Byram, M. (2012) Conceptualizing intercultural (communicative) competence and intercultural citizenship. In Jackson, J. (ed) *Routledge Handbook of Language and Intercultural Communication* (pp. 85–97). Abingdon, UK: Routledge.
Byram, M., Gribkova, B. and Starkey, H. (2002) *Developing the Intercultural Dimension in Language Teaching*. Strasbourg: Council of Europe, Language Policy Division.
Byram, M. and Morgan, C. (1994) *Teaching-and-Learning Language-and-Culture*. Clevedon: Multilingual Matters.
Byrnes, H. (2008) Articulating a foreign language sequence through content: A look at the culture standards. *Language Teaching* 41, 103–118.
Carmichael, L., Hogan, H. P. and Walter, A. (1932) An experimental study of the effect of language on visually perceived form. *Journal of Experimental Psychology* 15, 73–86.
Clarke, M.A., Losoff, A., Dickenson McCracken, M. and Rood, D. (1984) Linguistic relativity and sex/gender studies: Epistemological and methodological considerations. *Language Learning* 34, 47–67.
Cordier, R. W. (1946) Cultural understanding through social education. *Journal of Educational Sociology* 19(6), 359–364.
Deardorff, D. (2009) Synthesizing conceptualizations of intercultural competence: A summary and emerging themes. In Deardorff, D. (ed) *The SAGE Handbook of Intercultural Competence* (pp. 264–270). Thousand Oaks, CA: Sage Publications, Inc.
Deveney, B. (2007) How well-prepared do international school teachers believe themselves to be for teaching in culturally diverse classrooms. *Journal of Research in International Education* 6, 309–332.
García Canclini, N. (2006) *Diferentes, Desiguales y Desconectados. Mapas de la interculturalidad*. Barcelona: Ed. Gedisa.
Garner, P. (2008) The challenge of teaching for diversity in the college classroom when the professor is the 'other'. *Teaching in Higher Education* 13, 117–120.
Genetsch, M. (2007) *The Texture of Identity*. Toronto: TSAR Publications.
Goddard, C. and Wierzbicka, A. (eds) (1994) *Semantic and Lexical Universals. Theory and Empirical Findings*. Amsterdam: John Benjamins Publishing Company.
Hagood, M. and Skinner, E. (2012) Appreciating plurality through conversations among literacy stakeholders. *Journal of Adolescent & Adult Literacy* 56, 4–6.

Handsfield, L., Dean, T. and Cielocha, K. (2009) Becoming critical consumers and producers of text: Teaching literacy with Web 1.0 and Web 2.0. *The Reading Teacher* 63, 40–50.

Kramsch, C. (1993) *Context and Culture in Language Teaching*. Oxford: Oxford University Press.

Kramsch, C. (1995) The cultural component of language teaching. *Language, Culture, and Curriculum* 8, 83–92.

Kramsch, C. (1998) *Language and Culture*. Oxford: Oxford University Press.

Kramsch, C. (2003) The privilege of the nonnative speaker. In *The Sociolinguistics of Foreign-Language Classrooms: Contributions of the Native, the Near-Native, and the Non-Native Speaker. Issues in Language Program Direction*, A Series of Annual Volumes, pp. 251–262. ERIC Document ED481796.

Kramsch, C., Cain, A. and Murphy-Lejeune, E. (1996) Why should language teachers teach culture? *Language, Culture, and Curriculum* 9, 99–107.

Kramsch, C. and Whiteside, A. (2008) Language ecology in multilingual settings: Towards a theory of symbolic competence. *Applied Linguistics* 29(4), 645–671.

Lehrer, A. (1974) *Semantic Fields and Lexical Structure*. Amsterdam: Noth-Holland Publishing Company.

Loftus, E. (1979) *Eyewitness Testimony*. Cambridge, MA: Harvard University Press.

Palfreyman, D. (2005) Othering in an English language program. *TESOL Quarterly* 39, 211–234.

Ridgeway, C. (2006) Linking social structure and interpersonal behavior: A theoretical perspective on cultural schemas and social relations. *Social Psychology Quarterly* 69(1), 5–16.

Rollin, H. (2006) Intercultural competence for students of Spanish: Can we teach it? Can we afford not to teach it? *Language Learning Journal* 34, 55–61.

Rosaldo, R. (1993) *Culture and Truth. The Remaking of Social Analysis*. Boston: Beacon Press.

Salzmann, A. (1993) *Language, Culture, and Society: An Introduction to Linguistic Anthropology*. Oxford: Westview Press.

Sapir, E. (1963) *Language*. London: Rupert Hart-Davis.

Scarano, M. (2002) Leer/escribir/pensar la diversidad cultural latinoamericana desde la Argentina. *Anclajes* 6(6), 155–172.

Sharifian, F., Rochecouste, J. and Malcolm, G. (2004) 'But it was all a bit confusing. . .': Comprehending Aboriginal English texts. *Language, Culture and Curriculum* 17, 203–228.

Smith-Maddox, R. (1998) Defining culture as a dimension of academic achievement: Implications for culturally responsive curriculum, instruction, and assessment. *The Journal of Negro Education* 67(3), 302–317.

Steffensen, M., Joag-Dev, C. and Anderson, R. (1979) A cross-cultural perspective on reading comprehension. *Reading Research Quarterly* XV, 10–29.

Trujillo Sáez, F. (2005) En torno a la interculturalidad: Reflexiones sobre cultura y comunicación para la didáctica de la lengua. *Porta Linguarum* 4, 23–39.

Whorf, B. (1956) *Language, Thought and Reality: Selected Writings of Benjamin Lee Whorf*. Edited by John B. Carroll. Cambridge, MA: The M.I.T. Press.

Wierzbicka, A. (1986) Does language reflect culture? Evidence from Australian English. *Language in Society* 15(3), 349–373.

Wierzbicka, A. (1992) *Semantics, Culture and Cognition: Universal Human Concepts in Culture-Specific Configurations*. Oxford: Oxford University Press.

3 Using the *Model of Cultural Understanding* in Text Selection and Analysis

In this chapter we show how the *Model of Cultural Understanding* can be used to select, design or develop reading materials. To do this, we take the fragments from *Mi planta de naranja-lima*, *Cat's Eye* and *Desert Wife* and analyse them in terms of the levels in the model. The analysis shows the ways in which a text can be seen to illustrate the different levels in the model, and the kind of reflection and critical perspective that can be expected from student readers. This can then inform how teachers choose texts for reading.

The approach taken is illustrative and users of the model need to be sensitive to a number of factors. First, the 'meaning' of texts is complex and as Widdowson (2011, personal communication) says of the texts we use here:

> [literary texts] also tend to be thematically complex, so although each of the three dealt with here can be said to be 'about' Christmas, this may be of relative minor thematic significance. For this, and other reasons, literary texts are of their nature subject to variable and unregulated interpretation: what is significant for one reader may be very different from what is significant for another, depending (. . .) on a range of individual and social associations.

We shall return to this below. Second, there is no such thing as 'the reader' in an absolute sense and the user of the model needs to think in advance about which reader they have in mind in analysing a text. Allington and Swann (2009) and Jeffries (2001) highlight the importance of engaging in analyses of understanding by actual readers, as we do in this book. So this chapter is a starting point, and in the chapters that follow we will illustrate the multiple, simultaneous and complex readings that a single text can open up. Finally, it is important to note that our *Model of Cultural Understanding* is best used to capture how any text, short or long, operates at different levels simultaneously.

The Text Fragments

The fragments appear in Appendix I and are line-numbered. We begin with a brief summary of each before working with the model.

The novel *Mi planta de naranja-lima* by José Mauro de Vasconcelos narrates the experiences of the protagonist, Zezé, a five-year-old child who suffers due to extreme social and family circumstances. The story is set in San Pablo, Brazil, in the 1920s and 1930s and reflects the author's disturbing experiences during his childhood (Barroso, 1978). Zezé describes a Christmas celebration in the uttermost poverty in the shanty town of Bangu through his innocent but alert eyes. He describes the disappointment of the youngest members of his family because they will not receive Christmas presents, and there is no electricity and no food. The perception of inequality between the rich and the poor leads the characters to question Christianity, in particular the fairness of Jesus. The characters and their conflicts reflect a context of poverty and exclusion in which religion does not give peace or quiet. Zezé, because of his mischievous nature and the punishment he usually receives, identifies himself with Devil Child.[1] For this family, Christmas represents the death of Jesus rather than his birth. The child narrator tells us that happiness and rejoicing are for the others, for those who are well off and do not suffer deprivations; for them, God is present. For the poor, God exists but as an absence or punishment.

Cat's Eye is Margaret Atwood's seventh novel and it is considered her most autobiographical work (Aubrey, 2002; Bloom, 2000; Cooke, 1998; Flexner, 1996). It tells the story of Elaine Risley, a 50-year-old controversial painter who comes back to Toronto (where Atwood was schooled during the 1950s and the 1960s) for a retrospective of her work. Elaine struggles with disturbing memories from her childhood. An important part of the novel consists of Elaine's narration of this period of her life. In the centre of the story lies the cruelty that Elaine suffered as a child from her three friends.

The extract describes a Canadian family's Christmas celebration. As will be recalled from the previous chapter, the father of the family has invited Banerji, a student of his from India, who is alone, to share the celebration with them. Elaine is the narrator and at this point in the story she is the little girl of the house. The family sits around the table and the father sits at the head. He is compared to the Jolly Green Giant, a character that appears in publicity in the United States, particularly on a tin of vegetables of the same name. The family keeps the tradition of dining on roast turkey, to which they add a bittersweet cranberry sauce. The act of carving the turkey is a ceremony in itself, which is generally reserved for the head of the family, as in this case. In the presence of Banerji, Elaine remembers the Sunday school missionary paper with the images of Jesus sitting in a circle of children of different nationalities, from different parts of the world.

Desert Wife is based on Hilda Faunce's and her husband's experiences during four years they spent with the Navajos on the Covered Water reserve in Arizona. The story takes place at the beginning of the 20th century, but the book was first published in 1934 (Faunce, 1961: ix). Faunce came from the coast of Oregon State, a very green and wet place, completely different from the Arizona desert. She wrote letters from the reserve to her cousin Ruth Wattles that comprise the material from which the autobiographical text originates (Faunce, 1961: vii; ix).

The extract describes a Christmas celebration on a Native American reservation in the US through the eyes of the narrator, Hilda, and her husband

Ken, white Americans who work on the reservation and introduce the idea of Christmas to the inhabitants. As the Navajo and the American cultures mingle in the celebration, the cultural clash brings out many differences. Hilda is confronted by the different cultural codes of the Navajos, which create nostalgia and homesickness in her.

All three fragments contain key words that activate the Christmas schema and the Catholic church traditions. In *Mi planta de naranja-lima* some examples are: Christmas Eve dinner ("*cena de nochebuena*"), Santa Claus ("*Papá Noel*"), Jesus Child ("*Niño Jesús*"), He ("*Él*"), Father ("*Padre*"), Catechism ("*Catecismo*"), Devil ("*Diablo*"), angel ("*ángel*"), the birth of Jesus Child ("*nacimiento del Niño Jesús*"), Christmas Eve Mass ("*Misa de Gallo*"), God ("*Dios*"), miracle ("*milagro*"), new presents ("*regalos nuevos*") and church bell ("*campana de la Iglesia*"). Religious beliefs and practices are present throughout the fragment as characters mention the birth of Jesus, Christmas Eve Mass, Santa Claus, catechism, and the strong religious atmosphere implies that the family members are practising Catholics. Examples of words that activate the Christmas schema in *Cat's Eye* are "Christmas dinner" (lines 1, 4), "turkey" (l.11), "slices of dark and light" (l.28–29), "cranberry juice" (l.23), "cranberry sauce" (l.29–30), "Jello salad" (l.10–11) and "sit around the table" (l.1) for the Christmas meal, etc. In the first paragraph, the word "Christmas" is repeated three times. In *Desert Wife*, the title itself, in Navajo, "Kismas" (lines 4, 6, 34), activates the Christmas schema together with other instances such as "Christmas fires" (l.46) and "dancing" (l.55).

Analysing the Texts With the *Model of Cultural Understanding*

As explained in the previous chapter, the model, reproduced here for convenience, describes the ways in which readers approach cultural issues during reading and can be used to capture cultural understanding as a fluid process in a continuum of cultural familiarity and unfamiliarity. The model can be represented schematically as follows:

> Level 0. Erratic perception or omission of cultural aspects.
> Level 1. Perception/identification of cultural differences. Access to levels 2, 3, 4 and 5.
> Level 2. Identification of own values and ideas. Identification of the cultural assumptions behind one's own culture (insider perspective).
> Level 3. Perception of the cultural C2 from one's own frame of reference (C1) (outsider perspective). Stereotyped views of the cultural C2.
> Level 4. Perception of the cultural C2 from the frame of reference of members of culture C2 (insider perspective).
> Level 5. Perception of the cultural C1 from the perspective of the cultural C2 (outsider perspective).

38 *Using the* Model of Cultural Understanding

We now take each level and show how it can depict layers of potential comprehension of each text.

Level 0. Erratic Perception or Omission of Cultural Aspects

At this level readers may fail to perceive cultural aspects of a text, which leads to their omission, or they may perceive them erratically, either accepting or rejecting them. We identify these aspects in the next level.

Level 1. Perception/Identification of Cultural Differences.
Access to Levels 2, 3, 4 and 5

This level involves the perception of cultural differences, with identification of the different, or in some way striking, elements of a given culture. The perception of cultural differences through comparison, confrontation and contrast works as a bridge to the other stages in the model (levels 2, 3, 4 and 5). It is accessed through the identification of key vocabulary, words or phrases.

Interest in reading material often depends, *inter alia*, on its degree of surprise or novelty. Wade, Buxton and Kelly (1999) have argued that readers will be interested in material that they consider novel or abnormal; a completely familiar and predictable text will not catch the reader's attention. The effort to comprehend begins in this way, i.e., when a reader finds something that s/he considers weird, provoking, troubling or unsettling. Whatever amazes, surprises and/or challenges our schematic expectations and preconceptions will make us think. These feelings invite readers to dig deeper toward alternative, more profound ways of knowing and understanding. Bernhardt (1991) has suggested that, in general, readers tend to remember specific events when these events constitute exceptions to their rules or when they have a powerful or dramatic emotional meaning.

The three texts offer different views of Christmas, set in diverse contexts, and avoid total familiarity, transparency and predictability. The text in Spanish from *Mi planta de naranja-lima* portrays a Christmas celebration which is incongruent with a typical one in the sociocultural context of the readers in the research project. This fragment presents another view of the celebration: an extremely sad and poor ritual, with a religious component that challenges mainstream Catholic conceptions and views in Argentina (for instance, the questioning of the fairness of Jesus). In Atwood's text, the novelty is materialised mainly in the presence of a foreigner in the celebration together with the rich cultural details in relation to the food, the Christmas customs, the contrasts between the Canadian and Hindu cultures, and in the anecdotes referring to the manipulation of nature (turkey with four drumsticks, square tomatoes, chickens without feathers and cats without fur, etc.), among others. Finally, the variety and multiplicity of attractive episodes and elements in the Navajo text (dancing, wrestling, racing, cooking, dress, fires, music, etc.) portray a vivid and unusual world.

The perception of cultural differences, which occurs through the identification of key vocabulary and processes of comparison, confrontation and contrast, is a characteristic of level 1 in the model. The connection between key vocabulary and culture is close (Goddard and Wierzbicka, 1994; Kramsch, 2007; Wierzbicka, 1992, 1986) because

> some key words are particularly heavily connoted and reveal shared meanings of another society.
>
> (Alred and Byram, 2002: 342)

Explicit vocabulary referring to culturally specific phenomena might attract a reader's attention for a variety of reasons. A first step thus involves the identification of these elements as distinct from the reader's own realities. In *Mi planta de naranja-lima*, examples for Argentinean readers might include:

> *Rabanada mojada en vino; comida escasa; regalo viejo y usado; sin regalos nuevos de Papá Noel; nacimiento del Niño Diablo; velorio del Niño Jesús; Misa de Gallo; tío Edmundo pone dinero para la comida; tristeza de la cena; cenar en silencio; no esperar regalos para no decepcionarse; poner las zapatillas del otro lado de la puerta.*
>
> *Rabanada soaked in wine; scant food; an old and used present; without new presents from Santa Claus; birth of Devil Child; funeral of Baby Jesus; Christmas Eve Mass; uncle Edmundo gives money for the food; sadness of the dinner; eat in silence; not expect presents in order not to be disappointed; place the trainers on the other side of the door.*

The Portuguese word 'rabanada' refers to a slice of bread soaked first in milk and then in egg which is then fried; sometimes, after being fried, it is covered with syrup; it can also be soaked in wine rather than milk. In addition to some proper names that are quite common in the Argentinean setting (*Luis, Gloria, Lalá*), other names are specific to the Brazilian setting such as *Casino Bangu* (l.9) and terms of endearment (hypocorisms) like *Totoca, Zezé* (Beristain, 1995). In Portuguese, unlike Spanish, hypocorisms are based on processes of reduction (Luis-Lu), duplication (José-Zezé) or derivation (Antonio-Totoca).

In *Cat's Eye*, names, words and expressions with specific cultural connotations such as the Jolly Green Giant and the different food (the Jello salad, the cranberry juice, the turkey with bittersweet cranberry sauce, the sliced turkey—rather than in pieces—and the wine for the adults) might well attract attention from an Argentinean reader, as might some others in this list of ideas in the text:

> *Jello salad; Jolly Green Giant; enormous turkey; cranberry sauce; cranberry juice; variety and abundance of food; Sunday school; Sunday school missionary paper; Banerji as a strange creature; Elaine as a*

strange creature; family's hospitality; square tomatoes; turkeys with four drumsticks; chicken without feathers; cats without fur; classification of people (tame-wild); snakes as topic of conversation; turkey as topic of conversation; the turkey's stupidity; anecdote of drowned turkeys; Banerji's appearance.

Some foreign language words, for example from Latin ("*Meleagris gallopavo,*" 1.57), are likely to attract attention as culturally different. In addition, conceptual difficulties are likely to be found with such references like Sunday school, the Sunday school missionary paper, the oddities (square tomatoes, turkey with four drumsticks, etc.), the religious perspective and the voice like the BBC News. This reflects level 1 in the *Model of Cultural Understanding*.

Furthermore, these cultural phenomena and differences are perceived and identified from Elaine's perspective. Elaine mentions that in India, Christmas is not celebrated; there are no turkeys, there is no snow. She attempts to discover and analyse some aspects of Banerji's cultural background in order to make familiar what is strange for her. Cultures which are extremely divergent, such as Banerji's, may seem so exotic for people who do not belong that all aspects of daily life seem strange (Rosaldo, 1993). Social descriptions of divergent cultures require, from those who make them (in this case Elaine), a focus on familiarisation, so as to be able to make them emerge as distinct in their differences but at the same time recognisable as human in their similarities (Rosaldo, 1993). These processes are also associated with level 1 in the model.

In *Desert Wife* difference and strangeness is present directly and explicitly through the clear identification of cultural contrasts between the Navajos and the narrator, Hilda. This text includes several events that are described in detail through specific vocabulary and are consequently also relevant at level 1, such as the fact that this is a community celebration with 200 Navajos (the reader learns who is present and how they are related), the description of how Hilda and Ken cut wood and give it to the Navajos, the description of the dances, wrestling, coffee-making, dishwashing, etc. The elements in the following list might attract the attention of an Argentinean reader:

Desert landscape; Navajo dressed in their best clothes; 200 Navajos present; a community celebration; piñon smoke from Christmas fires; Native Americans stroll with raw beefsteaks; provision of wood by Hilda and Ken; dances and music for amusement; handmade musical instruments; wrestling and racing; early rising habits on Christmas; Navajos as efficient and ingenious; family groups eat together; Navajos eat and eat; candy bags; dishwashing; bread making description; stew preparation; coffee-making description.

In this case the reader's attention is drawn to the culturally different through Hilda's eyes. She mentions that the Navajos dress up for the occasion. There is a display of fashionable elements ("Everybody was dressed in his best: beads, bracelets and silver belts glistened against the bright-colored velvet shirts and glossy sateen skirts, with miles and miles of flounces", lines 16–19). She also points out the celebration size (200 people) and some other specific details. For example, women and children arrive in wagons and men and young people on horses; it is a community celebration (sons, daughters, grandchildren, husbands, wives, friends, relatives). As regards food, the narrator highlights the raw steaks, the fruit cake baked in the wood stove, the homemade bread, the meat roasted in big tubs with onions and potatoes, the flour to thicken the gravy, the salt, pepper and chilli. As regards dancing, the description of the music is important (clay water jar with water in it and rattles made of paper bags with beans in them). Hilda feels attracted by the fact that the dance is meant to be funny rather than solemn or ceremonial.

The cultural aspects of the fragment thus become evident in the vivid descriptions of places, characters and events. For instance, there is a colourful description of clothes (pearls, bracelets, silver belts, velvet shirts of brilliant colours, sateen skirts with flounces); a detailed description of the place (the hills, the wild reserve, big and small Christmas camp fires all along the area, full moon light, brilliant light that illuminates the landscape); and a detailed description of specific events (e.g., the dancing; the instruments such as the rattles made of paper bags with beans in them, or the clay water jar with water in it; wrestling and races). This is accompanied by auditory images (Indians yelling, songs, music, rattles, chattering teeth, loud sighs, Lady Betty growling) as well as olfactory images (pine tree smell and box boards burning on the fires).

So far we have referred to cultural phenomena that are explicitly mentioned in the texts. There exist however other cultural references that are implicit and are also associated with level 1 in the model. They emerge through the use of negative statements. For instance, in *Mi planta de naranja-lima*, the characters use denials to foreground aspects of the cultural reality that contradict their own ideas, expectations and suppositions about Christmas. Similarly, Argentinean readers might expect presents (rather than their absence), a religious spirit (rather than its questioning) as well as a festive spirit with happiness, hugs and eating (rather than silence, sadness and hunger).

Some examples are: "I am not going to get anything" ("*no voy a recibir nada*", l.14); "I dearly wish I didn't have the Devil inside" ("*querría tanto no tenerlo [el Diablo en la sangre]*", l.20–21); "I don't expect anything" ("*no espero nada*", l.27); "not even Jesus is as good as everybody says" ("*ni siquiera el Niño Jesús es eso tan bueno que todo el mundo dice*", l.28); "you didn't deserve a gift" ("*no merecías un regalo*", l.35); "And why isn't Baby Jesus good to us?" ("*¿Y por qué el Niño Jesús no es bueno con nosotros?*", l.55), "let's not talk about this anymore" ("*no hablemos más de eso*", l.62); "He didn't want to talk anymore" ("*no quiso conversar más*", l.64); "nobody talked to anybody else" ("*nadie hablaba con nadie*", l.71); "without saying goodbye or wishing Merry Christmas" ("*sin decir hasta luego ni desear felicidades*", l.74); "Nobody hugged or wanted to say something good" ("*nadie se abrazó ni quiso decir algo bueno*", l.82), "the little king . . . He was happy but we were not" ("*el reyecito . . . Sí era feliz [pero nosotros no]*", l.104–105); "I couldn't swallow anything" ("*no me dejaba pasar nada*", l.115–116), etc.

In *Cat's Eye*, examples of implicit cultural references include the family structure (a strong paternal figure: the father sits at the head of the table, he slices the turkey, the mother serves); hospitality as a value (even though it is a family celebration, they welcome Banerji in their house because he is alone and comes from another country); Christmas as a family celebration (discomfort due to the presence of a stranger); and the inappropriateness of certain topics of conversation at the table, for example about snakes (but it is accepted in order to help Banerji feel comfortable in the celebration, which in turn leads to the idea of hospitality).

As in the previous text, some of the implicit cultural aspects emerge through the use of negative statements. Elaine, Banerji, the father and the mother all make negative statements: [Banerji] "doesn't have a costume"; "he seems so unlike one" [a man]; "He has no idea"; "who's never seen snow before" (l.3–4); "they don't even have Christmas in his country" (l.5–6); "They care nothing for flavor" (l.94). Such statements reveal the assumptions of the speakers about the cultural reality they are speaking of, and it requires an effort on the part of the reader to make those assumptions explicit and consider their truth or otherwise.

Not all the elements of difference and/or strangeness appear explicitly in *Desert Wife* either. The use of implicit cultural information is important. In the family and social structure of the natives, the man is the head of the family and is in contact with horses. Polygamy is present (Little Bidoni has three wives). Women are sweet and speak softly and they do house chores (they cook, make bread, place stones about the cooking fires to set tubs with meat on, wash the dishes). There is also a hierarchical relationship revealed, for example, in the respect towards the eldest: the eldest are the best dancers as opposed to the young ones who know neither the dances nor the songs. An important issue is that through the narrator's feeling of discomfort about the Navajos, because they are all around, different conceptions of privacy in the two cultures are revealed.

Level 2. Identification of Own Values and Ideas. Identification of the Cultural Assumptions Behind One's Own Culture (Insider Perspective)

Comprehending the cultural C1 from an insider perspective means analysing one's behaviours, values, ideas, etc. in the light of one's cultural norms. Texts which include this level of insight, for example on the part of the characters, are challenging for the reader because they require the same process of analysis and because observing one's cultural reality is not easy. The use of the model is first to identify elements of a text which reach this level of analysis within the text itself about the cultural C2 and which therefore have the potential to stimulate reflection by readers about the cultural C1.

In *Mi planta de naranja-lima*, Zezé's profound reflections on the meaning of Christmas, and religion in general, is evidence of this level. The family's poverty leads to the religious questioning mentioned before, and the character's criticality and reflexivity in this respect represents a true insider perspective.

In the case of *Cat's Eye*, the text presents an insider perspective because Elaine is a participant, and not only an observer, in the Christmas celebration. At the same time, this is a limitation because the reader only has access to Elaine's vision, feelings and motivations through her own eyes, with the restrictions that this vision brings out. For example, the values, ideas and assumptions behind the Canadian culture, which represent level 2 in the model, come to the surface through the explicit mention of different aspects such as the variety and abundance of food for the Christmas dinner (the father eats up all his food and serves himself some more) and the association of Christmas with the snow typical of this time of the year.

The final part of the fragment from *Desert Wife* introduces the native Robert greeting Hilda in English rather than in Navajo, and this triggers a set of emotions in the narrator, who longs for her culture and her home away from the desert. The Christmas celebration with the Navajos, with the permanent comparing and contrasting between the natives' culture and the narrator's (manifested thoroughly and repeatedly in the text through various means, including the use of negative statements that make Hilda's own cultural assumptions explicit), closes with this greeting which makes Hilda reflect upon her own cultural background (level 2) and long for it.

Level 3. Perception of the Cultural C2 from One's Own Frame of Reference (C1) (Outsider Perspective). Stereotyped Views of the Cultural C2

This level involves comprehending the cultural C2 from an outsider perspective and requires becoming aware of how the behaviours, values and ideas of others are interpreted from the perspective of one's own cultural frame of reference (an observer perspective). Texts in which this level is present have the potential to lead readers to such insights and perspectives.

In *Mi planta de naranja-lima*, Zezé perceives the rich families mentioned in the text (Faulhaber, Villas-Boas, Adaucto Luz) from the perspective of everything that he and his family lack: a decent house, a decent meal at Christmas, light, fireworks, presents, nice clothes for the Christmas dinner, happiness.

The fragment from *Cat's Eye* offers an external perspective on Banerji's Indian culture, to which the reader has access through Elaine's vision. Banerji is marginalised in the family's celebration from the very first line, not taking part thoroughly: the inclusive "we" opposes the "he" of "young man" ("We sit around the table, eating our Christmas dinner. There's a student of my father's, a young man from India who's here to study insects and who's never seen snow before", lines 1–4). Elaine shows surprise, disbelief and attraction towards what is 'odd'. Banerji appears alien, not human, a strange creature since Elaine portrays him as part of the missionary paper depiction: Banerji appears as a postcard of the evangelized, with dark skin. This description is stereotyped and reveals Elaine's conception of her own culture as normal, and her difficulty in perceiving other cultures simply as different and not as inferior. Why should Banerji know the snow, for example? The snow represents normality for Elaine, a normality which Banerji does not understand. The underestimation of Banerji and his Indian culture is also shown in expressions such as "they don't *even* have Christmas" (1.6, emphasis added).

Elaine's vision of Banerji's foreign culture is also revealed through the use of negative statements, which indicate Elaine's prejudices and stereotypes, a characteristic of level 3 in the model. In India Christmas is not celebrated, there are no turkeys or snow. Banerji does not eat, speaks very little, there is silence. Banerji's voice sounds like the BBC News, that is, his English sounds unreal, bearing little resemblance to American English.

The prototypical aspects of a Christmas celebration in the Canadian context appear through Elaine's eyes as natural. How could all this be otherwise? This culture seems so natural for its members (in this case, Elaine and her family) that its common sense appears to be universal and part of human nature (Rosaldo, 1993). A stereotyped perspective and the naturalisation of one's cultural norms as universal are characteristic of level 3 in the model.

The use of negative statements is also present in *Desert Wife* in Hilda's and Ken's perceptions of the Navajos' culture, and reveals their preconceptions and stereotypes about such culture. For example, the appropriation or translation of the celebration by the Navajos is not solemn or cold (as Hilda and Ken believed) ("There was *nothing* cold or solemn about the gathering", l.77, emphasis added); coffee is not flavoured with cedar ("I was sure the whole dinner would be flavored with cedar, *but it wasn't*", lines 130–131, emphasis added).

Furthermore, the reference to novelty in "everything else was novel enough to make history" (lines 7–8) suggests that Hilda and Ken do not consider the Navajos' cultural practices similar to theirs. Hilda is surprised at certain Navajos' behaviours, such as the fact that women are efficient at baking bread ("By eleven o'clock Mrs. White Hat and Mrs. Japon began making bread and *the efficient way they went about it was a lesson to me*", lines 106–108, emphasis added); at peeling potatoes and onions ("Other women set to peeling onions and potatoes, and *very handy they were at it too*", lines 132–133, emphasis added); and that they have an ingenious way of preparing coffee. She is also surprised by the revelation of the Navajo women as hard workers (when cooking bread and meat). The view of the Navajos as clever and intelligent also attracts her attention (shown in the way they build the coffee pot with wood and the tubs to cook meat, etc.). A condescending tone towards the Indians' culture is also present on occasions. For instance, the change of the verb "beat" for "play" in "The music was made on a clay water jar with water in it and a rawhide stretched over the top. One fellow played this, or beat it" (lines 61–63) may suggest that their actions, in Hilda's view, do not deserve to be called music.

In short, the narrator perceives and judges behaviours of the Navajos from the perspective of the normality of her own culture (level 3). The comparison of the Navajos' yells to the Comanches' and pirates' is an example. Both Hilda and Ken feel uncomfortable with certain attitudes of the Navajos which are considered disrespectful or inconsiderate (for example, the proximity of the camp fires to their store, the burning of box boards on the fires, the lack of initiative to wash the dishes). Even though Hilda and Ken have lived in the reserve for a year, they do not belong to the Navajos' culture and act as observers. In other words, many times they are not able to express the motivations and values that would have helped them to explain certain of the natives' attitudes and deeds. What Hilda is unable to see is the motivation for the Indians' actions, which originate in their extreme poverty and hunger and which make them resistant and strong enough to live under such hostile circumstances in the middle of the desert.

Finally, stereotyping can be observed in the word *heathen*, in the fact that the Navajo women are treated as if they are unwilling to collaborate with the tasks, as well as in the cheating nature attributed by the narrator to the mothers when they induce their children to get more candy. The lexical choice 'heathen' has a strong symbolically loaded connotative value. From this position, the asymmetrical and commercial nature of the relations between the whites and the natives is naturalised, and features and manners of behaving, which are the product of history and subjection, are seen from Hilda's perspective as essence. The description of the relations in that peculiar community, the reserve, is naturalised by a narrator who is unable to fully understand the causality in the Navajos' behaviour. If they had not eaten a proper meal for a month, perhaps that is the reason why they agree to celebrate Christmas ("Some of the *heathen*, I know, *had not had a square meal for a month*", lines 150–151, emphasis added). If they suffer from scarcity of food, that is perhaps the reason why the children try to get a double ration ("Investigation revealed Mrs. Little Crank and a score of other mothers standing around the corner of the store, putting bags of candy into their blankets and sending the children back to stand in line for another. *There was a sort of appreciation in the Navajo, but it was the sort that wanted all they could get from anyone who wasn't looking*", lines 160–166, emphasis added). If they are guests, it is not to be expected from their perspective that they wash up ("They were willing enough to do it, though *they would have gone away and left everything dirty*, if I had not suggested the dishwashing. *I thought it best they do some little thing for their meal*", lines 154–157, emphasis added). In the reserve, there cannot be reciprocity in the nature of the relationships because they are imposed by the government and by the transactional and commercial nature of the relationship between Hilda, her husband and the Indians. It is from this positioning that what happens during the celebration is labeled as picturesque, exotic, ludicrous or outrageous.

Level 4. Perception of the Cultural C2 From the Frame of Reference of Members of Culture C2 (Insider Perspective)

This level involves the comprehension within the text of the cultural C2 from an insider perspective. How the members of another culture behave and what values they have are interpreted in the light of their own cultural norms. Where such a dimension is present in the text, there is potential for the reader to take the perspective and gain an insider understanding themselves, and perhaps also understand the significance of doing this in general.

In *Cat's Eye*, the family attempts to get closer to, and understand, Banerji's cultural reality from an insider perspective. First there are the processes of making the Other feel welcome. The topics of conversation at the Christmas table are modified, in relation to the Indian culture, and the characters talk about there being no turkeys in India and about there being poisonous snakes. Banerji also makes steps towards mutual understanding. In the social sphere, the family dominates discourse whereas he just answers the family's questions, without initiating discourse, but as regards biology and the scientific world, Banerji takes a more active role in the conversation and feels more at ease. He expands his contributions to small comments, he makes questions to show interest ("Indeed, sir?", 1. 83), and he makes some evaluative comments ("fooling with Nature", 1.99).

Elaine, the first-person narrator, compares herself with Banerji in the sense that she feels alien too ("Nevertheless I can hardly believe he's a man, he seems so unlike one. *He's a creature more like myself: alien and apprehensive*", lines 42–43, emphasis added). The processes of comparing and contrasting characteristic of level 1 in the model are also observed here. Both Elaine and Banerji are the Other. At the same time, while we referred to Elaine's prejudices and stereotypes before ("There's a student of my father's, a young man from India . . . *who's never seen snow before*", lines 1–4; "they don't *even* have Christmas", 1.6—emphasis added in both cases), characteristic of level 3 in the model, the text shows that Elaine fluctuates; she belongs to one group but identifies herself with the Other. These shifts in perception and this decentring are characteristics of levels 4 and 5.

Furthermore, in addition to the skills of observing, describing, analysing, comparing and contrasting, perspective-taking and decentring that we have just referred to, it is possible to observe other skills here such as critical thinking and reflexivity, which are also involved in cultural understanding and are characteristic of levels 4 and 5 in the model. For instance, Elaine tells the reader that she has developed a capacity to sniff unhappiness. She knows that Banerji is miserable. Even though she is a child, this narrator has the sensitivity and the discernment to be able to uncover veils (levels 4 and 5 in the model).

At other moments, Elaine becomes an observer at a great distance from the observed Other, Banerji; she becomes a non-participant spectator. This critical distancing (or decentring) is a necessary step in approaching the cultural, associated with levels 4 and 5 in the model. However, Elaine misses the point that Banerji may not feel lonely at all at Christmas simply because Christmas is not celebrated in his context. In this sense, she is not able to access a conception of the emotions experienced by Banerji in this context through Banerji's own world. In other words, she is not able to look at Banerji's reality from his own frame of mind, which is what level 4 in the model means.

In *Desert Wife*, the implicit and sometimes explicit contrast between the Navajos and the white couple traverses the whole narrative. It is present in the way they make food, in the ingredients, in the utensils used, in the furniture, in the way they sit and in many other examples. We have already referred to this as evidence of level 1 in the model. At some moments, the contrast between the visitors and those being visited is similar to a travel book which tries to attract the reader's attention to strangeness by emphasising the different elements of the place and of the people being visited, in order to arouse interest in those who remain at home.

Hilda describes the customs "of the others" as an outsider (level 3 in the model), and there is little in the text that can be easily associated with level 4 in the model. Hilda does not try to understand the feelings she attributes to the Indians. Why would the Indians feel in such a way? For example, there is no understanding of the reason why the Navajos feel outraged when Hilda's husband Ken makes them extinguish the campfires. The reader does not know if there is a ritual or a belief that motivates the feeling of outrage.

Thus, the way in which this narrator records these people's perceptions does not follow an ethnographic method. Although Hilda describes, analyses and records what attracts her attention about the Navajos, she does little to understand their meaning, purpose and intention. There is participant observation only on the surface. There is no real interest in Hilda to discover the hidden meaning, to discover why they do things the way they do them and what the meaning of things are for them. The meaning of such things derives from the social interaction that one has with others, but she makes no attempt to explain, capture or understand the motivations that the Indians give to their actions. In other words, Hilda does not go beyond the cultural preconceptions that cloud her view (level 3), and there is no attempt to understand the Navajos from their own mindset, a characteristic of level 4 in the model.

A reader who shows awareness of Hilda's positioning in his/her interpretation of this text, and who is able to discuss her positioning as we have just done here, is exercising the skills of cultural understanding involved in

48 *Using the* Model of Cultural Understanding

level 4 in the model. So identifying levels in a text, as we are doing here, is a beginning, but clearly the reader's role is then central.

Level 5. Perception of the Cultural C1 From the Perspective of the Cultural C2 (Outsider Perspective)

At this level, a text shows how the cultural C1 can be apprehended from an outsider perspective. There is awareness, for example on the part of a character in the text, of how his/her behaviour, values and ideas are seen through the eyes of members of other cultural groups. Where this happens, the reader too might gain insight into what level 5 experience consists of.

In *Cat's Eye*, Elaine sometimes analyses and questions the existence of a 'universal human nature'; this is associated with both levels 4 and 5 in the model. This analysis and questioning leads her to empathise with Banerji in the alienation that they share. At the same time, the sociocultural descriptions in the text, through Elaine's eyes as insider, involve an emphasis on defamiliarisation, that is, on the process to make strange what is familiar (Moreiras, 1991). Defamiliarising an event, such as a Christmas dinner, transforms its taken-for-granted routines and sees them from a distant position (Rosaldo, 1993). Thus, Elaine places herself at a distance from the intense emotions that a Christmas celebration may provoke.

The ability to identify one's own cultural parameters is a characteristic of level 2, but the ability to engage in processes of defamiliarisation and critical distancing is a characteristic of levels 4 and 5. Furthermore, the fact that Elaine feels alien just in the way that Banerji does allows her to consider how her own behaviour is interpreted according to other cultural parameters, in this case through Banerji's eyes. Level 5 is present here. At a formal level, there is a process of estrangement that allows a new and fresh view on something old. Elaine perceives her own cultural norms through the eyes of a foreigner, from an outsider perspective, and this facilitates the approach to a 'foreign culture', developing a critical appreciation of it. The decentralisation in relation to one's cultural codes allows individuals to become aware of their cultural relativity, since the critical reflection on one's cultural background as well as on others' contributes to relativising one's cultural assumptions and those of others.

In *Desert Wife*, the Navajo Robert approaches Hilda, wishes her Merry Christmas in English and calls her San Chee instead of Hilda. This translation of her name into Navajo triggers an estrangement in her, and she is driven to seek refuge in the known and familiar. She needs to protect herself in what is known to her. The Navajo appropriates her language and her name. By contrast, Hilda speaks the Navajo language, but her reason is utilitarian: Hilda and Ken work and trade on the reservation. The fact that the Navajo Robert uses English for civility purposes and not utilitarian ones seems to upset her. The strangeness has become nostalgia for the familiar and even rejection of everything that is "Indian" ("All day I had been too busy and excited to think, but that little attention [the greeting in English] *made me homesick for something not Indian*; and I stumbled into the store and hurried through to the living room, so Ken would not see *the tears in my eyes*", lines 175–179, emphasis added). The need to reaffirm her identity ("not Indian"), to avoid contamination is a result of the appropriation of her language and her name by the Navajo. This event is revealing of level 5, both from Hilda's perspective as well as the Navajos'.

The Model in Perspective

This chapter reflects the complexity involved in cultural understanding within a text as well as in attempts to analyse it using the model. For teachers or assessors selecting texts, the kind of analysis we have illustrated here reveals the complexity of the perspectives within a text and its potential to afford readers the opportunity to demonstrate their own levels of understanding.

The analyses also anticipate the main conclusion that we will put forward in this book, which is that cultural understanding is fluid, cannot be associated with isolated levels in any model of intercultural communication, as described for example in Spitzberg and Changnon (2009). This includes our own *Model of Cultural Understanding*, but we have above all emphasised how several levels can be observed simultaneously; this is not a matter of developmental stages such as one finds for example in Bennett (1993, 2009).

As we have seen, cultural understanding is related to the skills involved in approaching otherness, namely observing, describing, analysing, comparing and contrasting, perspective-taking, decentring, criticality and reflexivity. As we said at the beginning of the chapter, the complexity in interpreting literary texts adds further difficulty. On the other hand, a model such as the one used here is an aid in analysis because it provides criteria which users can discuss and apply in order to gain more agreement than would be possible otherwise. In practice, teachers or assessors might work together on the selection of texts as materials for teaching or assessment, analysing the different levels present in a text and coming to an agreed analysis which does however not exclude other interpretations by readers, as Widdowson said in the first quotation in this chapter. What would be important above all is that a selected text is 'rich' enough, has sufficient elements of all levels of understanding, for it to be valuable; texts which are 'poor' would be excluded. We shall see in later chapters how the potentials of the three texts analysed here helped learners to reach higher levels of understanding by critiquing the level of cultural understanding of a character in a story.

There are thus both pedagogical and research-oriented applications. In the former case, a teacher can clarify for themselves the degree of complexity and the intercultural depth of a text and how they might then bring their learners to those levels and beyond. In the second case, a researcher can establish how readers might be expected to respond to a text and use the

50 *Using the* Model of Cultural Understanding

criteria discussed and illustrated in this chapter to evaluate those they assess or who assess themselves, as we shall see in Chapter 8.

Note

1. Origin in Pastorelas: theatre representation of the birth of Jesus, the arrival of the Three Wise Men and the constant struggle between good and evil represented by angels and demons. Source: Candelaria, C., Aldama, A., García, P., and Alvarez Smith, A. (2004) *Encyclopedia of Latino Popular Culture.* Westport: Greenwood Publishing Group.

References

Allington, D. and Swann, J. (2009) Researching literary reading as social practice. *Language and Literature* 18, 219–230.
Alred, G. and Byram, M. (2002) Becoming an intercultural mediator: A longitudinal study of residence abroad. *Journal of Multilingual and Multicultural Development* 23, 339–352.
Aubrey, B. (2002) *Novels for Students.* The Gale Group. http://galenet.galegroup.com/servlet/LitRC?
Barroso, H. M. J. (1978) *Vida y saga de Jose' Mauro de Vasconcelos.* Buenos Aires: Editorial El Ateneo.
Bennett, J. M. (1993) Towards ethnorelativism: A developmental model of intercultural sensitivity. In Paige, R. (ed) *Education for the Intercultural Experience. Second Edition* (pp. 21–71). Yarmouth, ME: Intercultural Press, Inc.
Bennett, J. M. (2009) Cultivating intercultural competence: A process perspective. In Deardorff, D. (ed) *The SAGE Handbook of Intercultural Competence* (pp. 121–140). Thousand Oaks, CA: Sage Publications, Inc.
Beristain, H. (1995) *Diccionario de Retórica y Poética.* Mexico: Editorial Porrúa.
Bernhardt, E. B. (1991) *Reading Development in a Second Language.* Norwood, NJ: Ablex.
Bloom, H. (ed) (2000) *Margaret Atwood.* Modern Critical Views series, New York: Chelsea House.
Cooke, N. (1998) *Margaret Atwood: A Biography.* Toronto: E. C. W. Press.
Faunce, H. (1934) *Desert Wife.* Lincoln and London: University of Nebraska Press. Google Books. Last retrieved 6 May 2014.
Faunce, H. (1961) *Desert Wife.* Lincoln: University of Nebraska Press.
Flexner, E. (1996) *Century of Struggle: The Woman's Rights Movement in the United States.* Cambridge, MA: Belknap Press of Harvard University Press.
Goddard, C. and Wierzbicka, A. (eds) (1994) *Semantic and Lexical Universals: Theory and Empirical Findings.* Amsterdam: John Benjamins Publishing Company.
Jeffries, L. (2001) Schema affirmation and White Asparagus: Cultural multilingualism among readers of texts. *Language and Literature* 10(4), 325–343.
Kramsch, C. (2007) Classic book review. Re-reading Robert Lado, 1957. *Linguistics across cultures. Applied linguistics for language teachers. International Journal of Applied Linguistics* 17(2), 241–247.
Moreiras, A. (1991) *Interpretación y diferencia.* Madrid: Visor.
Rosaldo, R. (1993) *Culture and Truth: The Remaking of Social Analysis.* Boston: Beacon Press.

Spitzberg, B. H. and Changnon, G. (2009) Conceptualising intercultural competence. In Deardorff, D. (ed) *The Sage Handbook of Intercultural Competence* (pp. 2–52). Los Angeles: Sage.

Wade, S., Buxton, W. and Kelly, M. (1999) Using think-alouds to examine reader-text interest. *Reading Research Quarterly* 34(2), 194–216.

Widdowson (2011) Personal communication.

Wierzbicka, A. (1986) Does language reflect culture? Evidence from Australian English. *Language in Society* 15(3), 349–373.

Wierzbicka, A. (1992) *Semantics, Culture and Cognition: Universal Human Concepts in Culture-Specific Configurations*. Oxford: Oxford University Press.

4 Analysing Comprehension of Texts in Readers' First Language

In this chapter we illustrate our approach and some findings from our research with the text in the native language, Spanish, to show that the approach is relevant to the researcher and teacher of reading in a native as well as foreign language context. In the research project, we used a text in Spanish to take the notion of a continuum of cultural schemata into account. This text presents a cultural reality relatively familiar to the participants and the native language adds to this familiarity. The fragment from *Mi planta de naranja-lima* (Vasconcelos, 1971: 39–43) is set in Brazil and shows the Christmas celebration of a lower-class family narrated from the perspective of Zezé, one of the children in the family. Many elements of a Brazilian Christmas celebration are present, such as the reference to midnight mass, church bells and fireworks. The religious component is also normal in a Christmas celebration in Argentina. Zezé describes the bewilderment of the youngest members of the family, disappointed because, unlike those of the rich families in town, they are not to receive Christmas presents. The perception of such inequality leads the characters to question some ideas inherent in Christianity such as the belief in the fairness of Jesus, but this questioning makes the text less transparent for the Argentinean readers, as it may also for some Brazilian readers, and this is important in the investigation of reading because a completely stable and predictable text would pose no challenges. At the same time, the text includes information that the participants would be able to relate to or compare with their prior knowledge and their own experiences in some way, such as the explicit contrasts of rich families/poor families, abundance of food/lack or scarcity of food, good/evil, happiness/sadness, fireworks/silence and loneliness, presents/lack of presents.

  We illustrate with data from several participants in order to gain a broad sense of how cultural understanding took place, and the use of multiple excerpts from different data types allows us to achieve depth in the analysis of the individual cases. This approach is also intended to "make sure one has adequately understood the *variation* in the phenomena of interest in the setting" (Maxwell, 2002: 53, our emphasis). The excerpts appear in Spanish first, the language in which the data were collected, and then translations into English (provided later by the participants themselves) follow for the convenience of our readers. We add clarifying information between brackets and we italicise the evidence for the argument or point we wish to make in each case. Pseudonyms and data type appear between parentheses.

Using illustrations with several participants also focuses attention on the group phenomenon, on the question of the readers being from 'the periphery' as discussed in Chapter 1; the participants are a group of 'local' readers, where local refers to their being Argentinean and therefore 'periphery' readers. This is what Bishop (1999: 143) refers to as an "intrinsic case" which seeks understanding of "people in situations anywhere—including children and youth in schools—not just people who live in remote jungles or cosy peasant villages", the cases often considered by ethnographers. At the same time it provides details regarding the idiosyncrasies of the setting and socio-cultural context, as well as of the individual, what Rosaldo calls "the gradual thickening of symbolic webs of meaning" (1993: 2).

Our approach involved student volunteers reading three short text extracts and performing a number of tasks over a period of three weeks with one text per week. There was an initial 'prior knowledge' task before seeing the texts to establish what they already knew about the cultural context and contents in each case. They underlined the difficult or confusing parts and wrote a brief explanation of such difficulties in note form in each text itself. Then they wrote an immediate reflection log ('retrospective self-observation') referring to cultural aspects of the text and the comprehension difficulties they had found. After that, they responded to each text in their native language, Spanish, in a reading response task and a visual representation, which we describe in the following chapter. Individual semi-structured interviews were conducted, one week after the reading of each text, to encourage participants to comment upon their modes of response.

Comparing and Contrasting Within Familiar Knowledge and Experiences

Our readers interpreted all three texts by explicitly resorting to something familiar, either in the form of specific knowledge or personal experiences, and engaging in processes of comparing and contrasting. They made the connections very overt and put them in writing. In the case of the extract from *Mi planta de naranja-lima*, Tess, for example, in her reflection log explicitly mentioned her strategy of comparison and contrast ("por comparación con nuestra propia cultura"; "by comparison with our own culture"). She used her knowledge of the Three Wise Men in Argentina to understand the custom mentioned in the text of placing one's shoes outside the door to receive a present. Comparing and contrasting is essential in cultural understanding and gives an important place to the concept of 'difference'. Level 1 in the *Model of Cultural Understanding* refers to the identification of cultural similarities, differences and details through processes of comparing and contrasting.

Excerpt 1

Me parece que con los elementos que da el texto y *por comparación con nuestra propia cultura* podemos inferir lo no dicho o reconstruir cómo es la celebración de la navidad que se narra. Lo no dicho sería el 'background' de información que el autor puede dar por supuesto, por considerarlo parte del conocimiento compartido con el lector.

Podemos inferir que los niños tienen que dejar sus zapatos para que le dejen los regalos. Aunque no hacemos acá lo mismo, podemos entenderlo porque tenemos esa costumbre en el día de Reyes.

(Tess, reflection log)

English Translation of Excerpt 1

I believe that, with the elements that the text provides and *by comparison with our own culture*, we can infer what is not said, or reconstruct the Christmas celebration that is described. What is not said is the 'background' information which the author wouldn't provide, considering that this is part of the knowledge that he/she shares with the reader.

We can infer that the children have to leave their shoes around to get gifts. Although we don't do the same here, we can understand this because we have that very custom on Twelfth Night.

Tess then pointed out the difficulty of understanding this custom of the shoes for people with different backgrounds, and said that she got closer to the text due to the commonalities that exist between Latin American cultures and many Catholic traditions.

Excerpt 2

Seguramente *para lectores de otros orígenes el texto resultaría mucho más difícil*. Si pensamos que hay una *historia común entre las culturas latinoamericanas y muchas tradiciones católicas comunes, lo cual nos acerca al texto y probablemente no sería así para otros pueblos*.

(Tess, reflection log)

English Translation of Excerpt 2

Surely *for readers from other origins the text would turn out to be much more difficult*. If we think that there is *a common history amongst the Latin American cultures and many common Catholic traditions, which gets us closer to the text and it is not likely to be like that for other countries*.

When we asked in the interview what she meant by the expression "readers from different origins" ("lectores de otros orígenes"), Tess engaged in a discussion of terms like *origin, culture, country* and mentioned that she had thought about people from different *cultures*, especially remote cultures. She believed that Christmas can be a point of contact among people from some different cultures because it is an extended tradition at least in America, despite differences in how it is celebrated in each case. Tess was aware that she used comparison and contrast as a strategy of comprehension ("Se puede comparar por lo menos"; "At least they are comparable").

Excerpt 3

M.: . . . culturas.
TESS: Pero bien remotas, porque *la Navidad dentro de todo me parece como algo bastante extendido, por lo menos en todo América,* entonces tiene que ser algo *bien remoto.* Por eso no sabía bien si poner 'culturas', porque *puede ser de otras culturas diferentes pero que coincidan en eso, en cómo festejan la Navidad o . . . y que lo entiendan igual, aunque no sea exactamente lo mismo.*
M.: A vos, eso ¿qué motivó este comentario, el hecho de las zapatillas?
T.: (Pausa) *Sí, por ejemplo, y que no es exactamente lo mismo cómo se dejan los regalos . . . pero la idea es más o menos la misma.*
M.: Hm.
T.: *Se puede comparar por lo menos, no es tan distinto . . .*

(Tess, interview)

English Translation of Excerpt 3

M.: . . . cultures.
T.: But really remote ones, because *Christmas all in all seems to me something that is present everywhere, at least all over America,* so it has to be somewhere *remote.* That's why I didn't know whether to write 'cultures', because *they may be from different cultures but share that, how they celebrate Christmas or . . . it may be that they understand it anyway, although it may not be exactly the same.*
M.: To you, what has motivated this comment, the part about the shoes?
T.: (Pause) *Yes, for instance, and that it is not exactly the same how the gifts are left there . . . but the idea is more or less the same.*
M.: Hmm.
T.: At least *they are comparable, it is not so different . . .*

Distancing and Stereotyping

At times this process of comparing and contrasting revealed the participants' difficulty in distancing themselves from their own positions and understanding otherness from the point of view of the Other. This difficulty in decentring led to stereotyping. For instance, Tacuara said that poor people are uneducated and tend to become criminals. Similarly, Luz said that the concept of Santa Claus is less strong in the poor precisely because of their poverty. These are stereotypical generalisations that are not based on textual information and they represent level 3 in our *Model of Cultural Understanding*.

In her reading response task, Tacuara used her existing knowledge to interpret the text, in this case her knowledge of literary devices, in particular the synecdoche. She focused on the description of the society described in the text as "backward, behind and dispossessed." Here she brought in familiar knowledge from philosophy (for instance, Hegel) and this knowledge was quite detailed, sophisticated and complex in terms of the notions presented: "según la *teoría del absoluto Hegeliano* uno puede calificar a una cultura como más o menos atrasada según el *grado de autoconciencia* alcanzado (entendiendo como autoconciencia la idea de *pensarse como ser humano libre*, y demás)"; "according to *the Hegelian absolute* we can qualify a culture as more or less backward according to the *degree of self-consciousness reached* (understanding self-consciousness as the idea of *considering ourselves as free human beings* and so on)". She then connected the heavy religious component in the text with her evaluation of this society as backward: "considerando el fuerte peso que los aspectos '*milagrosos*' y '*religiosos*' tienen en el texto, teniendo en cuenta eso es que digo '*atrasado*'"; "considering the strong weight of the '*miraculous*' and '*religious*' aspects in the text, considering all that is the reason why I say '*backward*'". Her view of the family and this society as backward and dispossessed reflects a stereotyped conception of the poor as backward, diminished or disadvantaged in their religious conceptions as well as a stereotyped link among poverty, low education and religiosity.

Excerpt 4

El texto retrata a modo de sinécdoque (La sinécdoque es una licencia retórica mediante la cual se expresa la parte por el todo) a toda una sociedad o al menos una clase de ella (clase baja). Digo 'a modo de sinécdoque' porque es a través de una situación puntual (la navidad) y de un grupo (una familia) que la historia representa a un colectivo más amplio.

Yo calificaría a la sociedad, cultura retratada como desposeída y atrasada. En cuanto a este último *adjetivo ('atrasada'), no lo uso en un sentido peyorativo*, sino más bien Hegeliano, por así decirlo. Es decir, según la teoría del absoluto Hegeliano uno puede calificar a una cultura como más o menos atrasada según el grado de autoconciencia alcanzado (entendiendo como autoconciencia la idea de pensarse como ser humano libre, y demás). Teniendo estos conceptos presentes y considerando el fuerte peso que los aspectos 'milagrosos' y 'religiosos' tienen en el texto, teniendo en cuenta eso es que digo '*atrasado*'. Por ejemplo, al final del texto Zezé se levanta de la cama y cuando le preguntan adónde va, dice: 'a poner mis zapatillas del otro lado de la puerta ... a lo mejor sucede algún milagro'. A mi juicio, tanto este fragmento, como otros que tratan de justificar la ausencia de regalos y comida atribuyendo esta carencia a la falta de bondad en la persona, esos fragmentos para mí, *muestran lo sometida que está esa cultura. Sometida y hundida en la pobreza y la ignorancia. Ignorancia no en un sentido peyorativo, sino haciendo referencia a que ignoran que si están siendo castigados terrenalmente no es ni dios ni Jesús el verdugo. Digo despojados también porque se retrata en la historia la pobreza naturalizada.*

(Tacuara, reading response task)

English Translation of Excerpt 4

In a sort of synecdoche (the synecdoche is a rhetorical figure in which a part stands for the whole), the text portrays a whole society or at least a class within it (the lower class). I say 'a sort of synecdoche' because it is through a specific situation (Christmas) and of a group (the family) that the story portrays a wider population.

I would qualify the society, the culture portrayed as dispossessed and backward. As regards this last *adjective (backward) I am not using it in a pejorative sense* but rather with its Hegelian meaning, so to speak. That is, according to the Hegelian absolute we can qualify a culture as more or less backward according to the degree of self-consciousness reached (understanding self-consciousness as the idea of considering ourselves as free human beings and so on). Having these concepts in mind and considering the strong weight of the miraculous and religious aspects in the text, considering all that is the reason why I say '*backward*'. For instance, at the end of the text Zezé gets up from bed and when asked where he is going, he says: 'To put the shoes on the other side of the door ... maybe a miracle will come.' In my opinion, this fragment as well as others which try to justify the absence of presents and food, blaming this lack on the lack of goodness of people, these fragments *show, in my view, how submissive that culture is. Submissive and sinking in poverty and ignorance. Ignorance, not in a pejorative sense, but referring to the fact that they ignore that if they are being punished in this world, the executioner is neither God nor Jesus. I also say dispossessed because the story portrays naturalized poverty.*

In the last part of her reading response task Tacuara evaluated the text. She argued that texts which equate poverty and the lack of presents with the lack of goodness in people reveal the ignorance of the cultural group in question. She referred to the whole culture as ignorant and submissive and in this way she was generalising: "*A mi juicio*, tanto este fragmento, como otros que tratan de *justificar la ausencia de regalos y comida atribuyendo esta carencia a la falta de bondad en la persona*, esos fragmentos para mí, *muestran lo sometida que está esa cultura. Sometida y hundida en la pobreza y la ignorancia"*; "*In my opinion*, this fragment as well as others which try to *justify the absence of presents and food blaming this lack to the lack of goodness of people*, these fragments *show, in my view, how submissive that culture is. Submissive and sinking in poverty and ignorance*".

The most important point about Tacuara's reading response task and interview is the stereotyped and biased view that she projected of the poor and the dispossessed as well as the intricate line of argument in support of her position toward the textual content. At the same time, Tacuara missed the point that behind the possible religious questioning in the text, the adult characters wanted to give Zezé an innocent explanation for the lack of presents, electricity, food and their pervasive poverty. Tacuara's interpretation might have differed if she had positioned herself in the shoes of one of the adult characters for a second, but she did not and instead judged textual content from her own perspective, which resulted in this stereotyped and biased interpretation. Furthermore, Zezé was indeed aware of his reality and had a critical attitude toward it (revealed precisely in his continuous questioning of that reality in his interaction with these adults), but Tacuara did not notice this. These interpretations match level 3 in the *Model of Cultural Understanding*.

Despite these characteristics of level 3, there is also a lot of reflexivity and criticality in the thinking. Tacuara described the society portrayed in the text as "backward, behind and dispossessed" but argued that she did not intend her interpretation to be taken as stereotyped. The interpretation can be judged as biased and pejorative, but Tacuara was critical of her own views. In this sense, her reading response task simultaneously shows the dynamism and flexibility in how these readers approached otherness during reading. We see in Tacuara the critical and reflexive attitude that is typical of levels 4 and 5 in our model, which led her to produce a deep and well-argued social critique, revealing her awareness of social and cultural issues. We can also observe the simultaneous presence of levels 3, 4 and 5 of the model in the following interview extract, which confirmed our analysis of the reading response.

Excerpt 5

M.: Vos decís [in the reading response task]: "Teniendo estos conceptos presentes y considerando el fuerte peso que los aspectos milagrosos y religiosos tienen en el texto, teniendo eso en cuenta es que digo atrasado. Por ejemplo, al final del texto, él se levanta de la cama y cuando le preguntan hacia dónde va dice: A poner mis zapatillas."

(Pausa) ¿Por qué hacés tanto hincapié en lo milagroso y lo religioso? ¿Lo religioso es milagroso?

T.: Sí, lo veo muy parecido y . . . es que son . . . o sea, *me parece que es un bloqueo terrible, o sea, digo, por ejemplo, el querer que . . . ese esperar que las cosas cambien por sí solas, o sea . . . que hace sujetos completamente pasivos, resignados a . . . y más . . . digo, por ejemplo en esta familia y . . . creo que está muy ligado a eso, que mientras más humildes son, eh . . . más . . . se apoyan en una contención religiosa o . . . entonces esperar que, bueno, las cosas en algún momento van a cambiar, y si no es acá en otra vida, la vida será justa . . . tener que buscar otra vida, otro plano que excede a lo terrenal porque acá . . . o sea, ya está . . . las cosas son así, el pobre es pobre y . . . y hay que lidiar con eso y . . .* me parece que hace a eso.

(. . .) *el tema de la religión yo la veo que lleva a una resignación y a . . . qué sé yo, a aceptar un montón de cosas que no tendrían que ser así pero bueno, como a uno lo excede, deja todo . . . la justicia en manos de Dios.*

M.: Entiendo. (Pausa) "A mi juicio este fragmento y otros que justifican o tratan de justificar la ausencia de regalos y comida atribuyendo esta carencia a la falta de bondad de la persona muestran lo sometida que está esa cultura." No entiendo esto.

T.: Yo creo que era . . . sí, que decía . . .

M.: Los fragmentos que intentan mostrar . . .

T.: Sí, eran fragmentos, por ejemplo . . . cuando dice: '*Yo soy bueno . . .*' *o sea, como que si uno es bueno recibe, y si uno es malo no recibe.*

M.: Eso es lo que quiere transmitir el escritor, pensás vos.

T.: Claro, sí . . . en una parte . . . No, es . . . no, lo que los pensamientos, *cómo ellos mismos creen eso.* Por ejemplo, si yo soy bueno . . . O sea, '¿Yo soy malo, que no me van a traer regalos?', viste que pregunta.

M.: Sí.

T.: Es esa cosa de decir . . .

M.: Eso refleja que estamos hablando de una cultura sometida.

T.: Claro, para mí . . . tiene otra vez que ver con esto de que 'si soy bueno Dios me premia, y me va a dar.' En ese sentido, otra vez volver a caer en lo mismo, ¿entendés? O sea, *que nunca se planteó una cuestión de 'por qué no tengo'* y ver . . . qué sé yo, cuestiones más de . . .

M.: . . . profundas.

T.: Sí, pero profundas en el sentido de . . . de concretas, también, de cómo está organizada . . .

M.: . . . de la realidad.

T.: De la realidad, de cómo está organizada, de cuáles son las consecuencias, y no caer en . . .

M.: ¿Y qué tiene que ver eso con el sometimiento?

T.: Es que . . . es otra vez lo que decíamos hace un rato, con lo que yo . . . cómo lo entendía yo, 'atrasada' y . . . como el estar . . . *estar sometidos a creencias y a . . . estar otra vez estancado en ese lugar y esperando que las cosas cambien.*

(Tacuara, interview)

English Translation of Excerpt 5

M.: You say [in the reading response task]: "Having these concepts in mind and considering the strong weight of the miraculous and religious aspects in the text, considering all that is that I say 'backward'. For instance, at the end of the text Zezé gets up from bed and when asked where he is going, he says: 'To put the shoes out.' (Pause) Why do you emphasise the miraculous and religious aspect that much? Is the religious aspect miraculous?

T.: Yes, both are very similar and . . . these are . . . It seems to me that *these two imply a terrible block . . . that is, for example . . . wanting to . . . waiting for things to change on their own . . . that makes people be completely passive, resigned . . . for example, in this family and . . . I think that it's very related to this, the poorer they are, the more they look for . . . the support of religion or . . . to expect that . . . well, things will change at some point . . . and if not here, then in another life, life will be fair . . . having to look at another life, another level beyond this world because here that's it . . . things are like that, poor people are poor and have to put up with that and . . . I think it's related to that.*

I see that religion leads to resignation and . . . to accept a lot of things that shouldn't be like that. As people feel overwhelmed by the circumstances, people leave justice in God's hands.

M.: I understand. (Pause) "In my opinion, this fragment as well as others which try to justify the absence of presents and food, blaming this lack to the lack of goodness of people, these fragments show, in my view, how submissive that culture is. Submissive and sinking in poverty and ignorance." I don't understand this.

T.: I think that it was . . . Yes, it said . . .

M.: The fragments that try to show . . .

T.: Yes, these were fragments, for instance when it says: '*I am good*', that is . . ., *if one is good one gets things, and if one is bad one doesn't get anything.*

M.: Do you think that this is what the writer tries to say?

T.: Yes, sure, partly . . . No, it is . . . the thoughts, *how they believe that.* For instance, if I am good . . . That is, 'am I bad, and so that's why I won't get any present?' You know he asks . . .

M.: Yes.

T.: It is that thing of saying . . .

M.: That reflects that we are talking about a submissive culture.

Analysing Comprehension of Texts in Readers' First Language 61

T.: Sure, to me it is related once again to this idea that if I am good, God will give me a reward and he's going to give me ... In that sense it is going back to the same, do you see what I mean? That is, *they never thought why they didn't have things* and see ... I don't know, things ...
M.: ... deeper things.
T.: Yes, but deeper things in the sense of concrete too, of how it is organised ...
M.: ... of reality.
T.: Of reality, of how it is organised, of what its consequences are, and avoid falling in ...
M.: And how is it related to submission?
T.: It is again what we said earlier ... the way I understood it ... it is backward to ... *to be tied to beliefs ... and to be stuck again in that place waiting for things to change.*

Tacuara's visual representation shows the usefulness of having collected interview data in our research. In this case, the interview fulfilled a complementary rather than simply a supporting or confirmatory role in the data analysis phase because without the interview this visual representation would have been obscure.

Excerpt 6

Figure 4.1 Tacuara, visual representation, *Mi planta de naranja-lima*

English Translation of Excerpt 6

Waiting ... for the trainer to fly ...

Excerpt 7

M.: La representación visual, ¿qué significa?
T.: A mí me pareció . . . viste más o menos . . . el final del fragmento, que él deja la zapatilla y . . . una cuestión que todavía tiene esperanza pero . . . es, esperanza de que pase algo . . . no de una, o sea, *no hay una idea de que uno puede hacer o transformar de alguna manera, sino una idea de esperar algo más allá, esperar algo que venga de afuera* . . . Por eso en este dibujo me pareció que se reflejaba así un poco la pared y eso, relacionada con la casa precaria que me imagino en la que se vive, y . . . bueno, esa zapatillita así . . .
M.: ¿Ladrillos?
T.: Sí, son todos ladrillos.
M.: Entiendo.
T.: No tiene revoque.
M.: Ah, ladrillos . . . entiendo.
T.: Y . . . y la zapatilla . . .
M.: O sea que eso es importante, la zapatilla.
T.: Sí. Y está ahí como que . . . *esperando que vuele, o sea . . . que salgan solitas las alas* y . . . Y también lo que significa el volar . . . digo, todas las connotaciones o cómo uno asocia el hecho de volar, la libertad . . . qué sé yo.

(Tacuara, interview)

English Translation of Excerpt 7

M.: The visual representation, what does it mean?
T.: It seemed to me . . . You see, more or less . . . the end of the fragment, when he leaves his shoe outside and . . . He still has hope but it is . . . hope for something to happen, *the idea that we can do or transform things is not present, and we see the idea of waiting for something beyond that, something from outside*, so in this drawing I thought that the wall reflected it a bit . . . it's related to the precarious house in what I suppose that they live, and . . . well, that little shoe like that . . .
M.: Bricks?
T.: Yes, these are all bricks.
M.: I understand.
T.: Walls don't have plaster.
M.: Ah, bricks . . . I understand.
T.: And . . . and the shoe . . .
M.: So this is important, the shoe.
T.: Yes. And it is there . . . *waiting for it to fly . . . that is . . . that wings grow of their own accord* and . . . it is also about what flying means, that is . . . all the connotations or the things with which we associate the idea of flying, freedom . . . I don't know.

Critical Thinking, Cultural and Social Awareness

We have just shown how Tacuara fluctuated between stereotypical and critical interpretations in the tasks that she produced. The other participants also showed elements of criticality and reflexivity regarding textual content, combined with stereotypical views at times. In particular, the reading response and visual representation tasks brought to the surface the readers' critical cultural awareness, which the interviews served to confirm. For instance, Beryl questioned and criticised what she considered a materialistic view of Christmas and returned repeatedly to this topic in all her tasks. In her reading response task, Beryl used the term "social class" and emphasised the differences in social classes exclusively from an economic perspective. She argued that the text intends to portray this contrast between "those who have" and "those who do not have". Because she centred on this economic perspective (the presents and the food on the Christmas table are important), she concluded that the text offers a "materialistic" perspective. Her reasoning around this notion was very complex and presented a critical stance, an instance of level 4 in the model, while at the same time she seemed to be unable to see Christmas from the narrator's perspective, an instance of level 3 in the model. Zezé is a child, and it is not unreasonable that he wishes for a present and a nice meal for Christmas, but Beryl judged these wishes from the point of view of an adult, probably herself, and evaluated them as "materialistic."

Excerpt 8

La *cultura* presentada en el texto leído es, a mi entender, un reflejo de la *sociedad* actual, en la que vemos la distinción de *clase social* claramente marcada.

Es fácil determinar las contraposiciones que se hacen entre *quienes tienen (desde un nivel material y económico) y quienes no tienen*. El narrador mismo se coloca desde un punto *materialista, visto que para él/ella la Navidad tiene que ver con lo que Papa Noel puede traerle como regalo y lo que cada uno tiene en su mesa*.

Si bien esta familia *no parece pertenecer a una clase social alta*, o en todo caso *su clase social está en declive*, sus deseos parecen directamente relacionados con el *materialismo*.

(Beryl, reading response task)

English Translation of Excerpt 8

The *culture* portrayed in the text that we've read is, as I see it, a reflection of the current *society*, in which the distinction of *social classes* is very evident.

It is easy to determine the contrasts between *the better-off (from an economic and social perspective) and the poor*. The narrator places himself in a *materialistic* point of view *considering that Christmas, in his/her view, has to do with the presents that Santa can bring and with the things that one can put on the table.*

Even when this family *doesn't seem to belong to a high social class*, or at least *their social class is declining*, their wishes seem to be directly related to *materialism*.

Later in the interview Beryl attempted to define what she meant by low social class and materialism in her reading response task. She assumed that the family was not high class or middle class ('*quizás no* es de *clase alta* pero *tampoco* una *clase media*') but rather low middle class ('en la típica que se le llama hoy la *clase media baja*'). At this point she involved the social dimension, not only the economic, in her analysis of social classes ('mínimas referencias *sociales* y económicas').

Excerpt 9

B.: Entonces me parece que lo que surge es el *materialismo*, quizás por el hecho de que son una familia que se ve como que no . . . no es de . . . *quizás no es de clase alta pero tampoco una clase media, y por eso te decía que su sociedad . . . o sea, su clase está en declive.* Porque . . . *mínimas referencias sociales y económicas* que a mí me hacen ver que es como que *están en la típica que se le llama hoy la clase media baja.*

(Beryl, interview)

English Translation of Excerpt 9

B.: Then it seems to me that *materialism* is what comes up, *maybe because they are a family that we see as . . . they are not a high-class family but not either a middle-class family, and that's why I told you that their society . . . that is, their class is declining.* Because . . . there are *a few economic and social references* that make me see that *they are in what is now called lower middle class.*

In her visual representation, Beryl mentioned key concepts such as Christmas, happiness, presents, food and prosperity ('Navidad, felicidad, regalos, comida, prosperidad'), each one followed by a question mark.

Excerpt 10

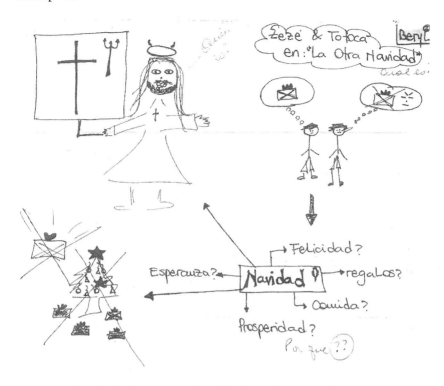

Figure 4.2 Beryl, visual representation, *Mi planta de naranja-lima*

English Translation of Excerpt 10

Zezé & Totoca in 'The Other Christmas'
Hope? Happiness? Presents? Food? Prosperity?

In the interview we asked about the meaning of the question marks and she responded that these concepts represent typical conceptions of Christmas as seen in advertising. She used the question marks as a way of showing that the text is in fact implicitly questioning where happiness, presents, food and prosperity can be found in Zezé's context. There is a lot of criticality and reflexivity in her thinking here.

Excerpt 11

M.: "¿Prosperidad?" [from the visual representation task] ¿Por qué con signos de pregunta? Eso era lo que te quería preguntar.
B.: Ah bueno . . .
M.: "Navidad, felicidad, regalos, comida, prosperidad."
B.: Precisamente porque . . . o sea . . . como *uno tiene las concepciones de que en la Navidad . . . hay alegría, hay abrazos, hay . . . prosperidad, que son los típicos advertisements que encontrás*, ¿no?
M.: Sí.
B.: Entonces mi pregunta creo que en base al texto, *lo que se pregunta el texto implícitamente es dónde está todo esto.*
M.: ¿Es un cuestionamiento entonces?
B.: *Es un cuestionamiento de dónde se encuentra . . . no dónde se encuentra presente en el texto sino lo que yo veo que se refleja en el texto.*

(Beryl, interview)

English Translation of Excerpt 11

M.: "Prosperity?" [from the visual representation task] Why did you write that with question marks?
B.: Ah, well . . .
M.: "Christmas, happiness, presents, food, prosperity."
B.: It is just because . . . *we have the idea that there should be happiness, hugs and prosperity at Christmas, all that is in the typical advertisements that we find*, right?
M.: Yes.
B.: Then my question, based on the text, *what the text implicitly questions, is where all that has gone.*
M.: Is it a questioning, then?
B.: *It is a questioning of where these things are, not where these things are in the text but what I see reflected in the text.*

For Beryl this text was difficult to understand because she did not agree with the commercial side of Christmas. In fact, being an atheist she had trouble seeing "what Christmas refers to exactly" in a religious sense as well.

Excerpt 12

B: A mí siempre me costó mucho porque *no entiendo precisamente la festividad de la Navidad*, no . . . *No entiendo a qué refiere exactamente la Navidad* y me parece *una cuestión totalmente comercial* y no . . . Si bien estoy bautizada no . . . *No practico la religión*, no me interesa, entonces . . .

(Beryl, interview)

English Translation of Excerpt 12

> B.: It was always a difficult topic for me since *I don't understand the Christmas celebration*, I don't . . . *I don't quite understand exactly what it refers to* and it seems to me *just a commercial issue* . . . Even if I am baptised, *I am not a practicing Christian*, I am not . . . I am not interested, then . . .

Beryl's difficulty in discovering the meaning of Christmas in the text may stem in part from the fact that religious social identifications, atheism included as in Beryl's case, are not only religious affiliations but also world views or general frameworks of understanding, as Ysseldyk, Kimberly and Anisman (2010: 65) explain:

> it could be argued that atheism, like religion, coincides with an epistemological and ontological framework through which to understand and interpret the world (. . .) Certainly, such a belief system also offers potential explanations regarding what can be known and what can exist and is likely to be of great import to those whose self-identification as an atheist is central.

In other words, Beryl interpreted the text from her atheist standpoint and in this sense, the philosophical notion that there is a limit to what can be known, that we described in Chapter 1, acquires importance here.

Victoria offers another rich example of a critical reading of this text, in particular of its religious content. She presented a "quasi-theological questioning" by addressing complex notions such as lack of reward, kindness and divine injustice ("aparente falta de recompensa a la bondad y la aparente injusticia divina"; "the apparent lack of reward for goodness and the apparent divine unfairness"). She said that Christmas has a more profound meaning, the religious, beyond the view of Christmas as a family gathering only ("no es sólo una reunión familiar"; "Christmas is not only a family reunion").

Excerpt 13

> Se añade aquí un *quasi cuestionamiento teológico*, planteado con absoluta inocencia por los más pequeños de la casa, sobre la aparente falta de recompensa a la bondad y la aparente injusticia divina (. . .) Para la lectura y plena comprensión de este texto es importante conocer *ciertos aspectos culturales concretos relacionados con la Navidad y sus usos, comidas y tradiciones*, pero es incluso más imprescindible comprender que la Navidad *no es sólo una reunión familiar*, porque las *disquisiciones quasi teológicas* de algunos de los personajes apuntan precisamente a *la parte subyacente y más profunda de esta fecha*.
>
> (Victoria, reading response task)

English Translation of Excerpt 13

Here a *quasi-theological questioning* is added, considered with absolute innocence by the youngest of the house, about the apparent lack of reward for goodness and about the apparent divine unfairness (. . .) To better understand this text, it is important to become familiar with *certain concrete cultural aspects related to Christmas, its customs, food and traditions*, but it is even more important to understand that Christmas *is not only a family reunion* because the *quasi-theological disquisitions* of some characters point out *the underlying, deeper aspect of this celebration.*

In her visual representation, which consisted of short phrases, perhaps owing to her being blind, the same concepts appear, together with new ones such as resignation and deception. The contrast poverty-richness is also present ("Reflejo del *nivel económico-social de la familia*, contraste con la *riqueza* en que viven otros"; "Reflection about the *economic level of the family*, contrast with the *wealth* of others"). Here she explicitly mentioned the critical position of Christmas offered by the text, from a social perspective. She added her own interpretation in that this social critical view centres on the injustice of the unequal distribution of money ("*Crítica social a la injusticia del dinero mal distribuido*"; "*Social criticism of the unfairness of badly distributed money*"), an injustice that is aggravated in her view by the fact that the protagonists are children.

Excerpt 14

Diálogo entre Zezé y Totoca, *cuestionamiento* sobre la *bondad del Niño Jesús, justicia o injusticia* de la *falta general de regalos*. Aparentes ventajas de la *resignación*, que evita *decepciones*. Reflejo del nivel económico-social de la familia, contraste con la riqueza en que viven otros. *Crítica social a la injusticia del dinero mal distribuido*. *Niños* como protagonistas, *mayor sentimiento de injusticia.*

(Victoria, visual representation task)

English Translation of Excerpt 14

Dialogue between Zezé and Totoca, *questioning* the *goodness of the child Jesus (sic), fairness or unfairness* of the *general lack of presents*. Apparent advantages of *resignation*, which avoids *disappointment*. Reflection about the economic level of the family, contrast against the richness of others. *Social criticism* of the unfairness of the badly distributed money. *Children* as main characters, protagonists' *greater feeling of unfairness.*

The point that these extracts illustrate is that all the participants positioned themselves as critical readers; this happened too with the other two texts as we shall see. This criticality was motivated by different and specific themes in each text, and led to reflections in which participants engaged in critical thinking defined as higher-order thinking (or the type of thinking that regulates and monitors itself), involving processes of analysis, synthesis and evaluation (Waters, 2006). However, these readers went beyond critical thinking in these terms, toward critical cultural awareness, or critical social awareness, that is, a criticality and reflexivity tied to a social dimension, issues of citizenship and of humankind and human nature from a philosophical perspective. Recurrent topics which led to this kind of response in the text in Spanish were the religious (and the questioning of the religious), accompanied by the related aspects of poverty, social injustice, socioeconomic inequality, submissiveness of the lower classes, taking action to fight this inequality (instead of accepting it) and criticisms toward the materialism associated with Christmas in capitalist societies.

Reflecting Upon Culture

In all data types, almost all the readers tended to include some sort of what we have decided to call *meta-cultural reflections*. These are reflections about the cultural aspects involved in communication in general, or about cultural practices in their own culture as well as in other cultures. In all cases, these reflections, which traversed all tasks and texts, were stimulated by textual content, and readers made this connection explicit.

Tacuara's reflection log and interview extracts below show not only this level of awareness of cultural issues but also the ability to compare and contrast that we referred to initially as well as an attempt to distinguish between related terms and define them. She analysed the concept of 'class' and revealed sophisticated cultural awareness (characteristic of levels 4 and 5 in the model) in her understanding that the concept of social class may transcend national boundaries (revealed by the use of a denial, which we mark in bold in the extract) and in her conclusion that commonalities and bonds are more likely to exist between people from a similar social class in different countries (even countries from different continents such as Latin America and Europe) than between people from the same country but belonging to different social classes.

> Excerpt 15
>
> Me parece que independientemente del origen del escritor o del lugar donde transcurre la historia, independientemente de eso, la problemática que está presente es una que también atraviesa nuestra *sociedad*, por lo cual el texto resulta más fácil de asimilar. (. . .) me parece que para abordar el texto hay que adoptar un punto de vista no sólo *cultural* sino también *clasista*.
>
> (Tacuara, reflection log)

M.: ¿Qué significa esto de 'clasista'?
T.: Ah, no, porque me pareció que . . .
M.: Vos distinguís entre algo clasista y algo cultural por lo que veo.
T.: Claro, es . . . una cuestión . . . es decir, **no sólo decir si es un país de Latinoamérica o no, o un país europeo** . . . o sea, por ese tipo de definición, y después que dentro también . . . que *dentro de un mismo . . . de distintos países, ya sea, un país más desarrollado o no, dentro de esos países también hay una división de clases,* y que esa división de clases para mí hace que por ejemplo . . . eh . . . *una persona de cierta clase social de la Argentina pueda tener más en común con una persona de cierta clase social de Europa que entre dos personas dentro de la Argentina, ¿me explico?* O sea, si yo comparo . . . a una persona de una familia más acomodada en un . . . con el otro extremo de la sociedad, tampoco tan extremo pero . . . o sea, no vayamos a un cartonero pero qué sé yo, una familia precaria, eh . . . qué sé yo, *por más que vivan dentro del mismo país, van a tener un montón de . . . van a estar separadas por un abismo* de . . .
M.: Sí. Sería más fácil para vos comprender . . . alguien de otro país o cultura pero del mismo . . .
T.: . . . *que comparta la misma clase, o sea, tiene por ahí las mismas dificultades* . . .

(Tacuara, interview)

English Translation of Excerpt 15

I think that regardless of the origin of the writer or the place where the story unfolds, the conflict of the story is also present in our *society*, which makes the text easier to understand. (. . .) Anyway, I think that to understand the text we have to see it not only from a *cultural* point of view but also from a *classist* one.

M.: What do you mean by 'classist'?
T.: Ah, no, because it seemed to me that . . .
M.: I see that you make a difference between something classist and something cultural.
T.: Sure, it is . . . that is, **not only to say whether it's a Latin-American country or not, or if it's an European country** . . . that is, about that kind of definition . . . besides the fact that within . . . *within the same . . . between different countries, no matter if it's a developed country or not, there is a class division within these countries* . . . and

to me, that class division makes, for instance . . . *a person that belongs to a certain Argentinian social class may have more things in common with a person from Europe who belongs to a certain social class, than between two people within Argentina*, am I being clear? That is . . . if I compare a person that belongs to a high-class family in a . . . with the other extreme of society, not that extreme but . . . I don't know, a precarious family . . . I don't know . . . *even if they live in the same country, they will have lots of . . . they will be separated by an abyss of . . .*

M.: Yes. To you, it'd be easier to understand . . . somebody of another country and culture but who shares the same . . .

T.: *. . . who shares the same social class . . . that is, maybe he'd have the same difficulties . . .*

Perspective-Taking

The participants did not favour the same themes in all the tasks they produced for the same text, and in the text in Spanish some readers focused their attention on the contrasts portrayed in the fragment (rural life/urban life, wealth/poverty, happiness/sadness, etc.); others focused on the religious content, and others on the Christmas celebration *per se* (with reference to the presents, the food, etc.). In addition, the tone of the tasks was very different depending on the enactments of these foci of attention. For instance, the tasks by Luz centred on the idea of hope while Enrique Alejandro focused on the negative aspects of the celebration (sadness, poverty, depression, etc.) and Tacuara engaged with the idea of religion as domination.

Scarlet Rose's visual representation, in the form of a cartoon, is rich in terms of cultural details (level 1 in the model) in areas such as the home, the community, food, dress, traditions, etc. It emphasizes some areas of attention such as food and the religious perspective. At the same time, Scarlet Rose adds layers of description and interpretation with the aim of leading to the identification of the value systems, social norms and expectations of the members of another culture. These layers are represented by the specific references to the poverty of the family, the religious perspective and the family members' view of Christmas, and illustrate level 4 in our model. This stage involves the comprehension of another culture from an insider perspective. In other words, how the members of another culture behave is interpreted in the light of their own cultural norms.

Excerpt 16

Figure 4.3 Scarlet Rose, visual representation, *Mi planta de naranja-lima*

English Translation of Excerpt 16

1. So, Santa is not going to bring me anything? Nothing new? Unique?
2. The doctor's family always receives something . . .
3. Why isn't Child Jesus good to our family? Here we're good . . . and, however . . . he only likes the rich people.
4. Look at us.
5. If you never expect anything, you won't be disappointed. Don't ask yourself these questions. It's not worth it.
6. I don't care. I'll put my shoes out anyway. Maybe miracles exist.

Another participant, Luz, began her reflection log dwelling on the confusion that the mention of the shoes in the text generated in her.

Excerpt 17

La dificultad se presenta cuando *el niño insiste en colocar sus zapatillas*, ilusionado con recibir un regalo de Papa Noel. *Según su cultura entiendo la idea ya que lo asocié con una parte de mi cultura (Los Reyes Magos).* Di por sentado esa relación. Igualmente creo que se me facilitó el entendimiento ya que son hechos o acciones que tenemos en común, pero se presentaría como un problema si la persona que lee el texto no realiza en su cultura un hecho familiar. Si en el país, región o lugar las personas carecen de ese ritual por llamarlo de alguna manera, no podría interpretar porqué el niño quiere poner las zapatillas del otro lado de la puerta.

(Luz, reflection log)

English Translation of Excerpt 17

The difficulty appears when *the boy insists on put his shoes*, getting excited about getting a Santa Claus present. *According to his culture, I understand the idea because I associate it with a part of my culture (the Three Wise Men)*. I assumed that relation. Likewise, I believe that it was easy for me to understand it because they are facts or actions that we have in common, but it will be presented as a problem if the person that reads the text does not realise [acknowledge] in their culture a similar event. If in the country, region or place people lack this ritual to name it anyway, I cannot interpret why the boy wants to put the shoes outside the door.

Luz attempts to interpret the reference to the shoes by relating this event to what she associated it with, namely the Three Wise Men (in italics in the extract). We see here the process of comparing and contrasting that we mentioned at the beginning, which is the point of departure for cultural understanding in level 1 in our model. But at the same time, Luz distances herself from this festivity in her own culture and makes an effort to reflect upon how somebody who did not have a similar festivity would interpret Zezé's actions ("pero *se presentaría como un problema si la persona que lee el texto no realiza en su cultura un hecho familiar*"; "but *it will be presented as a problem if the person that reads the text does not realize in their culture a similar event*"). There is here a trace of level 5 in the model, in the attempt to inspect one's cultural practices from the eyes of outsiders. Her perspective is sophisticated as she thinks about how someone in a C3 without the knowledge that she has as a member of her C1 would react to the text about C2. Luz concludes with a generalisable meta-cultural reflection about the need to anchor the protagonist's actions to something familiar in a reader's culture ("*Si en el país, región o lugar las personas carecen de ese ritual* por llamarlo de alguna manera, *no podría interpretar porqué el niño quiere poner las zapatillas del otro lado de la puerta*"; "*If in the country, region or place people lack this ritual* to name it anyway, *I cannot interpret why the boy wants to put the shoes outside the door*").

This reflection log supports what she had previously underlined in the text itself as problematic, and she provides a brief explanation in note form:

Excerpt 18

Entiendo que el nene quiere y espera el regalo de papá Noel y es por eso que coloca las zapatillas. *Nosotros lo hacemos no en Navidad sino cuando vienen los 'Reyes.'* En fin, lo entendí y *lo comparé y lo asocié con mi conocimiento sobre mi país y cultura, pero creo que si no tendría (sic) ese conocimiento previo hubiese sido muy difícil saber a qué hacía referencia y por qué el niño actuaba así.*

(Luz, note about the text underlined with difficulties)

English Translation of Excerpt 18

I understand that the boy wants and expects Santa's present and that's why that he puts his shoes. *We do that when 'the Three Wise Men' come, not at Christmas.* To sum up, I understood this and *compared and associated this with my knowledge about my country and my culture, but I think that if I didn't have that previous knowledge, it would have been very difficult to know what it referred to and why the boy acted like he did.*

Level 5 in the model crucially depends on the ability to assume different, sometimes conflicting, perspectives on a topic. In particular, it involves apprehending one's own culture from an outsider perspective, with awareness of how one's own behaviour is seen through the eyes of the members of other cultures. Below Luz is explaining, describing and informing about Christmas to her imagined reader, a reader who does not know what Christmas is, what it involves, who Santa Claus is, or what the Christmas Mass is intended to celebrate, among other aspects: a reader who is totally unfamiliar with the Christmas schema, its associated events and its connotations.

Excerpt 19

La historia refleja una familia muy ligada con la religión católica que esta por celebrar Navidad. Dicha familia parece encontrarse en una situación económica difícil, cosa que se ve reflejada en toda la historia.

El niño, personaje principal, piensa que no va a recibir ningún regalo. *En dicha cultura se ve que para Navidad suelen hacerse regalos por un tal Papa Noel.* Él asocia la falta de ese regalo con su comportamiento y relaciona el buen comportamiento con la religión, lo compara con el Niño Jesús, por el contrario el mal comportamiento está ligado con el diablo. Acá se ve claramente como *el niño está inmerso en una cultura donde la religión ocupa un espacio importante. Hace referencia también al Padre y el Catecismo, el primero se refiere a la persona que en la religión católica celebra la misa (también está a cargo de la Iglesia) y el segundo se refiere a un libro donde se encuentran las normas o esperados comportamientos de las personas*. Vendría a ser el ideal cristiano, por llamarlo de alguna manera.

Al momento de celebrar la Navidad la familia parece estar muy triste y asocian la falta de dinero con la cantidad de comida y cómo está su mesa en ese día tan especial. La familia demuestra su tristeza durante la cena, y la falta de entusiasmo y motivación en ese día tan importante. Nombran a *'La Misa de Gallo' que es una misa, celebración que se hace en la Iglesia tratando de imitar lo que fue el nacimiento de Jesús.* Al ser una familia católica es para ellos un evento muy importante y el hecho de no ir es visto de una mala manera. Esto suma al desgano, falta de interés por arreglarse y verse bien en esa celebración.

Finalmente el niño ve que la gente de su familia ni siquiera comieron por tal angustia. Aunque él sigue esperanzado que va a recibir el regalo, y se duerme con esa infantil e inocente esperanza.

(Luz, reading response task)

English Translation of Excerpt 19

The story shows a family too linked with the Catholic religion that is going to celebrate Christmas. This family seems to be in a difficult economic situation, that is shown in the whole story.

The boy, main character, thinks that he is not going to get any present. *In this culture, it seems that for Christmas, some presents are usually given by Santa Claus.* He associates the lack of the present with his behaviour and relates the good behaviour with the religious, he compares with Baby Jesus, on the contrary the misbehaviour is linked with the devil. Here it is seen perfectly well how *the boy is submerged in a culture where the religious occupies an important place. He makes also reference to the Father and the Catechism, the former refers to the person who in Catholic religion celebrates mass (he is also in charge of a Church) and the second refers to a book in which some norms or expected people's behaviours are found.* It is the Christian's ideal, to name it.

At the moment of celebrating Christmas, the family seem to be very sad and associate the lack of money with the amount of food and what their food is like on such a special day. The family demonstrate their sadness during the meal, and the lack of enthusiasm and motivation on that important day. They name *the 'midnight mass' that is a mass, celebration that is done on the Church trying to imitate what was the birth of Jesus.* As it is a Catholic family it is for them an important event and the fact of not going is seen as unacceptable. This adds the half-hearted, lack of interest on getting ready and looking nice in that celebration.

Finally, the boy sees that the people in his family do not eat because of such anguish. Even though, he is still hopeful that he will get a present, and he sleeps with that childish and naive hope.

The capacity to recognise and articulate the difficulties found in the process of perceiving a culture from inside is present here and is a characteristic of level 5 in the model. Luz resolved the difficulties successfully. This level matches Kramsch's "third perspective" (Kramsch, 1993: 210), which permits the adoption of insider, outsider and hybrid perspectives in the apprehension of C1 and C2. So Luz simultaneously took the perspective we have just described and at the same time she could not avoid filtering her own personal view toward textual content ("Vendría a ser el *ideal cristiano*, por llamarlo de alguna manera . . . en ese día *tan* especial . . . en ese día *tan* importante . . . se duerme con *esa infantil e inocente* esperanza"; "It is the *Christian's ideal*, to name it . . . on *such* a special day . . . on *that* important day . . . he sleeps with that *childish and naive* hope").

Luz explained the reference to the concept of the Christian ideal in the interview. This is evidence once again of the supporting function fulfilled by interview data.

Excerpt 20

L: trato de explicar el . . . o sea, qué es lo que . . . *el hecho de la Navidad que va más allá de* . . . *o sea* . . . *qué es lo que se hace, por ejemplo las comidas típicas*, y justo en esto . . . Más o menos trato de contar un poco la importancia de la parte religiosa que . . . que creo que es importante cuando el nene dice: 'Voy a ser una buena persona' o 'Voy a ser una mala persona', como que se hace replantear, 'Si soy una buena persona voy a tener un regalo; si no, no.'

M.: Entiendo. ¿*Cuál es el 'ideal cristiano'*?

L.: (Pausa) Eh . . . Y, *justamente eso, que estén . . . que el comportamiento de una persona sea el adecuado para llegar a ser como una persona buena . . . y justamente, bueno, los niños por ahí se plantean: 'Si soy una persona buena voy a tener un regalo.'*

(Luz, interview)

English Translation of Excerpt 20

L.: I try to explain the . . . I mean, what is the . . . *the fact that Christmas that goes beyond of . . . I mean . . . what is what it is done, for example typical food*, and just in that . . . More or less I try to tell a little the importance of the religious part that . . . that I believe that is important when the boy said: 'I am going to be a good person' or ' I am going to be a bad person', it is like he rethinks, 'If I am a good person, I am going to have a present; if not, I am not.'

M.: I understand. *Which is the 'ideal of a Christian'*?

L.: (Pause) Eh . . . *And, precisely that, that they are . . . that the behaviour of a person will be the correct one, to be like a good person . . . and precisely, well, children perhaps think about: 'If I am a good person, I will have a present.'*

Emotion in Cultural Understanding

The participants used affective terms frequently (in bold in the extracts). Miranda Dana's reading response and interview constitute an example.

Excerpt 21

Toda la celebración ocurre en *un clima de* **tristeza**. *Hay mucho* **silencio** *y* **hasta hay llanto**. *Parece como si no hay motivo para celebrar porque están rodeados de* **miseria**.

(Miranda Dana, reading response task)

M.: Acá no entiendo. ¿Por qué ". . . hasta hay llanto"? ¿Qué querés poner con el 'hasta'? Es representativo eso . . .
MD.: Como que . . .
M.: . . . lingüísticamente.
MD.: Claro. Eh . . .
M.: Porque en realidad lloran. ¿Por qué ponés "hasta lloran"?
MD.: Claro . . . *como que era un extremo, me pareció*.
M.: Un extremo . . .
MD.: *Que estaban todos que no comían, por ahí bueno, que estaban* **deprimidos**, *pero . . .* **hasta hay llanto**, *me pareció que era demasiado extremo quizás . . . la* **depresión**.
M.: Entiendo.
MD.: Por eso.
M.: Y . . . ¿y por qué demasiado extremo? ¿Vos qué harías en una situación parecida?
MD.: No sé, la verdad, no sé, pero . . . yo supongo que . . .
M.: Te parece muy extremo para lo que se refleja.
MD.: Claro, porque además *quizás . . . no es una situación que se dio de un momento para el otro: quizás la situación social de la familia ya es . . . viene hace un tiempo, no sé,* **me parece demasiado extraño que lloren así a tal extremo en una celebración** *. . . cuando tendrían que estar, no sé, más acostumbrados quizás*.
M.: Hm, entiendo.
MD.: Como que no es nada nuevo, entonces . . . me pareció eso.

(Miranda Dana, interview)

English Translation of Excerpt 21

The entire celebration takes place in *an atmosphere* **full of sadness** *where* **silence** *reigns and* **they even cry** *too. It seems as if there is no reason to be celebrating because they are surrounded by* **misery**.

M.: Here I don't understand. Why . . . "there is crying too"?
MD.: Well . . .
M.: . . . linguistically.
MD.: Sure. Eh . . .
M.: Because they cry actually. Why do you write that "they even cry"?
MD.: Sure . . . *it seemed to me that it was too extreme* . . .
M.: Extreme . . .

MD.: *The fact that they weren't eating, maybe . . . well, that they were* **depressed**, *OK, but . . . but* **they even cry too**, *I thought it was maybe too extreme . . . the* **depression** *. . .*
M.: I understand.
MD.: That's why.
M.: And . . . why "too extreme"? What would you do in a similar situation?
MD.: I don't know really, I don't know . . . but . . . I guess . . .
M.: You see it as too extreme for what is being reflected.
MD.: Sure, because, besides . . . *maybe* . . . *it's not a situation that came overnight. Maybe the social situation of the family existed . . . for some time, I don't know. . . .* **It seems too strange to me that they cry like that, to that point, in a celebration** *. . . since they should be . . . I don't know, maybe more used to the situation . . .*

In this interview extract, Miranda Dana explained her use of *even* in her reference to the action of crying. The use of this little word in this reading response task triggered a deep interpretation of one act, the act of crying. Here Miranda Dana made a deliberate effort to understand this action but did so from her own frame of reference. That is, her own understanding of a Christmas celebration as something festive (a characteristic of level 2 in the model) made her see this family's crying as *too strange* and *extreme*. This led to the naturalisation of poverty and therefore this family's apparent failure to be accustomed to their reality ("cuando *tendrían que estar, no sé, más acostumbrados quizás*"; "they should be . . . I don't know, maybe more used to the situation").

We observe Miranda Dana's difficulty in considering, judging and evaluating one action (only one action, the act of crying) within its cultural setting, or in other words, from the point of view of the members of another culture. This difficulty led her to interpret this part of the text as the naturalisation of poverty, i.e., because they have been poor for so long, they should be accustomed to it. This line of interpretation would be framed within level 3 in the model, which involves the perception of another culture from the reader's frame of reference, or in other words, approaching another culture from an outsider perspective as an observer. This approach helps comprehend another culture only superficially, analysing and explaining from the outside. The difficulty that Miranda Dana experiences in understanding the act of crying comes from her inability to put herself in the characters' shoes. There is no attempt to find the motivations (values and beliefs, for example) behind the family members' observable behaviours (a characteristic of level 4), which might help explain why the celebration is full of sadness.

Miranda Dana's lack of empathy to put herself in somebody's else's shoes is evidence of this level 3 but, at the same time, of the difficulty of reaching level 2, i.e., understanding her own culture from an insider perspective. It is the lack of cultural sensitivity and the prevalence of ethnocentric positions (which characterise this level 2) that do not allow her to understand the impossibility for the family to participate in the celebration as a time of festivity. All of this is revealed through her use of affective terms in her tasks.

What we have seen in this chapter, through this analysis of responses to a text in the readers' first language about a phenomenon not too distant from their own environment, is that different levels of understanding are achieved which can be analysed by reference to our *Model of Cultural Understanding*. It is therefore possible to use the approach taken here in classes where the language is the first language of learners. As mentioned in Chapter 2 when we introduced the model, it would also be possible to use texts which are in the L1 but from an earlier historical period, perhaps from the readers' own cultural inheritance, with similar questions of relative familiarity arising, but this is a facet we cannot develop in this book.

References

Bishop, W. (1999) *Ethnographic Writing Research: Writing it Down, Writing It Up, and Reading It*. Portsmouth: Boynton/Cook Publishers, Inc.

Kramsch, C. (1993) *Context and Culture in Language Teaching*. Oxford: Oxford University Press.

Kramsch, C. (2007) Classic book review. Re-reading Robert Lado, 1957. *Linguistics across cultures. Applied linguistics for language teachers. International Journal of Applied Linguistics* 17(2), 241–247.

Maxwell, J. (2002) Understanding and validity in qualitative research. In Huberman, A.M. and Miles, M. (eds). *The Qualitative Researcher's Companion*. California: Sage Publications Inc.

Rosaldo, R. (1993) *Culture and Truth: The Remaking of Social Analysis*. Boston: Beacon Press.

Vasconcelos, J. M. de (1971) *Mi planta de naranja-lima*. Translated by H. Jofre Barroso. Buenos Aires: El Ateneo.

Waters, A. (2006) Thinking and language learning. *ELT Journal* 60, 319–327.

Ysseldyk, R., Kimberly, M., and Anisman, H. (2010) Religiosity as identity: Toward an understanding of religion from a social identity perspective. *Personality and Social Psychology Review* 14(1), 60–71.

5 Developing New Instruments for Research and Teaching

Reading researchers stress the need for "consistency across L2 reading studies" that investigate the comprehension process (Brantmeier (2004: 52) with respect to the use of research instruments, and there is indeed widespread agreement in the research literature about the use of one instrument, the recall task or free recall protocol, for the investigation of cultural understanding in reading. We begin therefore with our reasons for ignoring the general agreement and avoiding the recall task. However, as well as recommending the use of recall, Bernhardt (1991, 2003), Brantmeier (2003, 2004), Heinz (2004), Klingner (2004) and others insist on the importance of using *multiple measures* when investigating reading comprehension. The recall is in general combined with other instruments such as multiple choice tests, probed recall, inference questions, open-ended questions, sentence completions, true/false, summaries and cloze tests. As we shall see below, we also avoid these instruments and propose the reading response and visual representation tasks instead.

One of the reasons why the recall task is inappropriate in the investigation of comprehension is that the kind of recall required in most cases is *verbatim*. For instance, Steffensen, Joag-Dev and Anderson (1979: 16) told their subjects to "maintain the same order and use the same words," to "write down every bit" they could remember, and if they could not remember the exact words, to write down the sentence "as close to the original as possible."

We already mentioned in earlier chapters the contradiction in the fact that comprehension is investigated using a task that emphasises memory. This contradiction is more apparent if we consider other instruments such as sentence completions, true/false, summaries (Yu, 2008) and cloze tests (Chihara, Sakurai and Oller, 1989; Sasaki, 2000). We agree with Klingner (2004: 59), who points out that:

> none of these [cloze task, multiple-choice, short-answer questions, etc.] are natural reading tasks nor do they reflect what we know about the reading process.

Instead of this, we propose a constructivist view of comprehension for which the alternative instruments, the reading response and visual representation tasks, are more appropriate.

Let us take a starting point in López Bonilla and Rodríguez Linares' (2003: 74) remark:

> In any case, what is at stake is what is understood by reading comprehension, a construct more and more slippery each time because of its fluid nature, situated in specific contexts (. . .) Contrary to traditional practices, in which the student selects an answer from a range of possibilities (multiple choice, true/false, matching), the alternatives require the construction of a response.
>
> (Our translation of the Spanish)

Furthermore, the complexity of studying comprehension has to be acknowledged, and part of this complexity stems from the fact that "almost 50% of the variability [in reader response] remains unexplained" (cf. Bernhardt, 1991; Sharp, 2002: 101; Smith-Maddox, 1998). The difficulty of accessing mental processes within human beings generally is another factor, but the use of a recall task implies a lack of concern for these considerations and there is instead a specific interest in how much is remembered from a text (or the *amount* of understanding). For instance, Khaldieh (2001) and Sharp (2002) equate remembering with comprehension, and Sharp (2002: 117) argues that:

> the assumption is that recall indicates something about the readers' assimilation and reconstruction of text information and therefore *reflects comprehension* (. . .) *Comprehension is therefore measured by the amount of information in the response.*
>
> (Our emphasis)

Similarly, Heinz (2004: 99–100) says

> the procedure [the recall task] allows misunderstandings and gaps in *comprehension* to surface (. . .) and stresses *the importance of understanding*. Students cannot simply guess at answers; they must attempt to form an *understanding* of the text.
>
> (Our emphasis)

Yet, we have suggested what Chang (2006: 522) also argues, that "comprehension does not necessarily equate with remembering" and on the basis of this distinction between recall and understanding, and a constructivist view of comprehension, we abandon the use of the recall protocol as a research instrument to investigate comprehension. Our decision is supported by Allington and Swann (2009: 224):

> psychological experiments on literary reading, with their 'think-aloud' protocols, their rating tasks, their tests of recalls, etc.—not to mention the exam-like environments in which they often take place, and the

bibliographically idiosyncratic texts (or 'textoids') at their heart—might be thought signally unsuited to the task of building up a model of 'ordinary reading': it may be better to treat such practices as indicative of the competencies on which particular groups or individuals *are able to draw when pressed* than of how reading 'normally' proceeds.

(Emphasis in original)

Reading Response and Visual Representation as Research Instruments

Instead, we adapt the reading response task from Ollman (1996). It goes beyond recalling and summarising by encouraging imaginative and personal responses to a text. It is also different from the summary, synthesis, academic essay and analysis paper frequently used in university settings. The instructions that the participants in our research received were:

> Make your own personal reading of the textual content. Put this response in writing using an essay/text format which answers these questions:
> How would you describe the culture reflected in this text?
> From a cultural perspective, what is the theme of the text?
> To do this task, imagine that you are going to prepare someone for reading this text. This person does not know the environment in which the fragment is set. What you write would be an introduction to the text telling the reader (who is not familiar with the context) what he/she needs to know, and what themes will come up in the text which are specific to the cultural setting.
> This is NOT a summary or a synthesis. You are not allowed to write a simple summary of the kind *The story begins with . . . follows with . . . and ends when . . .* You can illustrate your written task with events, situations, etc. taken from the story.

The second instrument is a visual presentation of textual content, undertaken by the reader, examples of which we have already seen in earlier chapters. It includes the combination of words, phrases and/or sentences with visual information in different formats (such as charts, tables, graphs, grids, mind maps, flowcharts, diagrams, drawings). It is different from *reformulation* in the classic sense, whereby a reader rewrites a text which is not their own, trying to adhere to the writer's assumed intended meaning (Cohen, 1983a, b, c, 1989, 2009 personal communication). The instructions that the participants in our research received to carry out this task were:

> Read this text and then portray it visually and in words. You may choose any format to do so (such as charts, tables, graphs, grids, mind maps, flowcharts, diagrams and drawings). The text is available to you at all times.

> A representation which is purely visual (only drawings) is not permitted. You are welcome to combine the visual with words, phrases or sentences. However, you are not allowed to write a traditional text in paragraph format.

These instructions do not require students to recall every bit of the texts and instead encourage them to focus on particular aspects that attract their attention. The reading response and visual representation tasks are thus clearly distinct from the *verbatim* recall generally required in the recall protocol, where exactitude in the reproduction of the original text is fundamental. Here, readers have to make sense of the cultural cues and the culturally situated information in a text, relate them to their own cultural parameters, and in this way bring their experiences, knowledge and background to their interpretation. Because readers vary in their attention to the same information in a text, the reading response and visual representation tasks include the individual dimension of reading, which is consistent with a view of reading as a multidimensional and multivalent process (Bernhardt, 2003; Paris and Paris, 2003).

Two Forms of Textual Intervention

Both the reading response and visual representation tasks presuppose some textual intervention, that is, an act of "transformation" that allows for a deeper understanding of a text (Pope, 1995: 1). They are new texts (Anstley and Bull, 2006), different from the fragments that served as reading prompts.

Based on Pope (1995), Carter (2010: 118) considers textual transformations for pedagogical purposes, referring to them as:

> processes of rewriting from different angles and positions by 'translating' the text from one medium to another along an axis of spoken to written, verbal to visual, textual to dramatic.

Carter identifies three types of textual transformations, and we suggest that the reading response and visual representation tasks as research instruments involve these three forms of transformations in different degrees:

> *Re-writing* involves making use of a different range of linguistic choices; *transformation* is the manipulation of some key design feature of the text such as its narrative organization; and *re-registration* involves a more distinct shift so that the same content is conveyed in a different genre.
> (Carter, 2010: 118; emphasis in original)

In writing responses to tasks, the participants in our research produced new texts, and in so doing, they engaged in processes of rewriting, transforming and re-registering.

The tasks reveal the repertoire of resources that the participants brought to bear on cultural understanding, ranging from their *knowledge about* cultural aspects to their *knowledge in action* about the cultural aspects in the prompt texts. 'Knowledge in action' refers to the participants' capacity to use cultural knowledge in new and concrete problem-solving situations, in this case the production of these textual interventions. Put differently, it involves the intercultural skills (Byram, Nichols and Stevens, 2001) set in motion while articulating knowledge about culture and cultural values. Thus, as textual interventions, both tasks captured the participants' cultural understanding at two points simultaneously: while reading a text, and while producing another text. Producing these interventions involved exploring each prompt text in order to rewrite it from alternative perspectives, perspectives that were always complementary or supplementary, but never identical to the original fragments.

Following Pope (1995: 5), intervening requires, initially, to ask oneself which "preferences" the writer creates, that is, which dominant reading is offered in a certain text. This can be complex in the case of literary texts because of their inherent ambiguity and aesthetic value (Widdowson, 2003). In addition, the fact that written language presents gaps of indeterminacy (not everything is spelled out) is not trivial because a high degree of participation is required of the reader in order to achieve meaning; the reader cannot check with the author but must supply the missing links. Playing with this indeterminacy, literary texts accomplish effects and allow varied readings through time and through readers.

Once a reader has identified what seems to them to be the dominant reading, the reading response and visual representation tasks encourage rewriting from alternative perspectives. The participants in our research had to make a decision as to how parallel, contrary or alternative their production would be in relation to each prompt text.

Both the reading response and the visual representation are re-centred textual interventions (Pope, 1995), the former from a new genre (short essay or composition) and the latter from an adaptation or change to a new medium (visual) with a narrative element. The task instructions made the participants incline toward an important narrative component, even in the reading response task. Because of the transformation that they involve, both tasks are also different from the re-tellings used by Martínez Roldán and Sayer (2006) and Van Hell, Bosman, Wiggers and Stoit (2003). Particularly in the case of the visual representation, because it presents a change of medium (from word to image-word), there is always transformation, never simply transfer.

Moreover, as Widdowson (2003: 89) points out:

> One area of linguistic experience, however, continues to be neglected, namely the imaginative and individual exploration of meaning potential that is characteristic of literature.

The reading response and visual representation tasks allow for such personal response to texts and in this way cater to the affective dimension involved in responses to literary texts. Because the tasks do not focus on exact recall but on personal responses to a text, they are congruent with the importance attributed in the scholarly literature to image and emotion schemata in cultural understanding (Sharifian, Rochecouste and Malcolm, 2004). Both tasks allow for emotional and imaginative responses in reading—an area in which schema theories have weaknesses (Sadoski and Paivio, 2004). Reading research has in general marginalised the role of imagery in comprehension (Alba and Hasher, 1983; Taylor and Crocker, 1981) and Sadoski, Paivio and Goetz (1991: 472) remark that "imagery (. . .) has generally been neglected by reading researchers." However, imagination is important to understand the Other because people usually feel and act in accord with their ethnocentric principles, and the outcome is a sort of "cultural egocentricity" (Byram, 1989b: 50). They "identify our [their] own local ways of behaving with Behaviour, or our [their] own socialized habits with Human Nature" (Benedict, 1935: 7). Bias, attitudes and prejudice result in honest and subtle differences of perception, and the reading response and visual representation tasks offer the possibility to reflect these through imagination.

Interpreting the Other thus involves the creative activity of building a shared territory: a community of beliefs, desires, meanings, values and real objects (Quintanilla Pérez-Wicht, 2004: 89). In other words, in order to understand the Other, readers need to perceive this Other as someone who is at once similar to, and different from, them (Byram, 1989a, b; Byram and Morgan, 1994; Quintanilla Pérez-Wicht, 2004) and to build a place, a third space, common to both, in which to interact and reformulate those parameters within which they interpret reality. This perception of otherness foregrounds ambivalences and points to a moment of disjunction that allows multiple visions, beyond dichotomies. In Chapters 6 and 7, we will show that the reading response and visual representation tasks, complemented by the interview, have provided this forum for students, and in so doing they have helped them move beyond stereotyped dichotomies.

This potential of textual interventions in the area of cultural understanding is strengthened by the property of the narrative genres which makes them a space with holes, an arena of conflict and negotiation of meanings about Others (Bruner, 2002). The creation involved in reading and intervening in a text, either with a reading response or with a visual representation, requires an exploration of the hybrid, fluid and dynamic nature of the voices and cultures present in a certain text. This exploration is different from the perception or understanding of a culture as a homogeneous entity, since writers give their characters voice in different sociocultural contexts. In order to produce these textual interventions, the participants had to identify the existing tension amongst the voices of Others in the texts and their own, which they portrayed in their reading response and visual representation tasks. As they did so, they brought in their own voice as well as the voices of Others in a way which was different from the writer's. Following Pope (1995), these textual interventions allowed students to turn into analysts, critics and writers themselves as they transformed the prompt texts in multiple and varied ways.

Imagination and Affect in Reading

The link that we have pointed out between cultural understanding, reading and imagination is relevant to all languages (whether foreign, second or native) and is summarised by Kramsch in this way:

> One of the major ways in which culture manifests itself is through language. Material culture is constantly *mediated, interpreted and recorded—among other things—through language*. It is because of that mediatory role of language that culture becomes the concern of the language teacher. Culture in the final analysis is always *linguistically mediated membership into a discourse community that is both real and imagined.*
>
> (1995: 85, emphasis in original)

Kramsch also emphasises the potential of literature to allow readers to imagine worlds different from their own as a consequence of the inherent ambiguity and aesthetic value of literary texts, and states (ibid.: 85):

> culture, then, constitutes itself along three axes: the diachronic axis of time, the synchronic axis of space, and the metaphoric axis of the imagination

and that:

> culture is therefore also literature, for it is literature that opens up 'reality beyond realism' and that enables readers to live other lives—by proxy.

Emotion and affect are a key aspect of this imaginative dimension of culture (Byram, Gribkova and Starkey, 2002; Guiora, 2005) and Shanahan (1997: 168) highlights the lack of attention to imagery, emotion and affect in language learning and the need to foreground it through literature:

> The cultural features of literature represent a powerful merging of language, affect, and intercultural encounters and often provide the exposure to living language that a FL student lacks.

Our research takes account of this imaginative dimension in two ways: through the use of literary texts as suggested by Kramsch (1995) and through one specific data collection instrument, the visual representation task. One reason for including visual representation as a mode of response is its usefulness in capturing emotional responses in reading. Brantmeier (2005: 54) cites one study specifically about foreign language learning which found that:

> imagery and affect were formed even in the absence of total understanding. This shows that they are fundamental variables in foreign language reading.

The visual representation is therefore conceived as a medium for the foregrounding of imagery and emotion in reading. Since the ability to put oneself in someone else's shoes is central in cultural understanding and requires imagination (Byram and Grundy, 2002; Kramsch, 1995), the visual representation task offers an opportunity for its manifestation (Burnett and Gardner, 2006), the idea being that readers react visually to textual content with the purpose of accessing their nonverbal imaginative systems (Arizpe, 2001; Pope Edwards and Mayo Willis, 2000; Sadoski and Paivio, 2004).

Images also serve as a strategy to recover textual information (Sadoski and Paivio, 2004) because the integration of textual information in visual format is related to the comprehension and appreciation of reading material (Pope, Edwards and Mayo Willis, 2000; Sadoski and Paivio, 2004).

In short, on the basis of the foregoing discussion, we suggest that the reading response task and visual representation, which have not been used in research investigating the cultural dimension of reading, can become useful instruments in reading research; there is also potential for pedagogic use.

Pedagogic Adaptations of the Reading Response and Visual Representation Tasks

The pedagogic value of the reading response and visual representation tasks resides in their being textual interventions (Pope, 1995), i.e., text transformations that allow students to turn into analysts, critics and writers themselves. We have shown in Chapters 2 and 4 that the reading response and visual representation tasks encouraged participants to transform the prompt texts in multiple and varied ways. Anstley and Bull (2006, 90–91) specifically suggest that such transformations can occur through:

- nontraditional uses of plot, characters and place, challenging the reader/observer to find different ways of reading/looking (for instance, the combination of image with text in the visual representations);
- unusual uses of the voice of the narrator, to make the reader/observer read/look in particular ways through the eyes of particular characters (for example, in transforming *Cat's Eye*, participants sometimes positioned themselves in Banerji's place while at other times they adopted the family's point of view);

- the mixing of styles of presentation of the visual, which requires a range of skills in how to read, using different techniques for different types of information (for instance, in the case of the visual representation, graphs, patterns, charts, etc.);
- changes of format from traditional to nontraditional, challenging the readings of the reader/observer of the narration (for instance, Scarlet Rose's choice of the cartoon format for her visual representations based on the three texts, illustrated in Chapters 2 and 4, this volume);
- intertextuality that requires a reader/observer to have access to and use other texts to reach available meanings (we illustrated this with the case of Tacuara and her reference to Hegel in the previous chapter and there is another example in the following chapter with the case of Beryl); and
- the availability of multiple readings and meanings for a variety of audiences.

More specifically, in intervening in each text, the participants used multiple techniques, such as:

- alternative reading responses and visual representations: drawing attention to different aspects, generating discourses with distinct value loads, establishing what each reader considers to be more or less central, etc. (this was revealed in our project through the different foci of attention that emerged in all the reading responses and visual representations based on the three texts);
- changes in the title, in the introductions (context of the narration) or in the beginnings with the purpose of creating different expectations in the reader (for instance, we will show in the following chapter that Beryl situated her reading response task to *Cat's Eye* in the context of Thanksgiving rather than Christmas);
- different endings to express a particular preference different from that of the original text;
- narrative intervention: changes in some central point of the narrative to explore alternative consequences;
- parody: exaggerating aspects of the original text to change its style or its concerns;
- exploring implied or partially explicit parts;
- centring the attention on a particular section of the text;
- focusing on central (essential) aspects, as well as on peripheral (secondary) information.

(These last three points were also illustrated in the different foci of attention that emerged in all the reading responses and visual representations based on the three texts.)

By means of these resources, the participants in this study produced multiple interpretations and questioned established characters, scenes and plots in the two types of task. These resources provided new and alternative interpretations of the narrative texts because they played a role in the ways in which each individual interacted with these texts. In this sense, both tasks allowed the exploitation of narrative devices in a process of construction. The texts were not considered simply as a final product, but rather as a continuous and active process that implied the recreation of the fragments in question by means of the textual intervention tasks; the pedagogic potential to help readers understand and not just recall the texts will be evident.

Reading Response and the Visual Representation in Assessment

As we have seen, standardised instruments to test comprehension for research purposes and also for pedagogic purposes include recall tasks, multiple choice tests, probed recall, inference questions, open-ended questions, sentence completions, true/false, summaries and cloze tests, but they focus on the memory factor, exact recall and the quantity of understanding. Klingner (2004: 59) has stressed the need for "innovative procedures that evaluate aspects of comprehension not assessed by standardized instruments" and in a similar vein, López Bonilla and Rodríguez Linares (2003: 74–75) have argued the need for alternative forms of assessment in reading comprehension, suggesting some examples which stress naturalness and authenticity:

> alternative evaluation can be understood as that which occurs on a daily basis in significant learning contexts. These practices reflect experiences that are conceived as 'authentic' and that are documented through, among other methods, observation, journal writing, portfolio writing, experiments and performance assessment. The emphasis here lies in the self-reflection of the person who undertakes each method as well as in the comprehension of what is done without taking into account the recall of isolated details.

The reading response and visual representation tasks are just such alternative assessment instruments. The illustrations we provide in Chapters 6 and 7 show their potential to encourage and assess the skills of intercultural understanding: observing, discovering, describing, analysing, comparing and contrasting, relating, interpreting, perspective-taking, adaptability, decentring, critical thinking, criticality and reflexivity, i.e., the elements of intercultural competence which are described in many models (Spitzberg and Changnon, 2009).

Simultaneously, in order to respond to the reading response and visual representation tasks, the productive language capacity of the student is important, and this means the instruments could be used in the assessment of writing too. For instance, in our investigation the completion of both tasks required the inclusion of a strong narrative component, given the narrative nature of the prompt texts. The narrative element required the integration of different kinds of knowledge, including linguistic, cognitive, social and discourse capacities (Allen, Kertoy, Sherblom and Pettit, 1994). At a linguistic level, it was necessary to have control over the logical and temporal organisation. At a cognitive level, it was necessary to use the typical elements in short stories such as events, aims, consequences, etc. and to know how these elements interrelate. At the level of social (cultural) knowledge, participants needed to explain the motivations and the behaviours of the characters and to include information about their mental states. At a discourse level, it was necessary to know how to create the frame or context for a story, to be able to distinguish the different voices present in a story (for instance, narrator and characters), to be able to distinguish the main and secondary characters and refer to them, to have the skill not to confuse their roles and activities, etc.

Furthermore, in Chapter 8 we present two examples of how students can self-assess by writing profiles of their cultural understanding using the *Model of Cultural Understanding*. There is then plenty of opportunity for alternative assessment products.

References

Alba, J. W. and Hasher, L. (1983) Is memory schematic? *Psychological Bulletin* 93, 203–231.
Allen, M., Kertoy, M., Sherblom, J. and Pettit, J. (1994) Children's narrative productions: A comparison of personal event and fictional stories. *Applied Psycholinguistics* 15, 149–176.
Allington, D. and Swann, J. (2009) Researching literary reading as social practice. *Language and Literature* 18, 219–230.
Anstley, M. and Bull, G. (2006) *Teaching and Learning Multiliteracies: Changing Times, Changing Literacies*. Newark, DE: International Reading Association.
Arizpe, E. (2001) 'Letting the story out': Visual encounters with Anthony Browne's The Tunnel. *Reading* 35, 115–119.
Benedict, R. (1935) *Patterns of Culture*. London: Routledge and Sons Ltd.
Bernhardt, E. B. (1991) *Reading Development in a Second Language*. Norwood, NJ: Ablex.
Bernhardt, E. B. (2003) Challenges to reading research from a multilingual world. *Reading Research Quarterly* 38, 112–117.
Brantmeier, C. (2003) The role of gender and strategy use in processing authentic written input at the intermediate level. *Hispania* 86, 844–856.
Brantmeier, C. (2004) Statistical procedures for research on L2 reading comprehension: An examination of ANOVA and regression models. *Reading in a Foreign Language* 16(2), 51–69.
Brantmeier, C. (2005) Effects of reader's knowledge, text type, and test type on L1 and L2 reading comprehension in Spanish. *The Modern Language Journal* 89(1), 37–53.
Bruner, J. (2002) *Making Stories*. Cambridge, MA: Harvard University Press.
Burnett, C. and Gardner, J. (2006) The one less travelled by . . .: The experience of Chinese Students in a UK University. In Byram, M. and Feng, A. (eds) *Living and*

Studying Abroad: Research and Practice (pp. 64–91). Clevedon: Multilingual Matters.

Byram, M. (1989a) Intercultural education and foreign language teaching. *World Studies Journal* 7, 4–7.

Byram, M. (1989b) *Cultural Studies in Foreign Language Education.* Clevedon: Multilingual Matters.

Byram, M., Gribkova, B. and Starkey, H. (2002) *Developing the Intercultural Dimension in Language Teaching.* Strasbourg: Council of Europe, Language Policy Division.

Byram, M. and Grundy, P. (2002) Introduction: Context and culture in language teaching and learning. *Language, Culture, and Curriculum* 15, 193–195.

Byram, M. and Morgan, C. (1994) *Teaching-and-Learning Language-and-Culture.* Clevedon: Multilingual Matters.

Byram, M., Nichols, A. and Stevens, D. (2001) *Developing Intercultural Competence in Practice.* Clevedon: Multilingual Matters.

Carter, R. (2010) Issues in pedagogical stylistics: A coda. *Language and Literature* 19, 115–122.

Chang, Y. (2006) On the use of the immediate recall task as a measure of second language reading comprehension. *Language Testing* 23(4), 520–543.

Chihara, T., Sakurai, T. and Oller, J. (1989) Background and culture as factors in EFL reading comprehension. *Language Testing* 6(2), 143–149.

Cohen, A. D. (1983a) Reformulating second-language compositions: A potential source of input for the learner. *Educational Resources Information Center*, ED 228 866, 20.

Cohen, A. D. (1983b) Writing like a native: The process of representation. *Educational Resources Information Center*, ED 224 338, 21.

Cohen, A. D. (1983c) Reformulating compositions. *TESOL Newsletter* XVII/6, 1, 4, 5.

Cohen, A. D. (1989) Representation: A technique for providing advanced feedback in writing. *Guidelines* 11(2), 1–9 (SEAMEO Regional Language Centre, Singapore).

Cohen, A. D. (2009) Personal communication.

Guiora, A. (2005) The language sciences—The challenges ahead. A farewell address. *Language Learning* 55(2), 183–189.

Heinz, P. (2004) Towards enhanced second language comprehension assessment: Computarized versus manual scoring of written recall protocols. *Reading in a Foreign Language* 16(2), 97–124.

Khaldieh, S. (2001) The relationship between knowledge of Icraab, lexical knowledge, and reading comprehension of nonnative readers of Arabic. *The Modern Language Journal* 85(3), 416–431.

Klingner, J. (2004) Assessing reading comprehension. *Assessment for Effective Intervention* 29(4), 59–70.

Kramsch, C. (1995) The cultural component of language teaching. *Language, Culture, and Curriculum* 8, 83–92.

López Bonilla, G. and Rodríguez Linares, M. (2003) La evaluación alternativa: Oportunidades y desafíos para evaluar la lectura. *Revista Mexicana de Investigación Educativa* 8, 67–98.

Martínez Roldán, C. and Sayer, P. (2006) Reading through linguistic borderlands: Latino students' transactions with narrative texts. *Journal of Early Childhood Literacy* 6(3), 293–322.

Ollmann, H. (1996) Creating higher level thinking with reading response. *Journal of Adolescent and Adult Literacy* 39(7), 576–581.

Paris, A. and Paris, S. (2003) Assessing narrative comprehension in young children. *Reading Research Quarterly* 38, 36–76.
Pope, R. (1995) *Textual Intervention: Critical and Creative Strategies for Literary Studies*. New York: Routledge.
Pope Edwards, C. and Mayo Willis, L. (2000) Integrating visual and verbal literacies in the early childhood classroom. *Early Childhood Education Journal* 27, 259–265.
Quintanilla Pérez-Wicht, P. (2004) Comprender al otro es crear un espacio compartido: Caridad, empatía y triangulación. *Ideas y Valores. Revista Colombiana de Filosofía* 125, 81–97.
Sadoski, M. and Paivio, A. (2004) A dual coding theoretical model of reading. In Ruddell, R. and Unrau, N. (eds) *Theoretical Models and Processes of Reading. Fifth Edition* (pp. 1329–1362). Newark, DE: International Reading Association Inc.
Sadoski, M., Paivio, A. and Goetz, E. (1991) A critique of schema theory in reading and a dual coding alternative. *Reading Research Quarterly* XXXI/4, 463–484.
Sasaki, M. (2000) Effects of cultural schemata on students' test-taking processes for cloze tests: A multiple data source approach. *Language Testing* 17(1), 85–114.
Shanahan, D. (1997) Articulating the relationship between language, literature, and culture: Toward a new agenda for foreign language teaching and research. *The Modern Language Journal* 81(2), 164–174.
Sharifian, F., Rochecouste, J. and Malcolm, G. (2004) 'But it was all a bit confusing . . .': Comprehending Aboriginal English texts. *Language, Culture and Curriculum* 17, 203–228.
Sharp, A. (2002) Chinese L1 school children reading in English: The effects of rhetorical patterns. *Reading in a Foreign Language* 14(2), 116–135.
Smith-Maddox, R. (1998) Defining culture as a dimension of academic achievement: Implications for culturally responsive curriculum, instruction, and assessment. *The Journal of Negro Education* 67(3), 302–317.
Spitzberg, B. H. and Changnon, G. (2009) Conceptualising intercultural competence. In Deardorff, D. (ed) *The Sage Handbook of Intercultural Competence* (pp. 2–52). Los Angeles, LA: Sage.
Steffensen, M., Joag-Dev, C. and Anderson, R. (1979) A cross-cultural perspective on reading comprehension. *Reading Research Quarterly* XV, 10–29.
Taylor, S. and Crocker, J. (1981) Schematic bases of social information processing. In Higgins, E., Herman, C., and Zanna, M. (eds) *Social Cognition: The Ontario symposium* (Vol.1, pp. 89–134). Hillsdale, NJ: Erlbaum.
Van Hell, J., Bosman, A., Wiggers, I. and Stoit, J. (2003) Children's cultural background knowledge and story telling performance. *International Journal of Bilingualism* 7(3), 283–303.
Widdowson, H. G. (2003) 'So the Meaning Escapes': On literature and the representation of linguistic realities. *Canadian Modern Language Review/ La Revue Canadienne des Langues Vivantes* 60(1), 89–97.
Yu, G. (2008) Reading to summarize in English and Chinese: A tale of two languages? *Language Testing* 25(4), 521–551.

6 The Reading Response Task and Foreign Language Texts

We introduced our *Model of Cultural Understanding* in Chapter 2 and illustrated it with a foreign language text, the fragment from *Cat's Eye*, in English. We applied our approach using an L1 text in Chapter 4 with the fragment from *Mi planta de naranja-lima*, in Spanish. Summaries of these extracts were provided each time. In this chapter, we introduce data based on the texts in English, a foreign language in our context.

Drawing on Familiar Knowledge to Reflect on Cultural Issues

Regarding *Cat's Eye*, the participants in our research were quite knowledgeable about the celebration of Christmas in a Canadian context because of its similarity with the North American setting, as revealed by the prior knowledge task, and they all said that their knowledge came from films, books, cartoons, TV and magazines (for instance, *The Simpsons* TV cartoon, the film *Home Alone*). The majority believed that the celebration would be similar to theirs in Argentina.

All of them resorted to familiar knowledge and experiences in their understanding of this text but also showed an ability to reflect critically on their prior knowledge and assumptions. For instance, in her reflection log Beryl questioned the truth of what television shows about cultural issues on the basis that she did not know that people in the US have turkey for Christmas (although the story is set in Canada); she had assumed that this was the case only for Thanksgiving Day (here as in previous chapters we italicise the elements to which we wish to draw attention):

> Excerpt 1
>
> Me sorprende saber que para navidad en EE.UU., de donde asumo que proviene originalmente este relato, se coma pavo. Siempre consideré que era una tradición de Acción de Gracias, la cual tengo entendido no es lo mismo que la Navidad. Creo que este descubrimiento radica en el hecho de que, *usualmente, uno solo se queda con las 'verdades' televisivas y éstas, muchas veces, forman parte de la ficción, no de algo cierto y real.*
> (Beryl, immediate reflection log, *Cat's Eye*)

English Translation of Excerpt 1

I was surprised to find out that at Christmas in the USA, from where I guess that the narration comes originally, they eat turkey. I always thought about it as a Thanksgiving tradition, which is not the same as Christmas, from what I understand. I think that this finding has to do with the fact that *we believe 'the truths' shown on TV, and many times those are just fiction, not something real.*

Then in her reading response task (Excerpt 2), she confuses both celebrations.

Excerpt 2

Desde mi punto de vista, la cultura reflejada en este texto es meramente estadounidense. *Asumo que es así porque se describe mucho la cena típica de Acción de Gracias.*

El tema del texto parece reflejar una cena navideña que, en comparación, con el texto anteriormente leído, de un grupo de personas de clase media. Infiero que es así por el hecho de que el protagonista/narrador comenta que están cenando un pavo que, evidentemente, se encuentra abundantemente relleno. Además, las bebidas que se describen no denotan una carencia dentro de tal familia, visto que no solo se toma vino sino también jugo de frutas.

El texto comenta el choque de culturas entre una familia clase media estadounidense y un estudiante extranjero, posiblemente de la India, *que comparte con ellos la cena navideña.* El evento transcurre con preguntas respecto a las tradiciones del extranjero y con comentarios sobre el pavo doméstico en contraposición con el salvaje.

Las contraposiciones entre tipos de pavo parecen ser una analogía entre culturas, pero también parecen mostrar una postura diferente sobre *la navidad*: es a partir de la simple cena como el protagonista arriba a conclusiones inesperadas que parecen reflejar algo más allá de la simple lectura. Hay un mensaje escondido entre líneas que el lector debe dilucidar.

(Beryl, reading response task, *Cat's Eye*)

English Translation of Excerpt 2

From my point of view, the culture portrayed in this text is typically American. *I think so because the typical Thanksgiving dinner is described at length.*

The topic of the text seems to reflect a Christmas dinner of a middle-class group of people, compared against the text we've previously read. I guess that it is like that because the main character/narrator comments that they are having an abundantly stuffed turkey. Besides, the drinks described don't show the lack of anything in that family, considering that they are not only having wine but also fruit juice.

The text portrays the clash of cultures between an American middle-class family and a foreign student, possibly from India, that shares *the Christmas dinner* with the family. During the meal, questions are asked about the foreigner's traditions and comments are made about tame turkeys as opposed to wild ones.

The contrasts between kinds of turkey seem to be a sort of analogy between cultures, but they also seem to show a different attitude about *Christmas*: it is the very meal that makes the main character arrive at unexpected conclusions that seem to reflect something beyond a simple reading. There is a message hidden between the lines that the reader has to discover.

In Excerpt 2 we see the connection that Beryl made between Christmas and Thanksgiving, and we also see the presence of contradictory information in the second and third sentences of her reading response task; this celebration is either one or the other, and cannot be both simultaneously. When we pointed out this inconsistency to Beryl in the interview (Excerpt 3 below), she recognised that there was an incongruence and admitted feeling surprised by the fact that turkey is eaten in both celebrations ("No sabía que para Navidad también era una especie de tradición el pavo . . . *me sorprendió* en sí cuando me di cuenta"; "I didn't know that the turkey was also a sort of tradition for Christmas. . . . *I was surprised* when I realised that"). The expression of surprise is evidence of decentring from what is familiar and of new insights gained about others. However, Beryl favoured her own interpretation ("No se si Navidad . . . Porque yo los veía como celebridades aparte con diferentes rituales en todo caso"; "Not sure if Christmas, because I saw them as different celebrations with different rituals"), which shows the strength of existing schemata, and the difficulty of accommodating and assimilating new knowledge to prior frames of reference. Beryl also explained that the source of her knowledge for her interpretation of the turkey came from her experience with 'Crusades for Christ' in Argentina:[1]

Excerpt 3

M.: Esto es nuevo para vos, que se come pavo en Navidad.
B.: Sí, *creí que sólo era en Acción de Gracias*. Hay uno de los chicos que están en *ese grupo en Argentina de Crusades for Christ* . . .
M.: Ah, sí.
B.: Bueno, *uno de ellos me comentó más o menos la diferencia entre . . . o sea, me dijo que había una diferencia entre Navidad y Acción de Gracias, yo no estaba muy familiarizada con el tema, y creí que el pavo era sólo para Acción de Gracias, que es una festividad aparte.*
M.: Claro.
B.: *No sabía que para Navidad también era una especie de tradición el pavo.*
M.: O sea que eso te generó dificultades.

B.: Sí, sí, me sorprendió en sí cuando me di cuenta.
M.: En la respuesta textual (pausa) Vos ponés que describe mucho la cena típica de Acción de Gracias.
B.: Sí.
M.: Y yo te pongo: 'Bueno, pero es Navidad'.
B.: Exactamente, precisamente porque me llamó la atención lo de que... lo de que se comiera pavo, me parecía que la acción, o sea, y además decía que había un 'stuffing' en el...
M.: O sea que...
B.: ...en el pavo...
M.: O sea que no te quedó claro que era de Navidad.
B.: *Me quedó claro que era de Navidad, pero me parecía que reflejaba más que nada Acción de Gracias.*
M.: Entiendo.
B.: *No sé si Navidad.*
M.: Entiendo.
B.: *Porque yo los veía como celebridades aparte con diferentes rituales en todo caso.*

(Beryl, interview, *Cat's Eye*)

English Translation of Excerpt 3

M.: This is new to you, that people eat turkey for Christmas.
B.: Yes, *I thought it was only for Thanksgiving*. There is a young man who belongs to *this group in Argentina of Crusades for Christ* ...
M.: Ah, yes.
B.: Well, *one of them told me, more or less, the difference between ... that is, he told me that there was a difference between Christmas and Thanksgiving. I was not familiar with the topic, and I thought that the turkey was only for Thanksgiving, which is a different celebration.*
M.: Sure.
B.: *I didn't know that the turkey was also a sort of tradition for Christmas.*
M.: So, this generated some difficulties for you.
B.: Yes, yes, I was surprised when I realised that.
M.: In the reading response ... (Pause) you wrote that the Thanksgiving meal is described.
B.: Yes.
M.: ... And I wrote: 'Well, but isn't it Christmas?'
B.: Exactly, just because it caught my attention, the fact that ... that people ate turkey, that is ... I thought that the action ... Besides, it said that there was some 'stuffing' in the ...
M.: So ...
B.: ... in the turkey ...

M.: So it was not clear to you that it was Christmas.
B.: *It was clear that it was Christmas, but it seemed to me that it rather reflected Thanksgiving.*
M.: I understand.
B.: *Not sure about Christmas.*
M.: I understand.
B.: *Because I saw them as different celebrations with different rituals.*

Particularly in the last three comments by Beryl, we can see her process of trying to accommodate new knowledge to an existing schema. In much the same way that she had attempted to understand what food is eaten at Christmas and at Thanksgiving by making a connection with knowledge gathered from 'Crusades for Christ', Beryl then tried to understand the concept of Sunday School and Sunday School missionary paper by tying it to her knowledge of *catecismo* in Argentina:

Excerpt 4

M.: Sunday school y Sunday school missionary paper, ¿a qué puede hacer referencia?
B.: Más o menos tengo una idea a lo que puede llegar a hacer referencia. Globalmente me parece que . . . es esta cuestión de que . . . generalmente *los estadounidenses tienen . . . eh . . . los domingos es muy típica la práctica de la misa, y que los menores a veces tienen . . . eh . . . como una Sunday school, a la que van y practican como el Catecismo para nosotros.*
M.: Ah, OK.
B.: *Es como la clase de Catecismo, ¿no?*
M.: Entiendo.
B.: Eh . . . pero no me pareció demasiado relevante porque me parece que el foco no estaba en sí, ¿no?, en ciertas cuestiones religiosas sino en el choque de culturas, no desde lo religioso.

(Beryl, interview, *Cat's Eye*)

English Translation of Excerpt 4

M.: Sunday school and Sunday school missionary paper, what could this be referring to?
B.: I know more or less what it might be referring to. In general terms I think that . . . it is that issue of . . . *usually the Americans have . . . ehm . . . Mass, it is very typical on Sundays, and then kids sometimes have . . . like a Sunday school, to where they go and practice something, as we do with Catechism.*
M.: Ah, OK.
B.: *It is like the lesson in the Catechism, right?*
M.: I understand.

B.: Ehm . . . but it didn't seem very relevant to me since I didn't think that the focus was placed on certain religious issues, right?, but on the clash of cultures, not from a religious perspective.

Simultaneously, Excerpt 4 shows Beryl's predominant use of generalisations in expressions like "*generalmente* los estadounidenses tienen . . . eh . . . los domingos es *muy típica* la práctica de la misa, y que los menores a veces tienen . . ."; "*usually* the Americans have . . . ehm . . . Mass, it is *very typical* on Sundays, and then kids sometimes have . . ."). These generalisations, as we mentioned in Chapter 2, are associated with a stereotyped approach to the cultural that attributes one cultural trait to a whole cultural group, and that is characteristic of level 3 in our *Model of Cultural Understanding*. There is some attempt to soften such generalisations with the use of an expression of frequency ("a veces"; "sometimes") but only in reference to "los menores" ("the kids") (and not "los estadounidenses"; "the Americans" for instance). All of this happens at the same time that Beryl shows a critical stance in her immediate reflection log (Excerpt 1) toward the truth of the representations of Christmas on television. Also worth mentioning here again is the fact that different foci of attention were revealed in the reading response tasks and the visual representations. In this case, Beryl focused on the theme of the clash of cultures (for instance, Banerji speaks with a BBC accent and doesn't know Christmas, in contrast to the family) rather than on the religious perspective and stated this explicitly in the interview ("*pero no me pareció demasiado relevante* porque me parece que *el foco no estaba en sí, ¿no?, en ciertas cuestiones religiosas sino en el choque de culturas, no desde lo religioso*"; "but *it didn't seem very relevant to me since I didn't think that the focus was placed on certain religious issues, right?, but on the clash of cultures, not from a religious perspective*"; Excerpt 4).

Similar phenomena were found in other data, and it is clear that the participants relied on familiar knowledge and experiences in their understanding of the texts, and that they also showed an ability to reflect critically on their prior knowledge and assumptions. They all interpreted the texts by explicitly resorting to something familiar, either in the form of specific knowledge or personal experiences. This knowledge and these experiences were not necessarily related to Christmas, and they were not necessarily related to the participants' own cultures either. On the contrary, many times they were free associations that the texts had triggered, tied to knowledge of different topics and the most diverse experiences.

Different Foci of Attention and Schema Processes

We illustrated above how Beryl's confusion between Christmas and Thanksgiving shows the strength of existing schemata as well as the difficulty of accommodating and assimilating new knowledge to prior frames of reference. Despite the presence of textual information that explicitly indicated that it was a Christmas celebration, Beryl chose to affirm that it was more linked to Thanksgiving.

Furthermore, participants omitted some themes and episodes altogether from the reading response and the visual representation tasks. For instance, Beryl decided not to focus on the religious perspective at all and focused instead on the theme of the clash of cultures as she stated explicitly in the interview ("pero *no me pareció demasiado relevante* porque me parece que *el foco no estaba en sí, ¿no?, en ciertas cuestiones religiosas sino en el choque de culturas, no desde lo religioso*"; "but *it didn't seem very relevant to me since I didn't think that the focus was placed on certain religious issues, right?, but on the clash of cultures, not from a religious perspective*"; Excerpt 4). She also omitted the anecdotes with the turkeys, the square tomatoes, the chickens without feathers and the cats without fur in *Cat's Eye*, and the dancing, wrestling, riding, music, bread-making, stew-preparation and coffee-making episodes in *Desert Wife*.

At other times, as we will show in Chapter 7 with the case of Enrique Alejandro, the participants elaborated on the textual content and attempted alternative interpretations. Enrique Alejandro attempted several interpretations to explain why the Navajo women would not have washed the dishes if they had not been told to do so.

These examples illustrate processes of assimilation and accommodation in schema theory operating within the process of cultural understanding. The notion of "schema affirmation" (Jeffries, 2001: 325) means that readers pay attention to textual information that relates to their prior knowledge and experience, at least in literary reading. The participants assimilated new information to their existing schemata, resulting in the elaboration of a schema through the inclusion of explanatory information, for instance (Bransford, 2004). They also accommodated new content by means of restructuring, consequently producing the modification of a schema; the new information led to change in their initial ideas (Bransford, 2004).

Drawing on Literary Knowledge

The participants all made a connection to their literary knowledge and skills in attempting to understand the texts. They made this connection very evident and put it explicitly in their writing. Pervasive in almost all cases was the idea that a text has a message that the reader has to discover, a message beyond the actual words on the page. The participants explicitly mentioned that there was something hidden for them to discover and that they had to read between the lines. Beryl, for instance, closed her reading response based on *Cat's Eye* in this way: "Las contraposiciones entre tipos de pavo parecen ser una analogía entre culturas, pero también parecen mostrar una postura diferente sobre la navidad: es a partir de la simple cena como el protagonista arriba a conclusiones inesperadas *que parecen reflejar algo más allá de la simple lectura. Hay un mensaje escondido entre líneas que el lector debe dilucidar.*"; "The contrasts between kinds of turkey seem to be a sort of analogy between cultures, but they also seem to show a different attitude about Christmas: it is the very meal that makes the main character arrive to unexpected conclusions *that seem to reflect something beyond a simple reading. There is a message hidden between the lines that the reader has to discover*" (Excerpt 2).

In another example, the participants associated the Jolly Green Giant mentioned in this fragment with the Grinch in the children's book by Dr. Seuss entitled *How the Grinch Stole Christmas* and the corresponding film, and then with American children's fables in general (without specific examples) and thirdly with children's stories in general (not necessarily American, and not necessarily fables). They considered that the anecdotes of the chickens without feathers, the cats without fur, the drowned turkeys and the snakes resembled fantastic stories. Beryl saw connections between this fragment and *The Great Gatsby* by Scott Fitzgerald that she had read as part of a language course at the University of La Plata.

Excerpt 5

> B.: Más o menos sé que para ciertas cosas . . . o sea, para ciertas situaciones necesitás . . . tener como una información previa, ¿no? Y me parece que en realidad es para la mayoría de los textos, y *lo más gracioso es que yo me acordaba de algo que vimos en Lengua 2 con The Great Gatsby.*
>
> (Beryl, interview, *Cat's Eye*)

English Translation of Excerpt 5

> B.: I know, more or less, that to do certain things . . . that is, in certain situations we need a sort of previous information, right? And I think that it's necessary in the majority of the texts, and *the funniest thing is that I remembered something we saw in Language II about The Great Gatsby.*

Another kind of intertextuality was evidenced too, an intertextuality that connected the three prompt fragments we used in our research. Beryl for instance made intertextual connections between the fragments from *Mi planta de naranja-lima* and *Cat's Eye*:

Excerpt 6

> El tema del texto [*Cat's Eye*] parece reflejar una cena navideña que, *en comparación, con el texto anteriormente leído* [*Mi planta de naranja-lima*], es de un grupo de personas de clase media.
>
> (Beryl, reading response task, *Cat's Eye*)

English Translation of Excerpt 6

The topic of the text [*Cat's Eye*] seems to reflect a Christmas dinner of a middle-class group of people, *compared against the text we've previously read* [*Mi planta de naranja-lima*].

Victoria also made such connections. She started her reading response based on the Navajos text with a comment on intertextuality between this fragment and that from *Cat's Eye*. She analysed both texts with reference to the concept of integration (who was being integrated in each Christmas celebration), and this prompted her to compare both texts using the concepts of 'local culture' and 'minority group'.

Excerpt 7

Me permito en primer lugar *establecer una mínima comparación con el texto anterior. En ambos casos se observa la integración (o intento de tal) de un extranjero en una fiesta navideña celebrada en una cultura que le es extraña. En el caso del texto anterior* [*Cat's Eye*], el que intentaba integrarse era un hindú, cuya cultura no considera las fiestas navideñas, a un entorno en el que la Navidad es relevante y muy popular como celebración. *En el texto presente*, un grupo de representantes de una cultura en que aparentemente también se celebra la Navidad (sospecho que la norteamericana, aunque los datos son pocos) se integran (o intentan hacerlo) a las celebraciones navideñas de un *grupo minoritario*: una tribu de navajos.

(. . .)

remitiéndome nuevamente a mi comparación con el texto anterior, no se ven en el caso presente (al menos no de manera tan marcada), el recelo y el prejuicio que sí se observaban en el texto anterior, sobre todo de parte de la 'cultura local'.

(Victoria, reading response task, *Desert Wife*)

English Translation of Excerpt 7

To begin with, I allow myself to *establish a comparison with the previous text. In both cases we can see the integration (or attempt of such) of a foreigner in a Christmas meal celebrated in a culture which is strange to that foreigner. In the previous text* [*Cat's Eye*], an Indian, whose culture doesn't celebrate Christmas, was integrated to an environment in which Christmas is relevant and a very popular celebration. *In the present text*, a group of representatives of a culture where Christmas is apparently celebrated (the American culture, I guess, even when there is not much information) are integrated (or tried to do so) to the Christmas celebration of a *minority group*: a Navajo tribe.

(. . .)

going back to my comparison with the previous text, we can't see in this case (at least not so evidently) the mistrust and prejudices that we observed in the previous text, mainly from the 'local culture'.

Other students also resorted to their literary knowledge and skills to understand cultural aspects in the texts and drew on an ability to make similar intertextual connections that included the prompt texts themselves but also others referring to books, stories and films from elsewhere.

Critical Cultural Awareness

Victoria's response to the prior knowledge task was particularly rich and revealed the criticality and reflexivity that are associated with levels 4 and 5 in our model. It included a reflection regarding Native Americans' struggles for their lands and rights, and she explicitly mentioned that a Christmas celebration by the Navajos had to be imported from the American culture, i.e., it could not be a native celebration. She evaluated her own interpretation as "paradoxical", based on her belief that the "Indians want to differentiate from that culture".

Excerpt 8

Lo único que considero que acaso pudiere ser relevante para la lectura del texto es recordar las *luchas de los indios por sus tierras y derechos*. Sospecho que la Navidad debe de ser para ellos una celebración *no autóctona, entendiendo por 'no autóctono' algo que han debido de tomar de la cultura norteamericana*. Esto resulta *paradójico* siendo que, por lo poco que sé al respecto, existe la intención de los indios de *diferenciarse de dicha cultura*. Por tanto, deduzco que las celebraciones navideñas deben de *tener diferencias bastante importantes* con respecto a las que se enmarcan en la cultura norteamericana.

(Victoria, prior knowledge task, Desert Wife)

English Translation of Excerpt 8

The only thing that I consider that might be relevant to reading the text is to remember *the struggles of the indigenous communities for their lands and rights*. I suspect that Christmas can't be an *autochthonous* celebration, *understanding 'not autochthonous' as something that they must have been taken from the American culture*. This is *paradoxical* since, from what I understand, there is an intention of the indigenous people *to differentiate themselves from that culture*. Therefore, I can infer that the Christmas celebration must *be somehow very different* from those framed within the American culture.

Prompted by a question in the prior knowledge task that required her to imagine what a Christmas celebration by the Navajos might be like, she repeated the idea of the standard American culture influencing minorities and emphasised two notions: the assimilation of both cultures and the idea of difference.

Excerpt 9

Imagino que las fiestas de Navidad de los navajos habrán *asimilado elementos de la cultura norteamericana*, pero también sospecho que en tales celebraciones se deben de haber *incorporado además rituales y tradiciones típicas de esta tribu*. No puedo suponer demasiado porque desconozco absolutamente el tema e ignoro, entre otras cosas, *la influencia que la cultura norteamericana estándar ejerce hoy día sobre estos grupos minoritarios*; pero sí tengo la idea de que las celebraciones navideñas de los navajos deben de ser *bastante diferentes a todo lo que conozco*.

(Victoria, prior knowledge task, *Desert Wife*)

English Translation of Excerpt 9

I imagine that the Navajo Christmas celebration must have *assimilated elements from the American culture*, but I guess that they must have *also introduced typical rituals and traditions of this tribe in such celebrations*. I can't go very far in my assumptions since I know nothing about the topic and I am not aware, amongst other things, of *the influence that the standard American culture exercises over these minority groups nowadays*, but I believe that the Navajo Christmas celebrations must be *very different from everything I know*.

Perspective-Taking and Decentring

As we saw in Chapters 2 and 4, sometimes the process of comparing and contrasting that characterised their approach to the cultural revealed the participants' difficulty in distancing themselves from their own positions and in understanding otherness from the point of view of the Other, something that led to stereotyping on occasion. By contrast, at other times the process of comparing and contrasting resulted in the adoption of different perspectives in understanding the cultural. This was the case for Victoria and her development of the topic of domination, which we analyse later in this chapter.

In general, in taking new perspectives Victoria was aware of, and explicitly stated, whose view the text portrayed. She also provided details regarding what perspective Hilda, the narrator, adopted in her description of the Navajos, with reflections about the fact that she was an outsider, an external observer who was also a participant but not a true participant, whose perceptions were not value-free ("*de ahí la importancia del juicio que ella pueda tomar de esto*, porque quizás para muchos va a ser el único contacto con la cultura navaja que tengan"; "*consequently the importance of the judgement that she can take from this*, because perhaps for many readers it's going to be the only contact with the Navajo culture that they have"; Excerpt 10). In spite of this, Victoria saw the text as offering a relatively objective account of the Navajos, despite the unavoidable lens through which the narrator observed them. In her approach to analysis Victoria supported her assertions with quotes from the text (we use underlining to signal quotes).

Excerpt 10

M.: ¿Cuál era la 'cultura local'? . . .

V.: La cultura local en aquel texto era la cultura del narrador, es decir, el *punto de vista del narrador del texto.*

(. . .)

M.: Hablás también de introducir . . . que 'la narradora quiere introducir al lector a las costumbres navajas.'

V.: No, lo que quiero decir con eso es que *si el lector desconoce, como me pasa a mí, las costumbres navajas, las vemos a partir de los ojos de la narradora.*

M.: Hm.

V.: O sea, *de ahí la importancia del juicio que ella pueda tomar de esto*, porque quizás para muchos va a ser el único contacto con la cultura navaja que tengan.

M.: Sí, pero *también decís que hay cierta objetividad.*

V.: A eso voy.

M.: O sea que *es una buena lectura, o una buena introducción.*

V.: A eso voy, exacto, o sea, incluso ahí está la conclusión, donde ella dice: 'No *hay nada frío, ni nada solemne, ni nada acartonado, nada almidonado en esto, la gente es feliz, son gente amable* . . .' O sea, si bien el aspecto . . . Por eso digo que me parece que *está narrado con bastante objetividad, dentro de lo que no puede evitar* . . .

(Victoria, interview, Desert Wife)

English Translation of Excerpt 10

M.: Which was the 'local culture?'

V.: The local culture in that text was the narrator's culture, *the narrator's point of view.*

(. . .)

M.: You're also talking about introducing . . . that 'the narrator wants to introduce the readers to Navajo customs.'

V.: No, what I mean by that is that *if the reader is unaware, as was the case with me, of Navajo customs, we see them through the eyes of the narrator.*

M.: Hm.

V.: That is, *consequently, the importance of the judgment that she can take from this*, because perhaps for many readers it's going to be the only contact with the Navajo culture that they have.
M.: Yes, but *you're also saying that there is certain objectivity*.
V.: *That's what I mean.*
M.: That is, *it's a good read or a good introduction.*
V.: That's exactly what I mean, that, even if there is the conclusion, where she says: 'There is nothing cold, nor solemn, nor stiff, nothing stuffy in this, the people are happy, they are friendly . . .' rather . . . That's why I say that it seems that *it's narrated with objectivity, including that which she can't avoid* . . .

Much discussion emerged about this issue of objectivity and the inevitability of bias and subjectivity in entering another culture. Victoria used the idea that Hilda learned from the Navajo women as evidence of the objectivity of the narrator's perception of the Navajos:

Excerpt 11

M.: Y relacionado con esto, mi pregunta es, ¿existe . . . o vos ves de parte de la narradora una visión peyorativa o denigratoria de los indios por racista?
V.: En ciertos casos . . . no sé si denigratoria, sí veo quizás algo condescendiente, y sí veo . . . Digamos . . . A ver, veo *una objetividad bastante marcada* a pesar de . . . veo . . . incluso ahí abajo pongo que hay un *interés incluso de aprender* de la cultura aborigen, esa cosa de . . . O sea, veo que está *bastante objetiva* la cuestión. Lo que sí creo es que *hay cosas que quizás no pueda evitar*.

(Victoria, interview, Desert Wife)

English Translation of Excerpt 11

M.: And with respect to this, my question is: Is there, or do you see on the part of the narrator, a derogatory or racist view of the Indians?
V.: In some cases . . . but I don't know if derogatory, I guess I do see something patronizing, and I do see . . . let's call it . . . I see *a marked objectivity* in spite of . . . I see . . . including below where I put that there is *even an interest in learning* the native culture, the thing that . . . that is to say, I see that the question is *pretty objective*. What I do believe is that *there are things that perhaps she cannot avoid*.

Victoria then generalised on the basis of this fragment (for instance, she mentioned that the US dominates the world) and she presented her ideological position toward this hegemony. The issue of the inevitability of certain attitudes and behaviours that Victoria explored before in talking about Hilda appear in Excerpt 12 linked to one specific country, the US.

Excerpt 12

V.: Ella [Hilda]. O sea, quizás como prototipo de *una cultura* que está dominando justamente, y que *domina no solamente al aborigen sino que casi como que al mundo*, digamos . . .
M.: Sí.
V.: *Quizás no puede evitar esa actitud de dominador*, ¿no?, de . . . o de *conquistador dondequiera que pongo el pie*.

(Victoria, interview, *Desert Wife*)

English Translation of Excerpt 12

V.: She [Hilda]. That is to say, perhaps as a prototype of *a culture* that is justifiably dominating, and that *dominates not only the natives but practically the whole world*, we could say . . .
M.: Yes.
V.: *Maybe this dominant attitude can't be avoided*, right?, that attitude of . . . of *conqueror wherever they put their feet*.

The episode of the candy bags (offered by Hilda as a Christmas treat), where the reader sees the Navajo children queuing up more than once to get several bags, prompted Victoria to reflect on the universality of certain cultural practices on the basis of the idea that people take more than what they need when others are not looking. More specifically, she argued that much of the narrator's culture is based on this precept. Through this generalisation, she was naturalising her own view of the American culture. She seemed to have missed the fact that the text was not contemporaneous with her times—the participants were not given the dates of texts—and that indeed Hilda might not have held such a negative view of her own culture. We see Victoria's own biases and prejudices in operation here. The use of a proverb, which is a Christian biblical allusion, to capture this complex idea is interesting and efficient ("está mirando la paja en el ojo ajeno y se olvida de la viga en el propio"; "She's seeing the mote in another's eye and forgets the beam in her own"; Excerpt 13). Worth noticing is the tentativeness that Victoria revealed in her linguistic choices, which we signal in bold in the extract.

Excerpt 13

V.: . . . yo hablaba del aspecto negativo de este episodio de los niños tomando las bolsas de dulce.
M.: Ah, sí.
V.: Yo pongo que se pasa por alto, es decir, *la narradora de nuevo* **parece** *olvidar*, en un punto de vista casi . . . **casi como** . . . **no sé si condescendiente o hasta** . . . **hasta negativo** de ese aspecto de la cultura Navaja, **parece** olvidar *que su cultura, mucho de su cultura se basa en esa cosa de hacer o de tomar lo que el otro no ve que le estoy tomando*. O sea, si es que . . .

M.: Eso es fuerte, lo que estás diciendo.
V.: O sea, lo planteo desde el punto de vista de que está . . . o sea . . . lo está . . . **digamos**, la narradora lo está poniendo desde el punto de vista de 'ellos, lo que hacen, mirá, ellos están . . . cuando nadie los ve están sacando cosas'. Bueno, **sospecho que muy sutilmente, si mis sospechas son ciertas y . . . y la voz narradora se inserta en la cultura norteamericana típica** . . .
M.: Sí, es así.
V.: Eh . . . **sospecho, bueno, que** . . . que hay una . . . o sea . . . hay una omisión de una información . . . **no sé si** deliberada o **quizás** porque no está mirando . . . *está mirando la paja en el ojo ajeno y se olvida de la viga en el propio*, **una cosa así**.

(Victoria, interview, *Desert Wife*)

English Translation of Excerpt 13

V.: . . . I spoke about the negative aspect of this episode with the children taking the candy bags.
M.: Ah, yes.
V.: I suggest that it's overlooked . . . that is to say *the narrator again seems to forget*, in a view point almost . . . almost . . . **I don't know if** condescending **or even** . . . **even negative** about that aspect of the Navajo culture, **seems** to forget *that her culture, much of her culture is based on getting or taking that which the other doesn't see that they are taking*. I mean, if it's that . . .
M.: That's strong, what you're saying.
V.: I mean, I explain it from the point of view that is . . . or rather . . . that it's . . . let's say, the narrator is showing it from 'the point of view of 'them', what they do; see, they are . . . when nobody sees, they are taking things'. Well, I suppose that very subtly, if my suspicions are correct and . . . and if the narrator's voice is placed in the typical North American culture . . .
M.: Yes, it is.
V.: Huh . . . I suppose, well, that . . . that there is a . . . rather . . . there is an omission of information . . . **I don't know if** it's deliberate **or perhaps because** she's not seeing . . . *if she's seeing the mote in another's eye and forgets the beam in her own*, **something like that**.

Excerpt 14 also shows Victoria's tendency to naturalise actions and behaviours as if they were universal, in particular in something as delicate as stealing. The point is important because she spoke of the idea of taking advantage as "intrinsic to human nature," irrespective of the prior and post softening of this assertion ("*No me atrevería a generalizar* porque sería por ahí ser injusto con quienes no lo hacen"; "Digamos, *no todo el mundo*"; "*I don't dare generalise* because that would be unfair to those who don't";

"Let's say *not the entire world*"; Excerpt 14). Softening the impact of her assertions in this way was characteristic for Victoria throughout her tasks. The switch to the first-person plural pronoun and references (in bold in Excerpt 14) to include herself in the generalisation is another important dimension of this. At this point her assertion also becomes more general as she refers to actions in general (not necessarily stealing or taking advantage) ("no creo que **todos** podamos decir que **nuestras** acciones a solas sean las mismas que **nuestras** acciones cuando **nos** están mirando"; "I don't think **we** could all say that **our** actions are the same when **we** are alone and when everyone is watching"; Excerpt 14). At the same time, she is able to see a behaviour (in this case, taking advantage) from a critical perspective, scrutinise it, and see herself as an exponent of it. In other words, her angles of vision of one event, the episode of the candy bags, were multiple and involved seeing the Navajos' actions from the point of view of an outsider (level 3 in the model), but also seeing her own actions (the possibility that she would also take advantage under some circumstances) from a distance (levels 2 and 4 in the model simultaneously).

Excerpt 14

> V.: Creo que es una *cuestión universal*, creo que *todo ser humano* hace un poco eso, ¿no? O sea, mientras lo dejen tomar ventaja quizás lo haga. *No sé si todos, pero una . . . una gran parte del género humano . . .*
>
> M.: Una universalidad ves ahí.
>
> V.: Sí, casi . . . Casi. No me atrevería a generalizar porque sería por ahí ser injusto con quienes no lo hacen, pero . . . sí creo que es *una cuestión casi, casi intrínseca de la naturaleza humana*, esa cosa de: 'No me miran . . .' Digamos, no todo el mundo . . . *no creo que todos podamos decir que nuestras acciones a solas sean las mismas que nuestras acciones cuando nos están mirando, por ejemplo.*
>
> (Victoria, interview, Desert Wife)

English Translation of Excerpt 14

> V.: I think that it's a *universal question*, that *every human being* has a little of that, right? Or that, as long as they are allowed to take advantage, perhaps they do so. *I don't know if everyone, but a . . . large part of humanity . . .*
>
> M.: You see something universal there.
>
> V.: Yes, almost . . . almost. I don't dare generalise because that would be unfair to those who don't, but . . . yes, I believe that it's almost, almost *an intrinsic question of human nature*, a thing of: 'they don't see me . . .'. Let's say not the entire world . . . *I don't think we could all say that our actions are the same when we are alone and when everyone is watching, for example.*

Summarising then, we have seen a process of comparing and contrasting underpinning the reference to prior and familiar knowledge in interpreting otherness. At times this process of comparing and contrasting revealed the participants' difficulty to distance themselves from their own positions and understand otherness from the point of view of the Other. This difficulty in decentring led to generalising and stereotyping, but at other times, the process of comparing and contrasting resulted in the adoption of different and multiple perspectives in the understanding of another culture.

Criticality and Reflexivity

The theme of domination constitutes a good example of the depth of criticality and reflection revealed in understanding the cultural in reading texts. Victoria explored the topic of domination through the dichotomy 'standard culture' vs. 'minority group', recurrent in a lengthy reading response task. The notion of integration is also present, evidenced in the contrast 'terreno ajeno—propio territorio' (foreign terrain—own territory). The domination is evident, according to Victoria, in the fact that the narrator attempts to dominate in a territory that is not her native land, in other words, on the Navajos' reservation. She quotes the cooking and dishwashing episodes as evidence of this domination (the cooking episode in which the narrator tells the Navajo women how best to cook for all, and the dishwashing episode in which the narrator tells the Navajo women to wash the dishes after the meal). We again underline Victoria's use of direct quotes and signal in bold the instances of doubt, hedging devices, modality, tentative language and vague and general language in her data samples. These instances reveal Victoria's decision not to take full responsibility for her interpretations; she decides to present her interpretations and then soften them, or distance herself from them, by recourse to these devices.

Excerpt 15

Me permito en primer lugar establecer una mínima comparación con el texto anterior. En ambos casos se observa la integración (o intento de tal) de un extranjero en una fiesta navideña celebrada en una cultura que le es extraña. En el caso del texto anterior, el que intentaba integrarse era un hindú, cuya cultura no considera las fiestas navideñas, a un entorno en el que la Navidad es relevante y muy popular como celebración. En el texto presente, un grupo de representantes de una cultura en que aparentemente también se celebra la Navidad (sospecho que la norteamericana, aunque los datos son pocos*) se integran (o intentan hacerlo) a las celebraciones navideñas de un grupo minoritario: una tribu de navajos.

*'*Christmas to us meant warm fires, red berries, gifts in tissue paper*'. Otro elemento que me permite sospechar que se trata de la cultura norteamericana es la posible proximidad geográfica y la expresión: *'that little attention made me homesick for something not Indian'*. El término 'homesick' no se relaciona, creo, aquí, con la lejanía del hogar sino de la cultura, y de ahí la especificación: *'. . . for something not Indian'*.

Ya desde el nombre, todo les resulta extraño: *'We found that the Navajo 'Kismas' included the warm fires, but everything else was novel enough to make history'*. Sin embargo, remitiéndome nuevamente a mi comparación con el texto anterior, no se ven en el caso presente (al menos no de manera tan marcada), el recelo y el prejuicio que sí se observaban en el texto anterior, sobre todo de parte de la 'cultura local'.

Por otro lado, **si mis sospechas son ciertas,** quienes intentan *integrarse* aquí forman parte de lo que **podríamos** considerar *'cultura estándar' (norteamericana),* **al menos** en relación a la *cultura del grupo minoritario de los navajos.* Quizás por eso, **incluso** en *'terreno ajeno'*, se generan escenas en que **aparentaría** producirse una *sutil dominación* por parte de quienes sin ser miembros de la tribu ni de la celebración que tiene lugar en ella, representan la *cultura estándar*:

'Other women I set to peeling onions and potatoes, and very handy they were at it too.'

'After the meal was over, the women cleaned the soot from the tubs and boiler with sand, while I scalded the spoons and pans. They were willing enough to do it, though they would have gone away and left everything dirty, if I had not suggested the dishwashing. I thought it best they do some little thing for their meal.'

Es como si, a pesar de hallarse inmersos temporalmente en otra cultura, *el hecho de pertenecer a la 'cultura estándar' concediera ciertos derechos implícitos de dominación,* **al menos** *sutil, y* **obligara** *implícitamente al grupo minoritario a aceptar el status quo incluso en su propio territorio.*

Ciertos factores contemplados desde el punto de vista de la 'cultura estándar' (cuya mirada, por otra parte, es la que conduce al lector a introducirse en la cultura de los navajos), focalizan en lo que podrían considerarse aspectos negativos de la tribu: *'What they did not eat at once they were afraid to put down because some one would steal it, so all the evening they strolled about with great raw beefsteaks in their hands'*. (. . .) *'There was a sort of appreciation in the Navajo, but it was the sort that wanted all they could get from any one who wasn't looking'*.

La narradora pasa por alto el hecho de que, al menos en este último caso, tampoco su cultura queda excluida de esta conducta negativa.

Se observan (aunque no se comentan en el texto) otros factores que diferencian a ambos grupos, como la mención a vuelo de pájaro de la poligamia (*'the Little Bidoni and his three wives'*).

De todos modos, también se consignan elementos positivos relacionados con la tribu (*'They were a most fun-loving people'*), y ciertos elementos parecen unir a ambos grupos (*'and they laughed at the same things we thought funny'*), e incluso se ve un interés genuino por parte de la narradora de aprender cosas de los navajos (*'Mrs. White Hat and Mrs. Japon began making bread and the efficient way they went about it was a lesson to me'*).

La descripción de los festejos resulta, por su contenido, novedosa tanto para el lector como para la propia narradora al momento de presenciar tales festejos. El punto de vista de la 'cultura estándar' guía al lector que desconociere las costumbres de los navajos para introducirse en ellas, al menos en lo que respecta a las celebraciones navideñas, y por tanto me resulta interesante esta cita del texto, que acaso resuma brevemente las impresiones de la narradora: *'There was nothing cold or solemn about the gathering; every one was laughing and happy'*.

(Victoria, reading response task, Desert Wife)

English Translation of Excerpt 15

To begin with, I want to establish a comparison with the previous text. In both cases we can see the integration (or attempt to integrate) of a foreigner in a Christmas meal celebrated in a culture which is strange to that foreigner. In the previous text, an Indian, whose culture doesn't celebrate Christmas, was integrated into an environment in which Christmas is relevant and a very popular celebration. In the present text, a group of representatives of a culture where Christmas is apparently celebrated (the American culture, I guess, even when there is not much information*) are integrated (or tried to do so) to the Christmas celebration of a minority group: a Navajo tribe.

**'Christmas to us meant warm fires, red berries, gifts in tissue paper.'* Another element that makes me suspect that this is the American culture is the possible geographical proximity and the expression: *'that little attention made me homesick for something not Indian.'* Here, I think, the term 'homesick' is not related to the geographical distance from home but from the person's own culture, and this makes necessary the specification: *'for something not Indian.'*

From the very name, all seems strange to them: *'We found that the Navajo 'Kismas' included the warm fires, but everything else was novel enough to make history.'* However, going back to my comparison with the previous text, we can't see in this case (at least not so evidently) the mistrust and prejudices that we did observe in the previous text, mainly from the 'local culture.'

Furthermore, **if my guess is correct**, those who try to be *integrated* here are members of what we **might** consider a *'standard culture'* (American), **at least** in relation to the *culture of the minority group (the Navajos)*. **Maybe** that's why, **even** in a *'strange territory'*, some situations take place in which we **can** observe a *subtle domination* from those who, yet not members of the tribe or the celebration within it, are representatives of the *standard culture*:

'*Other women I set to peeling onions and potatoes, and very handy they were at it too.*'

'*After the meal was over, the women cleaned the soot from the tubs and boiler with sand, while I scalded the spoons and pans. They were willing enough to do it, though they would have gone away and left everything dirty, if I had not suggested the dishwashing. I thought it best they do some little thing for their meal.*'

It seems that, despite *being temporarily involved in a different culture, the fact that they belong to the 'standard culture' granted certain implicit rights to dominate,* **at least** *subtly, implicitly forcing the minority group to accept this state of affairs even in their own land.*

Some factors observed from the point of view of the 'standard culture' (which introduces the reader to the Navajo culture), focuses on what might be considered as negative aspects of the tribe: '*What they did not eat at once they were afraid to put down because someone would steal it, so all the evening they strolled about with great raw beefsteaks in their hands.*' '*There was a sort of appreciation in the Navajo, but it was the sort that wanted all they could get from anyone who wasn't looking.*'

Here, the narrator misses the fact that, at least in this last case, her culture cannot be excluded from this negative behaviour either.

We can observe other factors (left unsaid in the text) that distinguish the two groups, such as the brief mention of polygamy ('the Little Bidoni and his three wives').

Anyway, there are also positive aspects related to the tribe ('*They were a most fun-loving people*') and certain factors seem to get the two groups closer ('*and they laughed at the same things we thought funny*'), and there is even a genuine interest from the narrator to learn things from the Navajos ('*Mrs. White Hat and Mrs. Japon began making bread and the efficient way they went about it was a lesson to me*').

The description of the celebration is novel because of its content, strange to the reader as well as to the narrator who witnesses such celebration. The point of view of the 'standard culture' guides the reader who didn't know the Navajo customs, being introduced to them, at least regarding the Christmas celebrations, and that's why I find this quotation from the text interesting, since it may be said to briefly summarize the impressions of the narrator: '*There was nothing cold or solemn about the gathering; every one was laughing and happy.*'

Victoria explains the idea of domination further in the interview (Excerpt 16), along the same lines: domination is subtle; there is an implicit privilege of domination in what she calls the "standard culture". She evaluates textual content by using adverbs such as "paradójicamente" ("paradoxically") and she comments on what attracted her attention as a point of departure for her interpretations.

Excerpt 16

M.: Hablás de dominación, eso es muy interesante.
V.: 'Dominación', me refiero a que en un momento dado, por ejemplo hay dos casos puntuales . . .
M.: Sí, los que citás acá.
V.: Los que cito ahí, en los cuales se genera una *sutil situación de dominación* en la cual *el que pone las reglas, o el que intenta ponerlas al menos, es el foráneo*, es decir, paradójicamente *ellos están en un . . . insertos en una cultura que no es la suya, y sin embargo están diciéndoles qué hacer.*
M.: Sí.
V.: Es decir, con su cultura, con sus costumbres.
M.: Sí.
V.: *Eso es lo que por ahí me llamó la atención.*
M.: Y ¿por qué los dominados aceptan?
V.: Y claro, o sea, por eso pongo más abajo que habría una suerte de cosa *implícita*, de . . . de . . . quizás *contacto implícito*, ¿no?, en el cual la . . . *la cultura mayoritaria* o la *cultura estándar, en este caso, que podemos llamar cultura estándar, tendría cierto privilegio de dominación*. Quizás por eso tampoco se genera ese recelo ante . . . Yo creo que el recelo incluso es . . . Estoy pensando en el término inglés 'take over', o sea, *esa cosa de . . . de que el foráneo o el extranjero pueda asumir el control.*

(Victoria, interview, *Desert Wife*)

English Translation of Excerpt 16

M.: You were talking about domination. That is very interesting.
V.: 'Domination', Yes, I meant . . . in a given moment, for example there are two specific cases . . .
M.: Yes, you quote them here.
V.: Those that I quoted there, in which *a subtle dominant situation is created* and in which *the one setting the rules, or who at least tries to set them, is a stranger, rather,* paradoxically *they are . . . inserted into a culture which is not their own; nevertheless, they are telling them what to do.*
M.: Yes.
V.: That is to say, with their culture, their customs.
M.: Yes.
V.: *That's what caught my attention.*
M.: And, why do those dominated accept that?
V.: Well, that's why I put that there was a sort of *implicit* issue, that . . . that . . . maybe *implicit contact*, right? in which the . . . *the majority culture or standard culture in this case, that we will call standard culture, would have a certain privilege of dominance.* Perhaps that's why that distrust isn't generated before . . . I think that distrust is

even . . . I'm thinking of the English term 'take over', or *that thing that . . . that the stranger or foreigner can assume control.*

We see then that Victoria's analysis focused on people taking more than what they need, quoting the extract portraying the Navajos strolling with raw beefs under their arms. She put this in perspective and criticised Hilda for not being aware that in her culture people also steal.

Excerpt 17

Ciertos factores contemplados desde el punto de vista de la *'cultura estándar'* (cuya mirada, por otra parte, es la que conduce al lector a introducirse en la cultura de los navajos), focalizan en lo que **podrían** considerarse aspectos negativos de la tribu: *'What they did not eat at once they were afraid to put down because some one would steal it, so all the evening they strolled about with great raw beefsteaks in their hands.' (. . .) 'There was a sort of appreciation in the Navajo, but it was the sort that wanted all they could get from any one who wasn't looking.'*
   La narradora pasa por alto el hecho de que, al menos en este último caso, tampoco su cultura queda excluida de esta conducta negativa.
(Victoria, reading response, Desert Wife)

English Translation of Excerpt 17

Some factors observed from the point of view of the *'standard culture'* (which introduces the reader to the Navajo culture), focuses on what **might** be considered as negative aspects of the tribe:
   'What they did not eat at once they were afraid to put down because some one would steal it, so all the evening they strolled about with great raw beefsteaks in their hands.' (. . .) 'There was a sort of appreciation in the Navajo, but it was the sort that wanted all they could get from any one who wasn't looking.'
   Here, the narrator misses the fact that, at least in this last case, her culture cannot be excluded from this negative behaviour.

We have thus shown so far that the participants' literary knowledge (for instance, that texts have a message that readers must discover) motivated them to inspect the texts in depth and select portions that they felt needed to be analysed further. They positioned themselves as critical readers of all texts, showing elements of criticality and reflexivity regarding textual content. Furthermore, many times they went beyond critical thinking understood as thinking that involves evaluation, analysis and synthesis (Waters, 2006) toward critical cultural awareness (Byram, 1997), or critical social awareness, that is, a criticality and reflexivity tied to a social dimension, issues of citizenship, of humankind and human nature from a philosophical perspective, as the illustration with the case of Victoria shows.

Emotions in Comprehension

We have shown that the reading response task, the visual representation and the interviews revealed varied affective reactions towards textual content. For instance, in *Cat's Eye*, Beryl's confusion between Christmas and Thanksgiving shows how the initial confrontation with what is different can produce feelings of disorientation, rejection, disbelief, surprise, excitement or attraction before what is different and unknown. This kind of reaction is natural and important because it constitutes the first step towards the appreciation of the unknown (level 1 in the *Model of Cultural Understanding*). Beryl's example also illustrates that when certain textual information did not match the readers' available schemata or was too divergent (such as the fact that Christmas and Thanksgiving are indeed different celebrations), it was ignored or rejected, even though it was noticed. Beryl realised that the celebrations are different but still included contradictory information in her reading response task in this respect (see Excerpt 2 in this chapter). In the interview she added, "Me quedó claro que era de Navidad, pero me parecía que reflejaba más que nada Acción de Gracias"; "It was clear that it was Christmas, but it seemed to me that it rather reflected Thanksgiving" (Excerpt 3). She admitted feeling surprised by the fact that turkey is eaten in both celebrations ("No sabía que para Navidad también era una especie de tradición el pavo . . . *me sorprendió* en sí cuando me di cuenta"; "I didn't know that the turkey was also a sort of tradition for Christmas. . . . *I was surprised* when I realised that"; Excerpt 3).

When participants felt an emotional commitment to certain text topics, they favoured them in their productions. Victoria's lengthy reading response (Excerpt 15) on the topic of domination in the Navajos text, described above, is a clear example. This topic was important to Victoria since she made it her focus and consequently led to deep reflection and critical analysis. Similar emotive themes for at least some participants were, in *Mi planta de naranja-lima*, the extreme poverty, the unequal distribution of wealth in society, and the scrutiny and questioning of the religiosity associated with Christmas; in *Cat's Eye*, the topic of hospitality, the meaning of Christmas beyond the festive aspect, the feelings of loneliness and nostalgia, and the manipulation of Nature; and in *Desert Wife*, the lack of religious connotation in the celebration by the Native Americans as well as the theme of authority, paternalism and condescension.

In summary, in this chapter we have seen that the students relied on familiar knowledge and experiences in their understanding of the texts by engaging in processes of comparing and contrasting. At times these processes revealed their difficulty in distancing themselves from their own positions and understanding otherness from the point of view of the Other. This difficulty to decentre led to generalising, stereotyping, bias, prejudice and 'schema affirmation', showing the strength of existing schemata as well as the difficulty of accommodating and assimilating new knowledge to prior frames of reference. At other times, however, the processes of comparing and contrasting resulted in the adoption of different and multiple perspectives in the understanding of the cultural as the participants positioned themselves as critical and reflective readers.

Note

1. Crusade for Christ (http://www.cru.org/about-us/index.htm) is a Christian missionary organization that has ministries in more than 190 countries around the world, including Argentina.

References

Bransford, J. (2004) Schema activation and schema acquisition: Comments on Richard C. Anderson's remarks. In Ruddell, R. and Unrau, N. (eds) *Theoretical Models and Processes of Reading. Fifth Edition* (pp. 607–619). Newark, DE: International Reading Association Inc.

Byram, M. (1997) *Teaching and Assessing Intercultural Communicative Competence*. Clevedon: Multilingual Matters.

Jeffries, L. (2001) Schema affirmation and White Asparagus: Cultural multilingualism among readers of texts. *Language and Literature* 10(4), 325–343.

Waters, A. (2006) Thinking and language learning. *ELT Journal* 60, 319–327.

7 The Visual Representation Task and Foreign Language Texts

The task which asked students to produce visual representations of their understanding of a text is important both as a research tool and because of its potential use in teaching and learning. In this chapter we illustrate the tool with two representations based on the texts in English, which are complemented and enriched by drawing on interview data.

Personal Themes

As mentioned in the previous chapter, the participants did not develop the same themes in all the tasks they produced based on each text. They seemed to follow their attraction to certain topics as they encountered them, and the visual representation in particular was a private endeavour, a deeply engaging personal act, a vehicle for self-expression, for researching the cultural through analysis, reflection and introspection, even in the text in the native language. For instance, some participants revealed their attraction to the contrasts in *Mi planta de naranja-lima* (rural life/urban life, wealth/poverty, happines/sadness); others focused on the religious content; yet others on the Christmas celebration *per se* (with reference to the lack of presents and of food). Areas of interest in the fragment from *Cat's Eye* revealed by the visual representation were the clash of cultures (Canadian, Hindu and their own); the scientific discourse (biology); Elaine or Banerji and their cultures; the turkey and the overarching contrasts (animals/humans, capitalism/nature, artificiality/naturalness). In *Desert Wife*, readers' focus also included their attention to contrasts (reservation/civilization, English/Navajo language, dirtiness/cleanliness, standard culture/primitive culture); to the clash of cultures (the Navajo's, the narrator's and their own); or to the common bonds among the cultures portrayed.

118 *The Visual Representation Task and Foreign Language Texts*

The starting point of cultural understanding in the visual representation was themes in participants' own cultural realities. Relying on comparison and contrast, they began with what was familiar to them in order to explore difference. In Excerpt 1, for instance, Tess combined drawings and short phrases structured around the contrast 'the Hindu' versus 'the family'. Despite this opposition, the centre is occupied by an emphasis on commonalities and underlying bonds ("Algunos puntos de contacto", "Some points of contact"); she mentioned barriers in communication and the desire to achieve such bonds ("Barreras: Deseo de complacer al otro, algunas adaptaciones, palabras e ideas"; "Barriers, desire to please the other person, some adjustments, words and ideas"). The idea that courtesy dominates behaviour is represented by a rope ("El indio atado para no faltar a la cortesía", "Tied to comply with politeness rules").

Excerpt 1

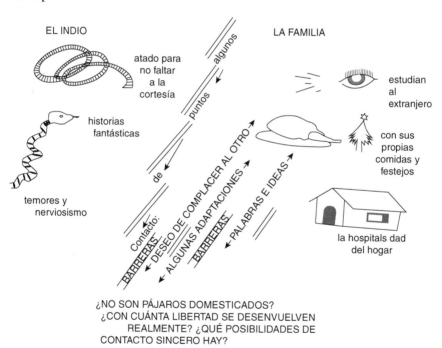

Figure 7.1 Tess, visual representation, *Cat's Eye*

English Translation of Excerpt 1

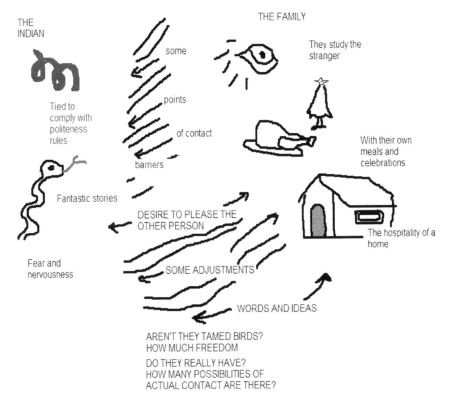

Figure 7.1 Continued

Tess introduces the idea that Elaine and the rest of the family are 'studying' Banerji, and represents this idea with a scrutinising eye ("estudian al extranjero", "they study the stranger"). This eye indicates the comparison and contrast between Elaine's and Banerji's cultures, which leads to the identification of cultural similarities and differences. Such processes are a preliminary in the contact with otherness, which involves the perception of the attractive, exotic, peculiar or different aspects of another culture and corresponds to level 1 in the *Model of Cultural Understanding*. The theoretical notion of difference described in Chapter 1 gains importance at this point because it is helpful in making cultures visible to external observers, for instance, those who read a text from another cultural background as in this case. Readers see what is 'different' from what they know in their own culture and tend to overlook everything else.

Tess also drew a Christmas tree with a star at the top, which can be seen as an elaboration of the Canadian Christmas or as a stereotyped intrusion from her own culture. The visual representation by itself was insufficient to clarify how Tess herself saw her inclusion of the Christmas tree, and the follow-up interview here, as in other cases described in earlier chapters, fulfilled a key function in accessing the students' perspectives.

Stereotypes, Generalisations and Reflections

It is interesting that in Excerpt 1, Tess does not mention Banerji's name at all and refers to him as "the Indian" or "the stranger" ("el indio", "el extranjero"). This avoidance is revealing because names are one of the most obvious and strongest markers of identity. Who is this 'Indian' or 'the stranger' then? Tess took the specific case portrayed in the fragment, represented by Banerji and the Canadian family, to move beyond Banerji and the family as individuals and to make stereotyped generalisations about both. Not referring to Banerji or any family members by name (simply referring to "la familia", "the family") can be seen as evidence of her intent to go beyond the specific case and to generalise to the social and cultural groups that the characters represent. This was confirmed by extracts from the interview that we quote below.

Tess rounded off her visual representation by formulating some questions that the text had triggered and had left unresolved ("¿No son pájaros domesticados? ¿Con cuánta libertad se desenvuelven realmente? ¿Qué posibilidades de contacto sincero hay", "Aren't they tamed birds? How much freedom do they really have? How many possibilities of actual contact are there?"). These questions show that Tess's responses were characterised by critical thinking, reflection, critical cultural awareness and social awareness, through simultaneous and alternative interpretations of textual content.

In Excerpt 2 (from the interview based upon the visual representation presented in Excerpt 1), Tess expanded on how she had conceived of this task, in particular in reference to the idea of courtesy (in italics in the extract). In bold, we highlight the adjectives she used to describe Banerji, which bring to the surface a stereotyped view of the Indian; this represents level 3 in our model. We underline a meta-cultural reflection which illustrates her ability to reflect upon culture—something that other participants also showed. In this case, Tess reflected on the link among culture, thinking, behaviour and language (specifically, speech). The final reflection questions in the visual representation, as well as her references in this task to "Some points of contact, barriers, desire to please the other person, some adjustments, words and ideas", reveal that Tess did not see the characters as individuals only, but as representatives of their own cultural groups, which suggests that her initial approach to the interpretation of this text was stereotyped.

Excerpt 2

> M.: En la representación visual dibujás una soga, eso es muy interesante. "Está **atado** para no faltar a la cortesía."
>
> T.: Por ahí *cortesía me suena muy poco a lo que yo quería decir. Yo quería dar la sensación . . . o da la sensación el texto, que él está*

*como **quieto**, como si estuviera **momificado** y que no se anima a decir ni hacer nada porque no sabe cómo van a reaccionar los otros.*

M.: Hm.

T.: Por eso puse como que estaba atado.

(Tess, interview, Cat's Eye)

English Translation of Excerpt 2

M.: In the visual representation you have drawn a rope; that is very interesting. "**Tied** to comply with politeness rules."

T.: *Maybe politeness sounds very little like what I wanted to say. I wanted to suggest . . . or the text suggests, that he is like **still**, as if he were **mummified** and that he dares not say or do anything because he doesn't know how the others will react.*

M.: Hm.

T.: That's why I wrote that he was like **tied**.

In Excerpts 3 and 4 below, other meta-cultural reflections (in bold) also show Tess's awareness of the interrelationships among language, culture, thought and behaviour. One key idea is that people are tied or limited, both in behaviour and language use, when confronted with otherness. Another is that the possibility of genuine contact is limited. These meta-cultural reflections were prompted by the questions that the text had left unanswered in Tess's opinion, which we highlight in italics in the extract. In all cases, Tess refers to the characters as exemplars of the larger cultural groups she identifies them with ("son culturas diferentes"; "la familia tenía sus propias costumbres, festejos, y le costaba desde esa visión ver al indio"; "están como que su propia cultura los limita"; "they are from different cultures"; "the family had their own customs, celebrations, and from that standpoint they find it difficult to see the Indian"; "like their own culture limits them").

Excerpt 3

M.: Acá concluís con pregunta. Te pregunto por qué pregunta, por un lado, y qué significa "¿No son pájaros domesticados?" ¿Quiénes? "¿Con cuánta libertad se desenvuelven realmente?" ¿Quiénes? "¿Qué posibilidades de contacto sincero hay?" *¿Quiénes son pájaros domesticados?*

T.: Para mí tanto el niño como la familia, pero . . . *serían como las preguntas que me quedaron después de leer el texto.*
Me parecía que cualquier persona se puede preguntar eso, a pesar de que el nene decía que ellos eran salvajes, no domesticados, por ahí en el sentido de que no . . . de que cuestionaban más las cosas o que tenían más inteligencia, **parece que ellos siempre están limitados a lo que tenían que hacer, cómo actuar, qué decir, estaban un poco también** . . .

M.: La familia y el hindú, todos . . .

T.: Sí, todos.

M.: O sea que a eso hace referencia "*¿Con cuánta libertad se desenvuelven realmente?*", que no habría una libertad genuina de manifestarse. Y "*¿Qué posibilidad de contacto sincero hay?*", no hay, estás cuestionando que haya la posibilidad de un contacto sincero.

T.: *Para mí hay posibilidad pero está limitada.*
Por ahí justamente con ese diálogo como que **ellos un poco se van desmitificando, cómo ven al otro.**

English Translation of Excerpt 3

M.: Here you've ended with questions. I'm asking why a question, on the one hand, and what it means. "Aren't they tamed birds?" Who? "How much freedom do they really have?" Who? "Is actual contact possible?" *Who are tamed birds?*

T.: For me both the boy [Elaine] and the family, but . . . *they would be like questions that I still had after reading the text.*
I thought that any person may ask him or herself that, in spite of the fact that the boy said that they were savages, not tamed, maybe in the sense that . . . that they questioned things more or that they were more intelligent, it seems that **they were always limited by what they had to do, how to act, what to say, that they were also a bit** . . .

M.: The family and the Indian, everyone . . .

T.: Yes, everyone.

M.: So that is what is being referred to with "How much freedom do they really have?", that there wouldn't be genuine freedom . . . And "*Is actual contact possible?*" Is it? Are you questioning the possibility of actual contact?

T.: *For me there is a possibility but it is limited.*
Maybe it's right with that dialogue that **they in some way undo some myths, the way they see the other.**

In the continuation (Excerpt 4), Tess introduces another dimension, that there is a lack of ability to decentre: "*No se ponen a pensar que para el indio es un día común*"; "*They don't stop to think that for the Indian it's just a normal day*". We again show meta-cultural reflections in bold.

Excerpt 4

M.: ¿Y está limitada por qué, porque son de culturas distintas o por otra cosa?

T.: En parte sí me parece porque son culturas diferentes, y también . . . por el temor a cómo va a reaccionar el otro, por ser corteses, por . . .

M.: Sí.

T.: Y en parte por su propia cultura, como el que ponía que **la familia tenía sus propias costumbres, festejos, y le costaba desde esa visión ver al indio, porque no se ponen a plantearse** . . . Por ejemplo,

pensaban que ellos lo invitan a Navidad para que no esté solo. No se ponen a pensar que para el indio es un día común . . .
M.: Claro.
T.: No es que se va a sentir más ni menos solo, **entonces están como que su propia cultura los limita en la relación.**

(Tess, interview, Cat's Eye)

English Translation of Excerpt 4

M.: And why is it limited, because they are from different cultures or because of something else?
T.: Partly I think that yes, because they are from different cultures, and also . . . for fear of how the other person will react, to be polite, to . . .
M.: Yes.
T.: And partly because of their own culture, for instance that **the family had their own customs, celebrations, and from that standpoint they find it difficult to see the Indian,** because they didn't stop to think . . . For example, *they thought that they invited him on Christmas for him not to be alone. They don't stop to think that for the Indian it's just a normal day . . .*
M.: Sure.
T.: He's not going to feel more or less lonely, so they are . . . **like their own culture limits them in that relationship.**

In the following interview extract (Excerpt 5), Tess explained what she meant by the phrase "words and ideas" that she had used in the visual representation (Excerpt 1). For her, the conversation at the dinner table represented a point of contact. This is revealing again of her view that there is a link between language and culture, specifically language as a bridge to culture ("vía de contacto", "channel for contact").

Excerpt 5

M.: "*Palabras e ideas.*" Esto no lo entiendo, ¿qué significa o a qué te referís?
T.: Me parecía que por ahí ellos en el diálogo, *en la conversación que tienen en la mesa eso es una vía de contacto para ellos.*
M.: Una . . .
T.: *Vía de contacto.*
M.: Vía de contacto . . . Ah, que las palabras e ideas son el contacto, está bien.

(Tess, interview, Cat's Eye)

English Translation of Excerpt 5

M.: "*Words and ideas.*" I don't understand this, what does it mean or what do you refer to?

T.: It seemed to me that maybe they in the dialogue, *in the conversation they have at the table that is a channel to make contact for them.*
M.: Ah . . .
T.: *Channel for contact.*
M.: Channel for contact . . . Words and ideas are the contact, OK.

Tess attempted to understand how Banerji, as an Indian, felt in this celebration, and what he was like. In a process of decentring, Tess abandoned for a moment her own position and perspective to place herself in Banerji's shoes. For example, in her reading response task Tess mentioned that Banerji "feels uncomfortable and insecure", and is "timid", "humble", "demure", "quiet" and "alienated" ("la *timidez* que se ve en el extranjero"; "Es *amable* y trata de *complacer*, pero a la vez es *silencioso, casi no habla*"; "the foreigner's *shyness*; he is *polite* and tries to *please*, but at the same time, he is *quiet*, and *he barely talks*"). She attempted to explain these feelings, but in many cases, she did so from her own frame of mind ("Si bien gran parte de la timidez que se ve en el extranjero puede deberse a que la familia que lo recibe es la de su professor"; "Although the foreigner's shyness may, to a large extent, come from the fact that the family who receives him is his professor's"). This illustrates the notion of cultural bias (Bereday, 1964) and "cultural egocentricity" (Byram, 1989: 50). For Tess, being at a dinner table with a professor would make her feel shy, and she assumed that Banerji would feel the same way, even though this is not explicitly mentioned in the text.

Ethnicity was central for Tess in her understanding of the story since she saw Banerji as a representative of people from India in general—"creo que también se está *representando la personalidad de los indios como una de humildad y recatamiento*", "I also think that *the text is presenting Indian people's personalities as characteristically humble and demure*" (Tess, interview, *Cat's Eye*). However, as she admitted informally months after data collection, her knowledge of India was limited, and she was probably basing her generalisations on the stereotype of the indigenous populations living in Argentina or in the Latin American region. She explicitly took Banerji as a representative of people from India and consequently generalised easily by saying, for instance, that Hindu people are humble and demure. This generalisation process is a key characteristic of stereotyping (Byram et al., 2009) and is associated with level 3 in our model.

In the interview extract in Excerpt 6, Tess attempted to present her rationale for the stereotyped generalisation of Banerji as an exemplar or prototype from India, and expressed her uncertainty (highlighted in bold in the extract):

Excerpt 6

M.: Cuando ponés: "Las personalidades de los indios . . .", de los "indios", ¿querés decir de la India o de los indígenas?

T.: De la India.
M.: De la India. "*Como una humildad y recatamiento*". *¿Por qué pensás que es posible generalizar? ¿Por qué son los hindúes, o por qué asociás a los hindúes con la humildad y el recatamiento?*
T.: **No sé, me pareció** . . .
M.: Está bien, yo te pregunto . . .
T.: **No sé**, es que . . . *como en el texto él se presenta más como indio que como persona individual,* **me parece que** *todo lo que se dijera de él se aplicaba* . . . *desde la mirada del texto para la familia se aplicaba a toda la población de la India, en general. Él estaba representando a su cultura.*

(Tess, interview, *Cat's Eye*)

English Translation of Excerpt 6

M.: When you write: "Indian people's personalities . . .", "Indian", do you mean from India or indigenous?
T.: From India.
M.: From India. "*As characteristically humble and demure*". *Why do you think it is possible to generalize? Why are Hindu people, or why do you associate Hindu people with humbleness and demureness?*
T.: **I don't know, it seemed to me** . . .
M.: It's all right, I'm asking . . .
T.: **I don't know**, it's that . . . *since in the text he is presented more as an Indian than as an individual,* **it seems to me that** *all that was said about him could be applied* . . . *from the point of view in the text for the family, it could be applied to the whole of India's population, in general. He was representative of his culture.*

Tess's stereotyped assumption that Banerji is a representative of all Indians applies to the Canadian family as well. For her, the family represents the Canadian family in general as she expressed in a post-reading task written after the reading response and the visual representation tasks ("el fragmento nos muestra también que *se trata de una cultura hospitalaria la de la familia*, que se esmera por hacer sentir bien al invitado y que no pase solo las fiestas"; "the fragment also shows us that *the family's is a welcoming culture*, and that they do their best to make the guest feel good and not to leave him alone during the celebrations") (Tess, post-reading written response, *Cat's Eye*).

Perspective-Taking, Decentring and Critical Cultural Awareness

This kind of stereotyping was Tess's initial way of approaching otherness, associated with level 3 in our model. However, she also showed a high level of cultural awareness. Her cultural sensitivity emerged, for instance, in her reference to perspective-taking ("Por ejemplo, pensaban que ellos invitan a Navidad para que no esté solo. *No se ponen a pensar que para el indio es un día común . . .*"; "*No es que se va a sentir más ni menos solo*"; "For example, they thought that they invited him on Christmas for him not to be alone. *They don't stop to think that for the Indian it's just a normal day . . .*"; "*He's not going to feel more or less lonely*", Excerpt 4 above). There is a lack of empathy on the part of the family in assuming that Banerji would feel lonely at Christmas and Tess showed that she understood why ("la familia tenía sus propias costumbres, festejos, y *le costaba desde esa visión ver al indio . . . su propia cultura los limita en la relación*"; "the family had their own customs, celebrations, *and from that standpoint they find it difficult to see the Indian . . . their own culture limits them in that relationship*"; Excerpt 4). Worth noticing here is the centrality in the theoretical literature of the notions of empathy, perspective-taking and decentring in understanding otherness (e.g., Byram and Morgan, 1994; Quintanilla Pérez-Wicht, 2004).

For Tess, the fact that Elaine and her family thought that Banerji would feel lonely at Christmas was evidence of their inability to see things from his frame of reference instead of their own. He may not feel lonely at all simply because in his culture Christmas is not celebrated. It is important that the same point comes from a different source, in this case a reading task written after the reading response and visual representation tasks.

Excerpt 7

La situación se describe *desde la perspectiva* de uno de los hijos del anfitrión, que aunque parece ser un niño, tiene un gran poder de evaluar las sensaciones del invitado . . . el fragmento nos muestra también que se trata de una cultura hospitalaria la de la familia, que se esmera por hacer sentir bien al invitado y que no pase solo las fiestas. *Analizando un poco más esta actitud y las conversaciones en la mesa también podemos interpretar que hay falta de comprensión en la familia de la cultura del indio, y más que nada desconocimiento. Asumen que deben invitarlo en esa ocasión para que no se sienta solo en la navidad sin pensar que para él no debe tener ningún significado en especial esa fecha.*

(Tess, post-reading written response, *Cat's Eye*)

English Translation of Excerpt 7

The situation is described *from the point of view of* one of the host's children, who, although seeming to be a boy, has a remarkable ability to assess the guest's feelings . . . the fragment also shows us that the family's is a welcoming culture, and that they do their best to make the guest feel good and not to leave him alone during the celebrations. *Considering this attitude more in detail and the conversations at the table, we can interpret that there is a lack of understanding in the family of the Indian's culture, and especially a lack of knowledge about it. They assume that they should invite him on that occasion for him not feel alone on Christmas, and they don't stop to think that for him this date does not have any special significance.*

Overall then, the visual representation complemented by the interview revealed Tess's stereotyped perceptions of another culture, which correspond to level 3 in our model. At the same time, the visual representation and the interview have also revealed the elements of criticality, reflexivity and cultural awareness through the questioning of those stereotypes, and this is characteristic of the highest levels in the model (levels 4 and 5). The elements of criticality, reflexivity and critical cultural awareness reveal a conceptualisation of stereotypes as fluid and open categories instead. From this point of view, the visual representation, together with the interview, may become a pedagogically useful instructional tool for accessing and developing the students' critical cultural awareness. We have illustrated here how Tess's visual representation and interview offered her the chance to move away from fixed stereotyping, which constituted her point of entrance to the text towards a space of possibilities. Tess achieved this by acknowledging the importance of perspective-taking and decentring (How did Banerji actually feel?), difference and the relativity of values and ideas (Christmas meant different things for Banerji and the family) and empathy (Banerji felt lonely and afraid).

Finally, Tess's visual representation constitutes a clear example of the power of imagery in cultural understanding, e.g., drawings of a rope, an eye, a snake. The strength of emotion is also revealed here through the use of emotional terms—"quieto", "momificado", "atado", "temores y nerviosismo", "deseo de complacer", "están limitados", "se van desmitificando", "temor a cómo va a reaccionar el otro", "still", "mummified", "tied", "fear and nervousness", "desire to please the other person", "are limited", "they in some way undo some myths", "fear of how the other person will react" (Tess, visual representation and interview, *Cat's Eye*). The visual presentation is congruent with the importance attributed in the scholarly literature to image and emotion schemata in cultural understanding (Sharifian, Rochecouste and Malcolm, 2004). Furthermore, because the visual representation allows for emotional responses to emerge in reading, it may compensate for the weaknesses that schema theories have in this respect (Sadoski and Paivio, 2004). Considering the important role of emotions in language learning (Dewaele, 2013), it is clear that this is an area that deserves more investigation.

128 *The Visual Representation Task and Foreign Language Texts*

Focus on Dichotomies

We have illustrated in Chapter 6 how the participants focused on some themes in the tasks and disregarded others. Enrique Alejandro's visual representation based on the *Desert Wife* extract was simple and schematic and centered on dichotomies, captured by the graphic nature of the task. His representation focused on the contrast between Christmas in the narrator's own culture and in the Navajos' culture. He mentioned some characteristics of the Navajos' Christmas celebration in the form of generalisations (food, families, fires, dancing).

Excerpt 8

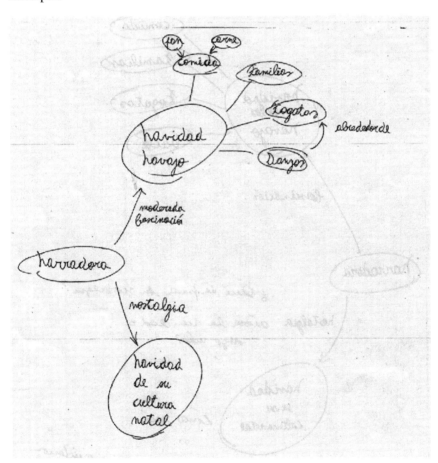

Figure 7.2 Enrique Alejandro, visual representation, *Desert Wife*

English Translation of Excerpt 8

The narrator

	Moderate fascination
Navajo Christmas	Food (bread) (meat)
	Families
	Fires around
	Dances

Nostalgia
Christmas in her native culture

In the interview extract below (Excerpt 9), Enrique Alejandro explained what he meant by the narrator's native culture ("Navidad de su cultura natal"). The use of evaluative and tentative language predominated, and we highlight expressions signaling this conjecturing in bold.

Excerpt 9

M.: Navidad en su cultura, ¿cómo será? ¿Vos decís que no podés identificarla con ninguna cultura en particular?

EA.: **Suena vagamente** occidental. Por lo que dice . . . la mención de las fogatas *medio me confundió, no sé de dónde pueda ser.* Pero **suena** . . . *de la zona europea, americana o . . . lo que sea.*

(Enrique Alejandro, interview, *Desert Wife*)

English Translation of Excerpt 9

M.: Christmas in her culture, what would it be like? Are you saying that you cannot identify this with any particular culture?

EA.: *She **sounds vaguely** occidental. Because of what she says . . . the mention of the fires confused me, I don't know where that might be. But **it sounds like** . . . some zone in Europe, America or . . . whatever.*

The feelings of fascination and nostalgia are important in the visual representation, and in the interview extract in Excerpt 10, Enrique Alejandro lifted a sentence from the text itself ("But we agreed we had never seen such a Christmas and would not see another in a lifetime") to argue that the white couple felt "fascinated" by the Navajo celebration (in italics in the extract). He also found this fascination to be contradicted by the objectivity he saw in the text:

Excerpt 10

M.: "Fascinación".

EA.: Eh . . . *otra vez con la falta de . . . de calificativos, lo dice en un momento que . . . o por lo menos describe . . . su . . . sentimiento,* eso como que: "Nunca habíamos visto nada parecido, nunca . . . nunca volveríamos a ver nada parecido", *lo que demuestra algún . . . grado de fascinación,* pero por otra parte el mismo texto, como dije, es objetivo. En un . . . por una parte dice: "Nos sentimos muy . . . impresionados", pero por otra parte no muestra ninguna impresión.

(Enrique Alejandro, interview, *Desert Wife*)

English Translation of Excerpt 10

M.: "Fascination".

EA.: *Ah, again with the lack of opinion, she says it in a moment that . . . or at least she describes . . . her . . . feeling,* that's like "we never saw something like it . . . we would never see something like it again", *which shows some degree of fascination,* but on the other hand the same text, as I said, is mostly objective. On the one hand she says "we felt very impressed", but on the other hand she doesn't appear to show being impressed.

With respect to nostalgia, he mentioned that the narrator missed her land, her celebration, her culture. This reference to nostalgia is important because it triggered a reflection about whether the celebration described is typical of the Navajos' background or Hilda's. Enrique Alejandro saw Hilda as an outsider (*"una fiesta a la que no pertenece"*; "*a festivity to which she doesn't belong"*) and mentioned that an interaction with one of the Indians created her feeling of homesickness ("supongo que es *uno de los indios, que . . . la saluda como alguien . . . de su propia cultura"*; "*I guess it's one of the Indians that . . . he greets her as someone . . . of her own culture"*). On this basis he interrelated concepts such as one's own land, Christmas celebrations and cultural background:

Excerpt 11

M.: ¿Qué dispara su nostalgia?

EA.: Ah, es un comentario de uno de los . . . supongo que es *uno de los indios, que . . . la saluda como alguien . . . de su propia cultura.*

M.: ¿Y qué significación tiene eso? ¿Por qué dispara semejante nostalgia?

EA.: Eh . . . bueno, *en el medio de una fiesta a la que no pertenece, repentinamente es tratada como si estuviera en la fiesta de su propia cultura. Por eso, repentinamente le hace recordar a su propia . . . a su propia tierra.*

M.: Añora . . . ¿Qué añora? La Navidad no porque ya me dijiste que no celebra la mujer la Navidad, pero ¿qué añora entonces? La nostalgia es la añoranza de algo . . .

EA.: Y sí . . . Eh . . . *¿Cómo que no . . . que no festeja la Navidad ella misma? ¿Yo dije algo parecido?*

M.: Yo creí entender que me dijiste que la Navidad es una celebración propia de los indios . . .

EA.: No, no, *esta celebración* . . .
M.: En particular.
EA.: *. . . es propia de los indios. Es la versión de la Navidad de los indios navajos.*
M.: Está bien. La narradora celebra en su . . .
EA.: *Evidentemente tiene una Navidad en su propia tierra. Por eso hace la comparación entre la Navidad de los navajos y la suya.*
M.: Y entonces ¿qué añora?
EA.: Añora . . . *directamente lo que añora es su propia Navidad. Indirectamente, probablemente sea la cultura entera.*

(Enrique Alejandro, interview, *Desert Wife*)

English Translation of Excerpt 11

M.: What triggers their nostalgia?
EA.: Ah, it's a comment of one of the . . . *I guess it's one of the Indians that . . . he greets her as someone . . . of her own culture.*
M.: And what does it mean? Why does it trigger such nostalgia?
EA.: Ah . . . well, *in the middle of a festivity to which she doesn't belong, suddenly she's treated as if she were in her own culture's festivity. That's why suddenly it makes her remember her own . . . her own land.*
M.: What does she miss? She does not miss Christmas because you have just told me that the woman does not celebrate Christmas, but what does she miss then? Nostalgia means missing something . . .
EA.: Yes . . . eh . . . *What about her not celebrating Christmas herself? Did I say something like that?*
M.: I understand that you told me that Christmas is a particular Indian celebration . . .
EA.: No, no, *this celebration* . . .
M.: In particular.
EA.: *. . . is particular to the Indians. It's the version of Christmas of the Navajo Indians.*
M.: It's ok. The narrator celebrates in her . . .
EA.: *Evidently she has a Christmas in her own land. That's why she makes the comparison between the Navajo Christmas and her own.*
M.: And so, what does she miss?
EA.: *She yearns . . . directly, what she yearns for is her own Christmas. Indirectly, probably her whole culture.*

The Complementary Role of the Interviews

If we look at Enrique Alejandro's visual representation in isolation, it is clear that the strong emphasis on dichotomies and generalisations can be associated with level 3 in the *Model of Cultural Understanding*, which reflects a stereotyped approach to another culture. However, this participant was simultaneously capable of the deep reflection and criticality that we saw in Tess and others. This became evident during the interview when he manifested, for instance, his ability to decentre in his analysis of the use of the word 'heathen' in the text from a perspective different from his own, the religious; he had said he was an atheist in the biographical questionnaire. In the following interview extract (Excerpt 12), he took the perspective of a pervasive and ingrained religiosity in the culture he imagined, thus distancing himself and his interpretation from a 21st century understanding of the word 'heathen'. The point of departure was what was different and this represents level 1 in our model: "*me pareció contradictorio . . . Esa contradicción me llevó a no . . . a no contarla porque . . . es tan raro que . . .*"; "*it sounded contradictory . . . That contradiction made me look it over since . . . it's so strange that. . .*".

Excerpt 12

EA.: 'Heathens', *cuando los llama 'herejes'. Eso también, otra cosa que me confundió.*

M.: No lo pusiste a eso.

EA.: No lo puse porque *me pareció contradictorio otra vez.* Durante el texto no menciona ninguna . . . *no hay ninguna otra mención despectiva de los indios.* Todo el resto [del relato] los trata como si fueran gente. Es más, dice que 'aprendí esto, les mostré esto' . . . No hay ninguna otra mención despectiva. *Quizás esto fue escrito en un contexto cultural en el que la religión era muchísimo más importante, los que no fueran cristianos eran herejes a pesar de que fueran perfectamente . . . normal.* Esa contradicción me llevó a no . . . a no contarla porque . . . es tan raro que no . . .

M.: Sí. ¿O sea que sería una visión . . . una posible visión nuestra, desde el siglo XXI?

EA.: Sí, precisamente, como que *no lo menciona de esa manera porque los desprecie, simplemente que los menciona . . . porque quien no es cristiano es un hereje, punto.*

M.: Sí, entiendo.

(Enrique Alejandro, interview, *Desert Wife*)

English Translation of Excerpt 12

EA.: 'Heathens', *when she calls them 'heathens'. That too, is another thing that confused me.*

M.: You did not write that.

EA.: I didn't put that in because, again, *it sounded contradictory.* During the text she doesn't mention any . . . *any other negative mention of the Indians.* The text treats them as if they were people. Moreover, she says 'I learned this, I showed them that' . . . there's no other negative judgement. *Maybe this was written in a cultural context*

> in which religion was much more relevant, those who were not Christians were heathens even if they were perfectly . . . normal. That contradiction made me look it over since . . . it's so strange . . .
>
> M.: Yes. You mean that it would be a view . . . a possible view from the 21st century?
>
> EA.: Yes, precisely, as if *she didn't call them that because she despised them, but rather because . . . because whoever is not Christian is a heretic, period.*
>
> M.: Yes, I understand.

This reflection was triggered by difficult textual content: the word 'heathen.' Enrique Alejandro states here that he had omitted this reflection on the word 'heathen' from his tasks because it was confusing and contradictory for him. But this interview extract shows that he is capable of deep criticality and reflexivity. The interviews thus served to enrich and complement the findings from other instruments at specific points in the process of understanding. It also shows that the process of comprehension was 'completed' later, after the reading of the text had finished, since the interviews for each text took place one week after the reading.

This extract is also rich in showing the *fluidity* of cultural understanding. By fluidity we mean that readers showed dynamism and flexibility in their approach to the cultural. In his visual representation Enrique Alejandro placed a strong emphasis on dichotomies and generalisations, and this is associated with level 3 in the *Model of Cultural Understanding*, reflecting a stereotyped approach to another culture. However, the discussion around the concept of 'heathen' in Excerpt 12 illustrates the reflection and criticality that characterises levels 4 and 5 in the model. Similarly, while Enrique Alejandro claimed that there was nothing pejorative in the view of the Navajos portrayed in the text, he himself referred to them in a fashion which could be interpreted as derogatory: "Todo el resto [del relato] los trata *como si fueran gente*"; "The text treats them *as if they were people*". The fluidity of participants' understanding, reflecting simultaneously various layers of comprehension as portrayed in our model, is something that we have also illustrated in previous chapters.

Alternative and Simultaneous Interpretations

All participants can be observed to have judged textual content as confusing at some point, and sometimes they spontaneously took the time and effort to think of explicit alternative interpretations, in particular in the immediate reflection logs and the interviews. By contrast, in the reading response tasks and in the visual representations, readers presented one interpretation and supported it at length. This finding points to the role of the different research instruments in revealing the characteristics of cultural understanding. Alternative interpretations in the reflection logs and interviews were not necessarily long, and often amounted to a brief succession of '. . . or . . . or . . .' sequences in the form of conjectures. For instance, many of the episodes in the Navajos text generated multiple possible interpretations, such as the dishwashing episode, the fact that the Navajos ate and ate or took more meat and candies than they needed, and Robert's greetings. Enrique Alejandro said the Navajos did not first wash the dishes because they expected someone else to do that job or because dishwashing was not an activity they were used to doing. Another participant, Lula, said that perhaps the Navajos thought they were guests and therefore did not have to do the dishwashing. Beryl said that maybe the Navajos left the dishes to be washed by the rain, or waited days before they actually washed them. Scarlet Rose resisted the idea that came to her mind that the Navajos were dirty. All the participants attempted explanations of this kind.

Enrique Alejandro invested time and effort in finding explanations for confusing textual information. In so doing, he constantly revisited conflicting content and entertained multiple interpretations (indicated in italics in Excerpt 13), and this revealed his ability to see through eyes different from his own. For instance, in connection with the dishwashing episode, Enrique Alejandro said "no puedo entender bien cómo es la situación", ("I can't really understand the situation"); and "No podría decir por qué los navajos no . . . no tienen la costumbre de lavar platos", ("I couldn't say why the Navajos don't have the habit of washing dishes"). Most instances of alternative interpretations were preceded by modality of some form or another ("*puede haber varias razones . . .*"; "*there could be various reasons . . .*").

Excerpt 13

> M.: Y no sé si recordás que hay una pequeña narración del lavado de los platos, donde la narradora sugiere el lavado de los platos.
> EA: Sí, ah . . .
> M.: Porque ellos no iban a hacer nada. ¿Eso te representó algo . . . te vino a la mente algo?
> EA: *¿Por qué ellas no iban a lavar los platos? No sé, puede haber varias razones . . . Eh . . . que esperen que alguien más los lave, que ellos no laven platos . . . no . . . no puedo entender bien cómo es la situación pero . . .*
> M.: Sí, no podés decir por qué es relevante o por qué está ahí mencionada.
> EA.: Sí, por qué . . . *No podría decir por qué los Navajos no . . . no tienen la costumbre de lavar platos.*
>
> (Enrique Alejandro, interview, *Desert Wife*)

English Translation of Excerpt 13

> M.: And I do not know if you remember that there is a little story related with washing up, where the narrator suggests washing up.
> EA: Yes, ah . . .
> M.: Because they would not do anything. Does that mean something to you . . . does something come to your mind?

EA: *Why they were not going to wash the dishes? I don't know, there could be various reasons . . . Ah . . . that they expect somebody else to wash them, that they do not wash the dishes . . . I can't . . . I can't really understand the situation but . . .*

M.: Yes, you can't say why it is relevant or why it is mentioned there.

EA.: Yes, why . . . *I couldn't say why the Navajos don't have the habit of washing dishes.*

We see therefore that, despite the fact that his visual representation was organised around dichotomies, there was a fluidity in Enrique Alejandro's approach to the cultural in this text as he moved beyond the binary divisions portrayed graphically and attempted multiple and critical interpretations.

Imagination in Cultural Understanding

The participants experienced difficulty in imagining some of the narrative or descriptive episodes in the prompt fragments. Enrique Alejandro had this difficulty with several elements in the fragment from *Desert Wife*, such as the clothing and the fires. In the interview he said that the clothing was something hard to imagine because it was not a familiar area for him and because he did not attribute importance to clothing. The fires were another because he only associated the fires at Christmas with Christmas fireworks. Again, comprehension proceeded by relating textual content to something familiar with a strategy of comparison and contrast:

Excerpt 14

M.: "Están vestidos con las mejores ropas" [dice el texto], ¿cuál es la dificultad en eso?

EA.: *Me cuesta un poco **imaginar** cuáles son las ropas.*

M.: Estaban descriptas ahí.

EA.: Sí, sí, pero no . . . Precisamente *no . . . no es algo que yo . . . considere como familiar. Precisamente no . . . **no lo registro** con facilidad.*

M.: Está bien.

EA.: *Tengo que ponerme a **imaginar**.*

M.: ¿Y los fuegos?

EA.: "Piñon smoke from the Christmas fires". *No estoy acostumbrado a fuegos en Navidad,* precisamente. Por eso el olor al humo no . . . salvo de la pirotecnia.

(Enrique Alejandro, interview, *Desert Wife*)

English Translation of Excerpt 14

M.: "They wear the best clothes" [the text says], what is the difficulty in that?

EA.: *It's a bit hard for me to **imagine** how they're dressed.*

M.: The clothes were described there.
EA.: Yes, yes, but . . . *precisely it's not something I. . . consider as familiar. I can't picture it easily.*
M.: Ok.
EA.: *I have to start trying to **imagine** it.*
M.: And the fires?
EA.: "Piñon smoke from the Christmas fires". *I'm not accustomed to Christmas fires.* That's why the smell of smoke isn't . . . well, *except for the smell of pyrotechnics.*

The visual representation task does not capture this difficulty of imagining certain episodes, but the interviews make it explicit. This is a phenomenon we have seen throughout this chapter that highlights the importance of multiple research instruments. It also suggests that in the use of such instruments for pedagogical purposes, there is a similar need to use a panoply of learning tasks and teaching techniques.

This chapter has shown that in the use of visual representation, the basis for understanding otherness rested on a process of comparing and contrasting, and in this process the participants resorted to what was known or familiar to them. Although the majority of the participants were interested in discovering alternative perspectives (as revealed by the pervasive presence of level 1 in the model in all tasks), their own frames of reference always mediated this interpretation. Even though this is expected and unavoidable in all comprehension, the characteristics of level 3 in the model (such as stereotyping, generalising and the prevalence of ethnocentric positions) were predominant kinds of response at times. Simultaneously, the cases of Tess and Enrique Alejandro in this chapter, as well as the illustrations with other participants in previous chapters, show that the confrontation with the values and ideas present in the perspectives of members of other cultural groups favoured a process of decentralisation or critical distancing from the participants' own perspective, and this is a characteristic of levels 4 and 5 in the model. The sliding back and forth among levels in the model (i.e., different layers of understanding) that we have illustrated in this chapter shows that cultural understanding was fluid as the participants showed a tendency toward stereotyping but at the same time also evidenced critical thinking, reflection and critical cultural awareness. They also offered simultaneous and alternative interpretations of textual content, revisiting and imagining that content, and a sophisticated ability to reflect upon the cultural. These are characteristics of levels 4 and 5 in the model based on an understanding of otherness that began with a process of comparing and contrasting.

References

Bereday, G. (1964) *Comparative Method in Education*. New York: Holt, Rinehart and Winston, Inc.

Byram, M. (1989) *Cultural Studies in Foreign Language Education*. Clevedon: Multilingual Matters.

Byram, M., Barrett, M., Ipgrave, J., Jackson, R., Méndez García, M. C., Buchanan-Barrow, E., Davcheva, L., Krapf, P., and Leclercq, J. M. (2009) *Autobiography of Intercultural Encounters: Context, Concepts and Theories*. Council of Europe, Language Policy Division. Available at http://www.coe.int/t/dg4/autobiography/Source/AIE_en/AIE_context_concepts_and_theories_en.pdf. Last accessed 6 May 2014.

Byram, M. and Morgan, C. (1994) *Teaching-and-Learning Language-and-Culture*. Clevedon: Multilingual Matters.

Dewaele, J.-M. (2013) Emotions and language learning. In Byram, M. and Hu, A. (eds) *Routledge Encyclopedia of Language Teaching and Learning. Second Edition*. Oxon: Routledge.

Quintanilla Pérez-Wicht, P. (2004) Comprender al otro es crear un espacio compartido: Caridad, empatía y triangulación. *Ideas y Valores. Revista Colombiana de Filosofía* 125, 81–97.

Sadoski, M. and Paivio, A. (2004) A dual coding theoretical model of reading. In Ruddell, R. and Unrau, N. (eds) *Theoretical Models and Processes of Reading. Fifth Edition* (pp. 1329–1362). Newark, DE: International Reading Association Inc.

Sharifian, F., Rochecouste, J. and Malcolm, G. (2004) 'But it was all a bit confusing . . .': Comprehending Aboriginal English texts. *Language, Culture and Curriculum* 17, 203–228.

8 Using the *Model of Cultural Understanding* in Self-Assessment

The question of assessment of intercultural competence or understanding is the subject of ongoing and complex debate (cf for example: Bennett, 2009; Scarino, 2009). There is some success in psychological testing (e.g., Alkheshnam, 2012; Antonenko, 2010; Nold, 2009), but high-stakes testing which is feasible and acceptable in education systems remains unresolved and beyond the scope of this book. Self-assessment and profiling is however possible and in this chapter we suggest that the *Model of Cultural Understanding* can be used in self-assessment and we give examples. Tess and Victoria self-assess using the model, and we show how the focus is on the skills of cultural understanding rather than on the achievement of levels in the model. These skills are the skills of observing, discovering, describing, analysing, comparing and contrasting, relating, interpreting, perspective-taking, decentring, critical thinking and reflexivity, all of which contribute to the development of intercultural competence. In previous chapters we illustrated how the participants in our research moved back and forth among the six levels in the model and displayed a range of skills of cultural understanding in their interpretations of text. This means that it would be misleading to associate cultural understanding predominantly with the highest levels in the model (levels 4 and 5) because each level involves specific skills and all are important. We suggest instead that students can create a profile of their reading as a form of self-assessment by reference to the model.

Self-Assessment Using the Model

We asked two of the students who participated in the research to write an analysis of their own understanding of the texts they had read, a document which could become part of a portfolio of their cultural understanding using the model as a structuring thread. We asked them to base their writing on their responses to the extract from *Cat's Eye*, chosen at random from the three extracts. The students received these instructions:

> Re-read the reading response and visual representation tasks that you produced based on this text, as well as the interview transcripts.

Using the Model of Cultural Understanding *in Self-Assessment* 139

> Read an abridged description of the model and the list of intercultural skills associated with it.
>
> Write a self-assessment reflection of your reading with a focus on the cultural dimension, i.e. go over your tasks considering the skills and levels of the model. This reflection can take the form of a stream of consciousness, or in other words you can write what comes to your mind without worrying about language or structure. We will consider this as a form of self-assessment of your cultural understanding.

Both Tess and Victoria wrote this self-assessment voluntarily and in English at the end of 2013, upon our request, and not as a part of any course requirement or research project. The interview, the reading response task and the visual representation had been collected, also voluntarily but in Spanish, in 2009–2010, when the research project on which this book draws was implemented. The use of Spanish then was intended to comply with the agreement in the relevant literature that research about reading in a foreign or second language be collected in the participants' native language. By 2013, Tess had already graduated and was no longer a student as in 2009–2010 but a teacher of English herself, and Victoria had made significant progress although she had not graduated.

We begin with Tess. Her self-assessment focuses on the interview she had at the time about the *Cat's Eye* extract as well as her own interpretations of the text in the reading response task and the visual representation. She reflects and comments on her responses to the tasks and supports her arguments with data from her interview about the text (in italics in Excerpt 1 below).

Excerpt 1. Self-Assessment by Tess

> Re-reading the tasks and the interview carried out for the research project some years ago, the main idea that comes to my mind is that my words and drawings reflect mainly the "dynamic interaction" between the levels of cultural understanding that is spoken of in the model. I feel that at times I could reach certain deeper level of comprehension and analysis of the C2 culture, but at the same time I believe that my interpretation is full of stereotyping and misinterpretations that result from my own cultural stance or perspective. Just as an example, in my interpretation I assigned the tale of the drowning turkeys to the Hindi man, since I felt that it was a fantastic story that had to be told from such a cultural background. However, I now quickly realise that in fact it was the professor who told this story. We can also see some stereotyping in my assigning the Hindi student some traits or qualities that would be representative of the cultural group as a whole instead of the individual: demureness and humbleness:

> M.: *When you write* [in the reading response task and visual representation]: *"Indian people's personalities," "Indian," do you mean from India or indigenous?*

T.: *From India.*

M.: *From India. "characteristically humble and demure." Why do you think it is possible to generalise? Why are Hindi people, or why do you associate Hindi people with humbleness and demureness?*

T.: *I don't know, it seemed to me . . .*

M.: *It's OK, I'm just asking . . .*

T.: *I don't know, it's that . . . since in the text he is presented more as an Indian that as an individual, it seems to me that all that was said about him could be applied . . . from the point of view in the text for the family . . . it could be applied to the whole of India's population, in general. He was representative of his culture.*

At passages such as these, I believe that I could place my thinking at level 3 of perception. Yet, I seem to oscillate between this lower level and a higher level of understanding, that I would place at about levels 4 or 5, when I analyze why the family has invited the student to their home, and what the significance of that day could actually have been for the young man.

M.: *And why is it limited, because they are from different cultures or because of something else?*

T.: *Partly I think that yes, because they are from different cultures, and also . . . for fear of how the other person will react, to be polite, to . . .*

M.: *Yes.*

T.: *And partly because of their own culture, for instance that the family had their own customs, celebrations, and from that standpoint they find it difficult to see the Indian, because they didn't stop to think . . . For example, they thought that they invited him on Christmas for him not to be alone. They don't stop to think that for the Indian it's just a normal day . . .*

At some points for instance in the following interview extract, I can identify a level 2 of understanding, when I relate the stories of genetically modified food to how the family sees the Hindi man, because I think I can identify my own prejudices or perception, from an insider's perspective, that is, I put my own perception or prejudices into words.

M: *Here you say that all the stories related to nature (the tomatoes, the chicken, the cats) are all important in the story, and at the same time you say that the scientific discourse about biology is something auxiliary. Isn't there a contradiction here? Aren't these examples of references to biology, or to scientific discourse?*

T.: *Yes, the thing is . . . I didn't relate it to scientific discourse, to biology and the examples but to showing what is strange, different . . . From that point of view.*

M.: *Ah.*
T.: *I associate it with the Hindi man, not so much with scientific discourse or biology.*
M.: *And why is it associated with the Indian?*
T.: *Because of that of finding something strange that seemed weird to them.*
M.: *To whom?*
T.: *To the family.*

As a conclusion to this analysis, I would say that I couldn't define my level of cultural understanding in the tasks as something stable or easy to categorize. I rather think that at times I was striving to be able to break free from my own perspective, to distance myself from the family's point of view, but that at times I presented a very stereotypical image of the Hindi student and that I misinterpreted some chunks of the text based on my own preconceptions. I would place myself in average around a level 3 or 4 of cultural understanding in these tasks. I have been able to experience some aspects of my own culture through the eyes of the student in some respects, but not to fully understand such a perspective without falling into the trap of prejudices and stereotypes.

Finally, what, in my opinion, this brief reflection can say about the Model of Cultural Understanding is that, as many other attempts to categorize reality, sometimes it is actually difficult to apply rigorously, and that the level of cultural understanding displayed by any individual will be fluctuating and ever-changing. Maybe what the model doesn't show is that behind an attempt to understand the "other" and adopt a new perspective, there will inevitably be some kind of "trace" of the stance that we regularly take, as if we were striving to get free from our prejudices but we could not get rid of them completely. As a result, I feel that I cannot place myself in a particular level of understanding. Otherwise, it would be either too good or too insufficient to describe what I think my actual level of cultural understanding is. I guess that even though we may make a conscious effort to try to adopt a different perspective, there is always a "hard core" of beliefs that we find difficult to change, and that at times come to the surface, unintended, just because they are deeply rooted in our perception of reality.

The comment in Excerpt 1 that "there will inevitably be some kind of 'trace' of the stance that we regularly take, as if we were striving to get free from our prejudices but we could not get rid of them completely" relates to the complexity and difficulty involved in cultural understanding, which we are finding throughout this book. Tess puts it in her own way: "I couldn't define my level of cultural understanding in the tasks as something stable or easy to categorise"; "the level of cultural understanding displayed by any individual will be fluctuating and ever-changing" (Excerpt 1). Part of this complexity stems, as we showed in previous chapters, from the impossibility of using one level in the model to characterise a particular interpretation: the participants showed evidence of all levels in almost all tasks. Part of the difficulty also comes from the theoretical notion of "cultural egocentricity" (Byram, 1989: 50), to which the words by Tess relate. There is always some kind of 'trace' of our own perspectives in text interpretation because we all feel and act in accord with our ethnocentric principles, or in other words, we "identify our own local ways of behaving with Behaviour, or our own socialized habits with Human Nature" (Benedict, 1935: 7). This results in honest and subtle differences of perception, or cultural bias, or in Tess's terms, the "traces" of one's stance.

We also see the skills associated with intercultural understanding all simultaneously at play in Tess's self-assessment:

- observing ("I now quickly realise that in fact . . ."; "We can also see . . .")
- discovering ("the main idea that comes to my mind is that my words and drawings reflect mainly the 'dynamic interaction' between the levels of cultural understanding that is spoken of in the model")
- describing ("it was the professor who told this story")
- analysing ("I put my own perception or prejudices into words")
- comparing and contrasting; also critical reflection ("Yet, I seem to oscillate between this lower level and a higher level of understanding")
- relating ("I feel that at times I could . . . but at the same time . . .)
- interpreting ("I misinterpreted some chunks of the text based on my own preconceptions"),
- perspective-taking ("I was striving . . . to distance myself from the family's point of view")
- decentring ("I was striving to be able to break free from my own perspective")
- critical thinking and reflexivity ("I guess that even though we may make a conscious effort to try to adopt a different perspective, there is always a 'hard core' of beliefs that we find difficult to change").

The self-assessment by Victoria is lengthy and rich. Precisely because her self-assessment is so long, we have decided to include it in full form at the end of this chapter (Excerpt 2), and we begin now with some observations based on sections of her writing. Victoria starts with some clarifications and caveats:

> I would like to start my comments with the caveat that my lack of experience working with the Model of Cultural Understanding might have made me miss many instances of different levels that an expert eye could spot in my reading response, visual representation and interview. Therefore, I have obviously signaled only those instances which were somehow visible to me, but I am sure that there is a lot more to say.

Using the Model of Cultural Understanding *in Self-Assessment* 143

In my tasks, I can observe instances of levels 3, 4 and 5 of the Model of Cultural Understanding. I list and explain these instances below, highlighting in bold, in each case, the words that I consider relevant.

One of the possible results of learners building up a portfolio of self-assessments might be that they become more aware and skilled—perhaps with the guidance of a teacher—and Victoria would be less self-conscious in later analyses.

Victoria analyses in great detail several elements of the work she did: reading response task, visual representation, post-reading reflection and interview. She finds multiple instances in these tasks for each level in the model, scrutinising her tasks and using them as data to support her views (highlighted in italics in the extracts below). For example, she writes the following, illustrating with data excerpts from her reading response (as we said, in italics), about what she considers the key indicators of level 3:

Instances of level 3, perception of culture C2 from one's own frame of reference (C1) (outsider perspective):
An apparently typical family (at least in their way of celebrating Christmas), receive a young Indian as their guest.
(reading response)

I consider this instance a level 3 one because I have used the word "typical" on the basis of my own perception and cultural knowledge about a Christmas celebration. For that matter, I have not questioned the fact that a Christmas celebration in the culture where the text is contextualised might be different, and just took for granted that it was a typical Christmas celebration only because it seemed typical according to my own cultural experience.

Another instance of level 3:
This fact introduces two different points of view in the story: on the one hand, we have what we might call the "local point of view," understanding as such the point of view of the culture in which the story takes place; on the other hand, we can observe the perspective of the foreigner who intends to integrate himself or to be integrated in such culture. On the one hand, the compassion ("We're having him to Christmas dinner because he's foreign, he's far from home, he will be lonely, and they don't even have Christmas in his country").
(reading response)

Other instances of level 3 identified by Victoria in her tasks, appear in Excerpt 2 in the appendix. Worth commenting on is her reflection on the theme of integration, which we highlight in bold in the extracts that follow. She addresses this topic in almost all her tasks: the reading response, the post-reading reflection, the visual representation and the interview. She sees this theme as evidence of level 3 in the model and explains why.

> I can observe another instance of level 3 in my reading response and visual representation, and then in my interview:
>
> We cannot deny that the text shows **an attempt at integration from both sides.** However, both cultures are strange to each other. To one of them (the local one) it is almost unacceptable that things might be so different in other parts of the world ("they don't even have Christmas in his country"). On the other hand, the young Indian accepts, without comments, the rules of the culture **in which he intends to be integrated** and whose rituals are completely strange to him and even the language might give him some troubles.
>
> (reading response)
>
> On the other hand, the foreigner accepts the local cultural norms and **tries to integrate himself to them,** or at least he does not refuse the responsibility of accepting the invitation to festivities whose significance is culturally foreign.
>
> (post-reflection written after the closure of data collection)
>
> Attempt at communication; brief, tense dialogues, based on the politeness of the Indian and on **an explicit intention from the local culture to integrate the foreigner.** Mutual observation.
>
> (visual representation)
>
> V.: Both are foreigners to each other, that is, that issue of being aliens.
> M.: Yes. Both are.
> V.: Both are, to each other, foreigners.
> M.: I see. [quoting from Victoria's reading response task] **"However, there is an attempt at integration from both sides."**
> V.: I mean, the foreigner wants . . .
> M.: **Does the foreigner want to be integrated, do you think so? You write there that he intends to be integrated.**
> V.: **At least he is using a . . . politeness that shows a subjection to the rules.**
> M.: Hmm.
> V.: I mean, in fact he is accepting an invitation to a celebration which is not even culturally familiar to him, that is, a celebration that is strange to him.
> M.: I see.
> V.: Maybe out of curiosity, maybe because he has been invited by his professor . . . but he is, in fact, moving . . . if we think of a chess board, he's moving a piece that means his acceptance of certain rules.
>
> (interview)

In this case, maybe on the basis of my own conceptions or on what I would do myself if I were in that situation, I take for granted the fact that the Indian guest accepts the invitation to celebrate Christmas **in an attempt of integration to the culture where he is currently living**, but I make no questionings about whether those are the real motivations of his acceptance.

Another instance of level 3:

M.: *"However, these two perspectives have something in common."* There you write a quotation.

V.: Yes, exactly. There . . . In fact this is a . . . a quotation that . . . I think there are two . . .

M.: Two, two quotations, indeed. *"I know he's miserable, underneath his smiles . . . "*

V.: Yes, in the sense that . . . Exactly. Despite belonging to the local culture, she can understand, the narrator, **certain feelings that go beyond any culture and any local or foreign frame** [the emphasis here belongs to Victoria], *maybe she can understand . . . There I wrote . . . I think that I wrote something such as that young people can realise . . . or something like that . . .*

(interview)

In this case, I just take for granted that there are things which go beyond any culture or local or foreign cultural frame, but my only basis for such assertion lies on my own perceptions of the world.

Victoria's basis for saying that these are instances of level 3 in the model is that she only considers her own point of view in interpretation ("maybe on the basis of my own conceptions", "but my only basis for such assertion lies on my own perceptions of the world"). This is of course a characteristic of level 3. However, she misses the point that she has in fact also attempted to put herself in the character's shoes, and this is evidence of level 4, i.e., perceiving another culture from the frame of reference of the members of that culture, from an insider perspective ("the Indian guest accepts the invitation to celebrate Christmas in an attempt of integration to the culture where he is currently living"). Whether this interpretation is appropriate, or intended, does not really matter. What is important in cultural understanding is that Victoria shows here the ability to position herself in somebody else's shoes ("what I would do myself if I were in that situation"). Furthermore, there is a lot of criticality and reflexivity in these extracts, which Victoria does not seem to recognise in this self-assessment and which are evidence of levels 4 and 5 in the model ("I just take for granted that . . .", "but I make no questionings about whether those are the real motivations of his acceptance").

Victoria then distinguishes level 3 from level 4 using an interview extract as a springboard and later illustrating with a post-reflection written after the closure of data collection:

> M.: *"The contact with the other culture, the Indian's culture, generates on the one hand, compassion"* . . . [The interviewer is quoting Victoria's words in one of her tasks]
> V.: *Hmm.*
> M.: *I don't understand very well why compassion.*
> V.: *Compassion in the sense that . . . he is somebody who is . . . I mean . . . let me see, no, sorry. When I write "On the one hand" I mean the first aspect, the local side.*
> M.: *Hmm.*
> V.: *I mean . . . because I think that at first . . . Here I am using a syntactic parallelism: "On the one hand," I started the parallelism on the local culture, "on the other hand," I pose again the issue of compassion and the . . . the local point of view, a foreigner who is alone, whose country doesn't even celebrate Christmas, and who is . . . I mean . . . he is invited just because he is going to spend a celebration that is relevant to them, to the local culture, and the foreigner is going to spend it alone.*
>
> (interview)

In this case I have perceived C2 from my own cultural framework, since I have not taken into account, at least to start, the possibility that, since they do not celebrate Christmas in India, the young Indian guest might not see this celebration as relevant and, therefore, he would not necessarily feel lonely being alone on that day.

However, I can observe an instance of level 4 (perception of culture C2 from an insider perspective) in my post-reflection, where I seem to take this fact into account:

At one point, the foreigner was a strange being who was contemplated with fascination that is related with the prejudice of the unknown (I seem to remember that stranger was qualified as "beautiful" in the text), or with the compassion of someone who doesn't conceive that there are people who live in countries where things happen differently than in his/her own country. The local culture (reflecting the narrator's point of view), considers inadmissible, for example, that the Hindu boy doesn't celebrate Christmas in his country, even pitying him for it (I mark a phrase here that seems relevant and that I almost remember verbatim, and in which I underline the word which I consider that represents my prior comment about compassion: "They didn't even have Christmas in his country.") It is supposed, also from the local point of view, that the foreign boy will feel alone at the Christmas celebrations if nobody invites him to spend them with their family; nevertheless, this

presumption ignores how badly one can feel during a Christmas celebration for whom Christmas does not signify a celebration.
(Post-reflection written after the closure of data collection)

When Victoria turns to the highest level, she takes an extract from the literary text, followed by her commentary in her reading response task, and then comments on her own use of language there:

"*Fooling with Nature, sir,*" *says Mr. Banerji. I know already that this is the right response. Investigating Nature is one thing and so is defending yourself against it, within limits, but fooling with it is quite another.*
(extract text)

*This might be considered just as a common topic: the young Indian is a student of biology and the narrator's father is his teacher. However, how symbolic can a comment like this be? It implies the idea of not experimenting with nature, of not trying to adapt it to man's needs, and we might wonder to which extent the fact of integrating a man to a foreign culture to the point of intending him to resemble that culture is not like wanting to adapt what is strange to **our** own needs, even if it is done with the best intentions.*
(reading response)

In this case, in my use of the first plural person "our" I seem to intend an observation of a possible attitude of my own culture as regards a culture C2.

She identifies other instances of level 5 in the interview and in the post-reflection written after the closure of data collection, and these can be found in Excerpt 2 in the appendix to this chapter.

Ultimately, Victoria echoes Tess in her formulation of one of the main ideas of this book:

The fact that I could observe various simultaneous instances of the levels in the Model of Cultural Understanding in my tasks implies, in my opinion, that the cultural understanding is not a one-stage process, since according to what I could grasp from my own experience, the same reader can reach different levels—degrees of depth—of perception along the same text. In my opinion, the Model covers and explains those levels. In fact, in my view this Model allows for a flexible process of cultural understanding and provides a realistic account of how this understanding is carried out. At least in my tasks, the Model has revealed what I have shown of the cultural understanding process carried out during my reading of the texts, without leaving anything aside. However, I want to

148 *Using the* Model of Cultural Understanding *in Self-Assessment*

highlight once again the fact that my knowledge and experience on the subject are limited enough as to constrain my conclusions.

As with Tess, it is also possible to observe the skills associated with intercultural understanding all simultaneously at play in her self-reflection:

- observing ("I can observe")
- discovering ("but my only basis for such assertion lies in my own perceptions of the world")
- describing ("In this case, in my use of the first plural person 'our' I seem to intend an observation of a possible attitude of my own culture as regards a culture C2")
- analysing ("I consider this instance a level 3 one because I have used the word 'typical' on the basis of my own perception and cultural knowledge about a Christmas celebration")
- comparing and contrasting ("However . . . in my post-reflection . . . I seem to take this fact into account)
- relating ("In this case, maybe on the basis of my own conceptions or on what I would do myself if I were in that situation")
- interpreting ("the foreigner accepts the local cultural norms and tries to integrate himself to them")
- perspective-taking ("I have not questioned the fact that a Christmas celebration in the culture where the text is contextualised might be different, and just took for granted that it was a typical Christmas celebration only because it seemed typical according to my own cultural experience")
- decentring ("In this case I have perceived C2 from my own cultural framework, since I have not taken into account, at least to start, the possibility that, since they do not celebrate Christmas in India, the young Indian guest might not see this celebration as relevant and, therefore, he would not necessarily feel lonely being alone on that day")
- critical thinking and reflexivity ("but I make no questionings about whether those are the real motivations of his acceptance").

In summary, what we have seen in this chapter is that students can reflect with insight on their own competence in interpreting and understanding texts such as the ones used in this book. Clearly this is time-consuming for all involved and crucially depends on the willingness and ability of each student to produce reflections of this kind, and more work would need to be done with students who are perhaps younger, less sophisticated in self-analysis and in need of teacher help. The creation of self-assessment profiles of reading is nonetheless feasible, at least by student-teachers like Tess and Victoria, but also perhaps by advanced language learners in general. The production of such self-assessments over a period of time, which might then be held in a portfolio, would in turn allow students to analyse change in their levels of understanding according to the model and develop a meta-analysis of their own progress.

Appendix. Excerpt 2. Self-Assessment by Victoria

I would like to start my comments with the caveat that my lack of experience working with the *Model of Cultural Understanding* might have made me miss many instances of different levels that an expert eye could spot in my reading response, visual representation and interview. Therefore, I have obviously signaled only those instances which were somehow visible to me, but I am sure that there is a lot more to say.

In my tasks, I can observe instances of levels 3, 4 and 5 of the *Model of Cultural Understanding*. I list and explain these instances below, highlighting in bold, in each case, the words that I consider relevant.

Instances of level 3, perception of culture C2 from one's own frame of reference (C1) (outsider perspective):

An apparently typical family (at least in their way of celebrating Christmas), receive a young Indian as their guest.

(reading response)

I consider this instance a level 3 one because I have used the word "typical" on the basis of my own perception and cultural knowledge about a Christmas celebration. For that matter, I have not questioned the fact that a Christmas celebration in the culture where the text is contextualised might be different, and just took for granted that it was a typical Christmas celebration only because it seemed typical according to my own cultural experience.

Another instance of level 3:

This fact introduces two different points of view in the story: on the one hand, we have what we might call the "local point of view," understanding as such the point of view of the culture in which the story takes place; on the other hand, we can observe the perspective of the foreigner who intends to integrate himself or to be integrated in such culture. On the one hand, the compassion ("We're having him to Christmas dinner because he's foreign, he's far from home, he will be lonely, and they don't even have Christmas in his country").

(reading response)

M.: *(. . .) "The contact with the other culture, the Indian's culture, generates on the one hand, compassion"* . . .
V.: *Hmm.*
M.: *I don't understand very well why compassion.*
V.: *Compassion in the sense that . . . he is somebody who is . . . I mean . . . let me see, no, sorry. When I write "On the one hand" I mean the first aspect, the local side.*
M.: *Hmm.*
V.: *I mean . . . because I think that at first . . . Here I am using a syntactic parallelism: "On the one hand," I started the parallelism on the*

local culture, "on the other hand," I pose again the issue of compassion and the . . . the local point of view, a foreigner who is alone, whose country doesn't even celebrate Christmas, and who is . . . I mean . . . he is invited just because he is going to spend a celebration that is relevant to them, to the local culture, and the foreigner is going to spend it alone.

(interview)

In this case I have perceived C2 from my own cultural framework, since I have not taken into account, at least to start, the possibility that, since they do not celebrate Christmas in India, the young Indian guest might not see this celebration as relevant and, therefore, he would not necessarily feel lonely being alone on that day.

However, I can observe an instance of level 4 (perception of culture C2 from an insider perspective) in my post-reflection, where I seem to take this fact into account:

At one point, the foreigner was a strange being who was contemplated with fascination that is related with the prejudice of the unknown (I seem to remember that stranger was qualified as "beautiful" in the text), or with the compassion of someone who doesn't conceive that there are people who live in countries where things happen differently than in his/her own country. The local culture (reflecting the narrator's point of view), considers inadmissible, for example, that the Hindu boy doesn't celebrate Christmas in his country, even pitying him for it (I mark a phrase here that seems relevant and that I almost remember verbatim, and in which I underline the word which I consider that represents my prior comment about compassion: "They didn't even have Christmas in his country.") It is supposed, also from the local point of view, that the foreign boy will feel alone at the Christmas celebrations if nobody invites him to spend them with their family; nevertheless, this presumption ignores how badly one can feel during a Christmas celebration for whom Christmas does not signify a celebration.

(Post-reflection written after the closure of data collection)

I can observe another instance of level 3 in my reading response and visual representation, and then in my interview:

We cannot deny that the text shows an attempt at integration from both sides. However, both cultures are strange to each other. To one of them (the local one) it is almost unacceptable that things might be so different in other parts of the world ("they don't even have Christmas in his country"). On the other hand, the young Indian accepts, without comments, the rules of the culture in which he intends to be integrated and whose rituals are completely strange to him and even the language might give him some troubles.

(reading response)

Using the Model of Cultural Understanding in Self-Assessment   151

On the other hand, the foreigner accepts the local cultural norms and tries to integrate himself to them, or at least he does not refuse the responsibility of accepting the invitation to festivities whose significance is culturally foreign.

(post-reflection written after the closure of data collection)

Attempt at communication; brief, tense dialogues, based on the politeness of the Indian and on an explicit intention from the local culture to integrate the foreigner. Mutual observation.

(visual representation)

V.: *Both are foreigners to each other, that is, that issue of being aliens.*
M.: Yes. Both are.
V.: Both are, to each other, foreigners.
M.: I see. "However, there is an attempt at integration from both sides."
V.: I mean, the foreigner wants . . .
M.: Does the foreigner want to be integrated, do you think so? You write there that he intends to be integrated.
V.: At least he is using a . . . politeness that shows a subjection to the rules.
M.: Hmm.
V.: I mean, in fact he is accepting an invitation to a celebration which is not even culturally familiar to him, that is, a celebration that is strange to him.
M.: I see.
V.: Maybe out of curiosity, maybe because he has been invited by his professor . . . but he is, in fact, moving . . . if we think of a chess board, he's moving a piece that means his acceptance of certain rules.

(interview)

In this case, maybe on the basis of my own conceptions or on what I would do myself if I were in that situation, I take for granted the fact that the Indian guest accepts the invitation to celebrate Christmas in an attempt of integration to the culture where he is currently living, but I make no questionings about whether those are the real motivations of his acceptance.

Another instance of level 3:

M.: "However, these two perspectives have something in common." There you write a quotation.
V.: Yes, exactly. There . . . In fact this is a . . . a quotation that . . . I think there are two . . .
M.: Two, two quotations, indeed. "I know he's miserable, underneath his smiles . . .
V.: Yes, in the sense that . . . Exactly. Despite belonging to the local culture, she can understand, the narrator, **certain feelings that go**

beyond any culture and any local or foreign frame, maybe she can understand . . . There I wrote . . . I think that I wrote something such as that young people can realise . . . or something like that . . .

(interview)

In this case, I just take for granted that there are things which go beyond any culture or local or foreign cultural frame, but my only basis for such assertion lies on my own perceptions of the world.

I can also observe an instance of level 5 (perception of culture C1 from the perspective of culture C2):

They talk about an empty turkey, devoid of stuffing, which is no longer the centerpiece of this Christmas meal. I propose that the final vision of the turkey is comparable to that of the foreigner (. . .) The turkey is compared to a "headless baby." The word "baby" makes us think immediately of a human being, and "headless" could symbolically represent the removal of such differences. The head contains the face, the features, a large part of what makes us unique and special at first glance. A "headless baby" could simply be a human being like any other, without its essential differences. This supports my idea that the vision of the foreigner has changed, passing from being observed like someone foreign and fascinating, distinct from everything that is already understood, to a being seen simply as human being, like any other . . . the same, even as the narrator.

(Victoria, post-reflection written after the closure of data collection)

M.: *(Pause)* "probable symbolic meaning related to the human being, naked of old prejudices and fascinations." Explain that to me, that is very interesting.
V.: After . . . after the Christmas meal . . .
M.: It says: " . . . seen now just as a creature equal to many others."
V.: The turkey is no longer considered as a Christmas meal.
M.: Hmm.
V.: There is a moment when the turkey is left naked of any stuffing and covering.
M.: Yes.
V.: In the case of the foreigner, I think that after meeting him, after having looked at him in a different way, maybe after mutual observation, after all this interaction . . . "Oh, he's a human being, just like me . . . "
M.: Sure.
V.: That is . . . they no longer see the . . . and anyway, if the turkey is a silly creature and the foreigner is a strange creature, maybe sillier than me, or more impolite or whatever, it happens to be that I am just like him.
M.: I see.
V.: As a human being, I mean.

Another instance of level 5:

"Fooling with Nature, sir," says Mr. Banerji. I know already that this is the right response. Investigating Nature is one thing and so is defending yourself against it, within limits, but fooling with it is quite another.

This might be considered just as a common topic: the young Indian is a student of Biology and the narrator's father is his teacher. However, how symbolic can a comment like this be? It implies the idea of not experimenting with nature, of not trying to adapt it to man's needs, and we might wonder to which extent the fact of integrating a man to a foreign culture to the point of intending him to resemble that culture is not like wanting to adapt what is strange to our own needs, even if it is done with the best intentions.

(reading response)

M.: *Yes. (Pause) "There is another factor that seems to be common to both cultures", and you write this issue of "fooling with nature."*
V.: *This fact that both agree on . . . well, on the idea that men should be careful about nature . . .*
M.: *Hmm.*
V.: *That's why I've also taken this issue a bit deeper from a symbolic point of view.*
M.: *That's fine.*
V.: *I mean, the man, let's say, with the foreigner . . . I am thinking of the fascination of looking . . . when they look at the foreigner, I mean, to what extent are they looking at him as a human being and not, in a sense, as an object under dissection.*

(interview)

In this case, in my use of the first plural person "our" I seem to intend an observation of a possible attitude of my own culture as regards a culture C2.

The fact that I could observe various simultaneous instances of the levels in the Model of Cultural Understanding in my tasks implies, in my opinion, that the cultural understanding is not a one-stage process, since according to what I could grasp from my own experience, the same reader can reach different levels—degrees of depth—of perception along the same text. In my opinion, the Model covers and explains those levels. In fact, in my view this Model allows for a flexible process of cultural understanding and provides a realistic account of how this understanding is carried out. At least in my tasks, the Model has revealed what I have shown of the cultural understanding process carried out during my reading of the texts, without leaving anything aside. However, I want to highlight once again the fact that my knowledge and experience on the subject are limited enough as to constrain my conclusions.

References

Alkheshnam, A. (2012) Intercultural competence: Components and measurement (PhD thesis, University of Surrey).

Antonenko, T. A. (2010) *Stimulating Intercultural Intellectual Capabilities in Intercultural Communication: Testing an Innovative Course Design.* Amsterdam: Universiteit van Amsterdam.

Benedict, R. (1935) *Patterns of Culture.* London: Routledge and Sons Ltd.

Bennett, M. J. (2009) Defining, measuring, and facilitating intercultural learning: A conceptual introduction to the intercultural education double supplement. *Intercultural Education*, 20(sup1), S1–S13.

Byram, M. (1989) *Cultural Studies in Foreign Language Education.* Clevedon: Multilingual Matters.

Nold, G. (2009) Assessing components of intercultural competence—reflections on DESI and consequences. In Hu, A. and Byram, M. (eds) *Interkulturelle Kompetenz und fremdsprachliches Lernen. / Intercultural Competence and Foreign Language Learning* (pp. 173–177). Tubingen: Gunter Narr Verlag.

Scarino, A. (2009) Assessing intercultural capability in learning languages: Some issues and considerations. *Language Teaching*, 42, 67–80.

9 Conclusions

Theoretical Perspectives: New Conceptualisations of Culture, Identity and Schema

The research on which this book is based investigates cultural understanding in EFL reading among college students, prospective teachers and translators of English in their early twenties at Universidad Nacional de La Plata in Argentina, and the data were collected in 2009–2010. The theoretical contribution lies in the conception of culture and identity we adopt and the acknowledgement of the complexity and importance of the sociocultural context in reading. All this is encapsulated in the *Model of Cultural Understanding* itself and in the way in which we—and students—have used it to capture the complexity, fluidity, criticality and reflexivity of cultural understanding.

We have addressed the need to "engage with the reality of language as experienced by users and learners" (Widdowson, 2000: 23), and in this sense, the Argentinean setting is important, justifies our case study and reveals how literacy in English was lived by this particular group of students.

There is also a significant methodological dimension for both research and teaching. The new instruments—the reading response and visual representation tasks—were developed in order to overcome the weaknesses of previous research on reading intended to investigate the process of comprehension, which relied so much on 'recall', in various forms, and which we showed to be inadequate. We have demonstrated that our instruments can be used in teaching too.

Contrary to much previous research on the cultural dimension of reading in particular, in this study the cultural is not limited to an isolated aspect of identity—such as race, ethnicity, nationality or religion—to be controlled as an independent variable as we have seen in laboratory-based experimental approaches. We have acknowledged the complexity of the sociocultural context through a sociocultural perspective on schema theory as an approach to the investigation of reading in classroom-based research. Schemata are seen as sociocultural and historical constructions that appear through transactions with others in real contexts and are mediated by cultural activities, materials and artefacts. We have shown that cultural understanding among readers in an Argentinean setting was linked equally to what the prompt texts had to offer and what these readers brought with them. This became evident in the re-visiting of textual content generated through the negotiation, interaction, reflection and critical analysis that the research instruments allowed for. What we have captured are the *developmental, social, cultural* and *functional* dimensions of schemata. We showed first what happened in readers' minds through interconnections with their prior knowledge and experiences at different points in their lifetimes (the *developmental* dimension), simultaneously linked to sociocultural assumptions and preconceptions.

Thus, although schemata are abstract knowledge structures that represent generic concepts stored in memory, our research has revealed their *functional* role in the relationships of individuals and the environment. This happened in two ways. First, they functioned as a means of relating to the situation proposed by the research context itself, whereby these participants had to respond to the specific reading experiences presented around the Christmas schema, evaluating and accommodating their understanding of what they thought they were required to do. Second, they functioned as a means of drawing on the Christmas schema itself, prompted by the confrontation of the Christmas visions offered by each text with their own understandings and experiences.

More specifically, this sociocultural perspective on schemata presents schemata as constructs which extend beyond the individual. Cultural schemata are not a static characteristic of an individual's cognition but instead they are shared by members of a cultural group—in this study, the group of student participants—and are constantly being negotiated and renegotiated through time and generations. In this case, the time span lasted for the length of our research and there was negotiation stimulated by the participants' interaction with ourselves in our role as interviewer. Our communication with the participants also continued after the closure of data collection, on occasion over a year afterwards, whereby students revisited their understandings of some data excerpts.

This book foregrounds the importance of *image* and *emotion* schemata within the cultural dimension of reading and highlights the difficulty and complexity of this imaginative and emotional dimension as well as the need for further research in these areas. The visual representations that the participants produced show the simplicity and power of visual imagery in capturing the cultural in reading. The interviews in turn served to show the depth, complexity, reflexivity and criticality behind the apparent simplicity of images.

The Model of Cultural Understanding

One of our main concerns has been to overcome the strong dichotomy *product vs. process* usually observed in the investigation of reading comprehension. This opposition is manifested theoretically in the static notions of culture and identity embraced in many studies of reading, where comprehension is assumed to have occurred when a text is recalled as accurately as possible in a recall task. In such studies, text comprehension is also determined by examining whether a reader's recall is consistent or inconsistent with the schema presupposed by a text, and this brings about a static conceptualisation of schemata as well: either a reader has the schema needed to understand a text, or not. We disagree with this view of comprehension because it emphasises the memory factor and relies on an essentialist view of culture, identity and schema. In contrast, our *Model of Cultural Understanding* is based on the notion of comprehension founded on flexible layers of understanding.

More specifically, our research emphasises the underlying centrality of cultural understanding as a *fluid process* in a *continuum* of cultural familiarity and unfamiliarity throughout, which is captured by our model. The emphasis on process reveals how participants moved freely back and forth over the levels in the model at many points during the reading process. There were indications of all layers of understanding in almost all the tasks the participants performed, but the majority of their responses were framed within levels 4 and 5. They demonstrated therefore their critical thinking, reflection, critical cultural awareness and social awareness, the entertainment of simultaneous and alternative interpretations of textual content, and a sophisticated ability to reflect upon culture. The confrontation with the values and ideas present in the perspectives of members of other cultures in the prompt texts favoured a process of decentring or critical distancing from the participants' own perspective.

Cultural Understanding and the Context of Reading

In approaching otherness, the participants resorted to what was known or familiar to them as Argentineans through an ongoing process of comparing and contrasting. They compared and contrasted, through various means and resources, the different cultural realities presented in the texts with their own. At times this process of comparing and contrasting revealed their difficulty in distancing themselves from their own positions and understanding otherness from the point of view of the Other. This difficulty to decentre led to stereotyping. At other times, however, the process of comparing and contrasting resulted in the adoption of different perspectives in the understanding of another culture.

Moreover, the participants inspected the texts in depth and selected portions that they felt needed to be analysed further. They all positioned themselves as critical readers of all texts, showing elements of criticality and reflexivity regarding textual content. At the same time, they reflected on cultural practices in their own culture as well as in other cultures. These reflections were rich and varied and were motivated by textual content, and the participants took the time and effort to think of explicit alternative interpretations when textual content was perceived as confusing. All this was facilitated by the instruments we developed and, we suggest, would not have been possible using existing instruments.

Thus, as these participants were confronted with certain topics in the texts, they were attracted to them from their particular context, but the reading response and the visual representation tasks were a private endeavour, a deeply engaging personal act, a vehicle for self-expression, for researching the cultural through analysis, reflection and introspection. The interviews, an established research instrument but used here in the specific combination with the two new tasks, were person-centred, involved these readers' sense of self, interests, beliefs, values, behaviours, actions, etc., and led to the identification of an individual's themes in connection with the cultural.

In short, our research shows how the context—in this case Argentina—and the cultural experience of readers impact on their reading, but at the same time we have seen how each individual has their own interests and foci when they read a text. The local and peripheral situate the analyses and interpretations we provide in the book.

Methodological Perspectives: The Reading Response Task and the Visual Representation

The reading response task and the visual representation contrast sharply with the immediate recall protocol and represent a development in reading research methodology. A reading response task allows readers to project their own interpretations of texts and is different from summaries and syntheses. A visual representation of textual content combines words, phrases, and/or sentences with visual information in different formats of varying complexity. In order to produce a reading response task and a visual representation, recalling and summarising alone are not enough. Readers have to make sense of the culturally situated information in texts, relate them to their own cultural parameters and, in so doing, bring their previous experiences, knowledge and background to their interpretations. The instructions do not require them to recall every bit of a text, and they are free to respond to whichever aspects attract their attention. They are not committed to reflecting the views of the writer or the narrator of a text. In both reading response and visual representation, readers produce a new "text" that is *different* from the prompt text (Anstley and Bull, 2006: 24) and in this respect both tasks are clearly distinct from *verbatim* recall where the exactitude and precision in the reproduction of the original text is fundamental. Both tasks thus take account of current sociocultural views on reading that rest, among other features, on the multidimensional and multivalent nature of its processes (Bernhardt, 2003; Paris and Paris, 2003). The fact that the visual representation allows for emotional responses to textual content is a further distinguishing feature not found in recall protocol-based research.

In addition, these instruments stimulate readers to put their knowledge about the cultural aspects of a text into action. 'Knowledge in action' refers to readers' capacity to use cultural knowledge in new and concrete problem-solving situations; they produce new texts in order to express their comprehension of the texts they read. From this perspective, the reading response and the visual representation tasks, as production of texts, capture readers' cultural understanding at two points simultaneously: while reading a text and while producing another one. Producing a text required our participants to comprehend the prompt texts in order to rewrite them from alternative perspectives, perspectives that were always complementary but never identical to the original fragments. The creation involved in reading and intervening in the prompt texts required an exploration of the hybrid, fluid, changing and dynamic nature of the voices and cultures found in them.

The Power of Writing and Speaking

The writing generated by both instruments was sufficiently long to avoid the superficial treatment of issues. Both the writing in these tasks and the speaking in the interviews involved a process of exploration of thoughts as our participants themselves discovered from the acts of writing and speaking what these thoughts were. The written and spoken engagement in critical analysis of their beliefs facilitated access to them. The acts of writing and speaking, by externalising thoughts, allowed them to contemplate, clarify, reconsider and revise those thoughts. Writing about and speaking about textual content facilitated the interaction with thought: participants manipulated ideas; they explored, opposed and made connections between propositions. Writing and speaking about the cultural was a discovery process as the writing and speaking themselves triggered insights and stimulated ideas. Writing ideas on paper made them want to reflect more as the physical act of writing created concrete examples to focus their attention on later during the interviews. Writing was generative as it led to the discovery of new ideas, which were then explored in the interviews. In this way, the participants engaged in experiential, expressive writing and speaking through reflection on self-generated topics. As the reading response task, the visual representation and the interview opened up a genuine investigation of such topics, hidden concerns were discovered and personal anecdotes, values and beliefs were revealed. Thinking became visible. Reflexive thinking involved participants in making a conscious effort to reflect on what they knew and thought. The depth of the reading response tasks, the visual representation tasks and the interviews revealed that these participants were capable of such critical reflection and analysis.

The Model, the Reading Response Task and the Visual Representation in Teaching

The pedagogic value of the reading response and the visual representation tasks, combined with a follow-up interview (and/or group discussion), resides in their being textual interventions, i.e., textual transformations that allow students to become analysts, critics and writers themselves. We have shown in this book that the reading response and visual representation tasks encouraged participants to transform the prompt texts in multiple and varied ways. These transformations can occur through nontraditional uses of plot, characters and place; unusual uses of the voice of the narrator; the mixing of styles of presentation of the visual; changes of format, e.g., from a narration to a simultaneous representation; the creation of intertextuality with allusions to texts associated in the mind of the reader; and the creation of multiple meanings. By means of such resources, readers can produce multiple interpretations and question established characters, scenes and plots.

The reading response and visual representation tasks can also be used as assessment instruments. The illustrations we provide in Chapters 6 and 7 show their potential to encourage and assess the skills of intercultural competence: observing, discovering, describing, analysing, comparing and contrasting, relating, interpreting, perspective-taking, decentring, critical thinking, criticality and reflexivity.

The model itself can be used in selecting teaching materials, in materials design and development, and in assessment. Teachers can use the model to select, or design and develop reading materials for specific contexts by analysing a text in terms of the levels of the model. By 'text' we mean anything that can be 'read' and 'interpreted' in a variety of semiotic systems and media, including print, nonprint, visual, digital, multimodal (Hagood and Skinner, 2012; Handsfield, Dean and Cielocha, 2009). We have shown in Chapter 3 how this can be done with the fragments from *Mi planta de naranja-lima*, *Cat's Eye* and *Desert Wife*.

The model can also be used in self-assessment, as we illustrated in Chapter 8, with a focus on the skills of self-analysis and the skills of cultural understanding, rather than emphasising levels of achievement in comprehension. We have shown that the participants in our research could analyse how they had moved back and forth among the six levels in the model and displayed a range of skills of cultural understanding in their interpretations of text. It would be inappropriate therefore to associate cultural understanding only with the highest levels in the model because each layer involves specific skills and all are important. Self-assessment is successful when learners are able to see this and express their insights, for example, in creating self-assessment profiles of their reading based on the model, of the kind presented in Chapter 8. The development of such alternative assessment products could be complemented by alternative approaches to grading by learner or teacher, and this is clearly an area that requires more exploration.

The focus of this book has been on an intensive investigation of cultural understanding in EFL reading in an Argentinean setting and thus emphasises the significance of the situation and situated reading. Participants revealed their understanding of the cultural by means of self-disclosure, self-report and self-revelation. The book, by placing the readers' responses to and perceptions of the cultural at the centre, reveals their sophisticated understandings regarding cultural comprehension by showing their own actions, thoughts and strategies in connection with the cultural dimension of reading. We consequently reject the idea that it is possible to identify, or determine, one dominant reading or preferred interpretation in the abstract, in particular with literary texts and also in cultural understanding, because "an abstract or ideal reader "has no 'specific cultural situation'—and indeed, no particular identity" (Allington and Swann, 2009: 220). By contrast, this book shows how this 'specific cultural situation' is present in the multiple and idiosyncratic interpretations that the participants provided in their reading responses, visual representations and interviews.

References

Allington, D. and Swann, J. (2009) Researching literary reading as social practice. *Language and Literature* 18, 219–230.

Anstley, M. and Bull, G. (2006) *Teaching and Learning Multiliteracies: Changing Times, Changing Literacies*. Newark, DE: International Reading Association.

Bernhardt, E. (2003) Challenges to reading research from a multilingual world. *Reading Research Quarterly* 38, 112–117.

Hagood, M. and Skinner, E. (2012) Appreciating plurality through conversations among literacy stakeholders. *Journal of Adolescent & Adult Literacy* 56, 4–6.

Handsfield, L., Dean, T. and Cielocha, K. (2009) Becoming critical consumers and producers of text: Teaching literacy with Web 1.0 and Web 2.0. *The Reading Teacher* 63, 40–50.

Paris, A. and Paris, S. (2003) Assessing narrative comprehension in young children. *Reading Research Quarterly* 38, 36–76.

Widdowson, H. G. (2000) On the limitations of linguistics applied. *Applied Linguistics* 21(1), 3–25.

Appendix
Literary extracts used in this book

This appendix includes the literary extracts used in the research on which this book draws, in this order: *Mi planta de naranja-lima*, *Cat's Eye* and *Desert Wife*. The fragments are an exact copy of the materials as the participants received them (for instance, layout, line numbers), except for their size, which is reduced here to fit the page. The numbers in the fragments indicate line numbers.

Copyright credits

Atwood, M. (1998). *Cat's Eye*. Bantam, Anchor Books.
Excerpt(s) from CAT'S EYE by Margaret Atwood, copyright © 1988 by O. W. Toad, Ltd. Used by permission of Bloomsbury Publishing Plc, and of Doubleday, an imprint of the Knopf Doubleday Publishing Group, a division of Penguin Random House LLC. All rights reserved.
Faunce, H. (1961). *Desert Wife*. Lincoln, University of Nebraska Press.
Reprinted from *Desert Wife* by Hilda Faunce Wetherill. Copyright 1928, 1934 by Little, Brown, & Company. Copyright renewed 1961 by Hilda Faunce Wetherill.
Vasconcelos, J. M. de (1971). *Mi planta de naranja-lima*. Jofre Barroso, H. (translator). Buenos Aires, El Ateneo.

Licencia de reproducción cortesía de Grupo ILHSA S. A. para su sello Editorial El Ateneo, © 2014

Literary extract from *Mi planta de naranja-lima*

En la cocina estaba Dindinha, que había venido para hacer "rabanada" mojada en vino. Era la cena de Nochebuena.

Le comenté a Totoca:

—Y mira, hay gente que ni siquiera tiene eso. El tío Edmundo dio el dinero para el vino y para comprar las frutas para la ensalada del almuerzo de mañana. Totoca estaba haciendo el trabajo gratis, porque se había enterado de la historia del Casino Bangu. Por lo menos, Luis tendría un regalo. Una cosa vieja, usada, pero muy linda y que yo quería mucho.

—Totoca.
—Habla.
—¿Y no voy a recibir nada, nada, de Papá Noel?
—Pienso que no.
—Hablando seriamente, ¿crees que soy tan malo como dice todo el mundo?
—Malo, malo, no. Lo que pasa es que tienes el diablo en la sangre.
—¡Cuando llega la Nochebuena, querría tanto no tenerlo! Me gustaría tanto que antes de morir, por lo menos una vez, naciese para mí el Niño Jesús en vez del Niño Diablo.
—Quién sabe si a lo mejor el año que viene...
—¿Por qué no aprendes y haces como yo?
—¿Y qué haces?
—No espero nada. Así no me decepciono. Ni siquiera el Niño Jesús es eso tan bueno que todo el mundo dice. Eso que el Padre cuenta y que el Catecismo dice.

Hizo una pausa y quedo indeciso entre contar el resto de lo que pensaba o no.

—¿Cómo es, entonces?
—Bueno, vamos a decir que fuiste muy travieso, que no merecías un regalo.
—Pero ¿Luis?
—Es un ángel.
—¿Y Gloria?
—También.
—¿Y yo?
—Bueno, a veces..., tomas mis cosas, pero eres muy bueno.
—¿Y Lalá?
—Pega muy fuerte, pero es buena. Un día me va a coser mi corbata de moño.
—¿Y Jandira?
—Jandira tiene ese modo... pero no es mala.
—¿Y mamá?
—Mamá es muy buena; cuando me pega lo hace con pena y despacito.
—¿Y papá?
—¡Ah, él no sé! Nunca tiene suerte. Creo que debe haber sido como yo, el malo de la familia.
—¡Entonces! Todos son buenos en la familia. ¿Y por qué el Niño Jesús no es bueno con nosotros? Vete a la casa del doctor Faulhaber y mira el tamaño de la mesa llena de cosas. Lo mismo en la casa de los Villas-Boas. Y en la del doctor Adaucto Luz, ni hablar.

Por primera vez vi que Totoca estaba casi llorando.

—Por eso creo que el Niño Jesús quiso nacer pobre sólo para exhibirse. Después El vio que solamente los ricos servían... Pero no hablemos más de eso. Hasta puede ser que lo que diga sea un pecado muy grande.

Se quedó tan abatido que no quiso conversar más. Ni siquiera quería levantar los ojos del cuerpo del caballo que pulía.

Fue una comida tan triste que ni daba ganas de pensar. Todo el mundo comió en silencio; y papá apenas probó un poco de "rabanada". Ni siquiera había querido afeitarse. Tampoco habían ido a la Misa del Gallo. Lo peor era que nadie hablaba nada con nadie. Más parecía el velorio del Niño Jesús que su nacimiento.

Papá agarró el sombrero y se fue. Salió, incluso en zapatillas, sin decir hasta luego ni desear felicidades. Dindinha sacó su pañuelo y se limpió los ojos, pidiendo permiso para irse en seguida con tío Edmundo. Y éste puso algún dinero en mi mano y en la de Totoca. A lo mejor hubiese querido dar más y no tenía. A lo mejor, en vez de darnos dinero a nosotros, desearía estar dándoselo a sus hijos, allá en la ciudad. Por eso lo abracé. Tal vez el único abrazo de la noche de fiesta. Nadie se abrazó ni quiso decir algo bueno. Mamá fue al dormitorio. Estoy seguro de que ella estaba llorando, escondida. Y todos tuvimos ganas de hacer lo mismo. Lalá fue a dejar a tío Edmundo y a Dindinha en el portón, y cuando ellos se alejaron caminando despacito, despacito, comentó:

—Parece que están demasiado viejitos para la vida y cansados de todo...

Lo más triste fue cuando la campana de la iglesia llenó la noche de voces felices. Y algunos fuegos artificiales se elevaron a otros cielos para que Dios pudiera ver la alegría de los otros.

Cuando entramos nuevamente, Gloria y Jandira estaban lavando la vajilla usada y Gloria tenía los ojos rojos como si hubiese llorado mucho.

Disimuló, diciéndonos a Totoca y a mí:

—Ya es la hora de que los chicos vayan a la cama.

Decía eso y nos miraba. Sabía que en ese momento allí no había ya ningún niño. Todos eran grandes, grandes y tristes, cenando a pedazos la misma tristeza.

Quizá la culpa de todo la hubiera tenido la luz del farol medio mortecina, que había sustituido a la luz que la "Light" mandara cortar. Tal vez.

El reyecito, que dormía con el dedo en la boca si era feliz. Puse el caballito parado, bien cerca de él. No pude evitar pasarle suavemente las manos por su pelo. Mi voz era un inmenso río de ternura.

—Mi chiquitito.

Cuando toda la casa estuvo a oscuras pregunté bien bajito:

—Estaba buena la "rabanada", ¿no es cierto, Totoca?
—No sé. Ni la probé.
—¿Por qué?
—Se me puso una cosa rara en la garganta que no me dejaba pasar nada... Vamos a dormir. El sueño hace que uno se olvide de todo.
Yo me había levantado y hacia barullo en la cama.
—Voy a poner mis zapatillas del otro lado de la puerta.
—No las pongas. Es mejor.
—Las voy a poner, sí. A lo mejor sucede un milagro. ¿Sabes una cosa, Totoca? Quisiera un regalo. Uno solo. Pero que fuese algo nuevo. Sólo para mí...

Miró para el otro lado y enterró la cabeza debajo de la almohada.

Seudónimo:

Literary extract from *Cat's Eye*

We sit around the table, eating our Christmas dinner. There's a student of my father's, a young man from India who's here to study insects and who's never seen snow before. We're having him to Christmas dinner because he's foreign, he's far from home, he will be lonely, and they don't even have Christmas in his country. This has been explained to us in advance by our mother. He's polite and ill at ease and he giggles frequently, looking with what I sense is terror at the array of food spread out before him, the mashed potatoes, the gravy, the lurid green and red Jell-O salad, the enormous turkey; my mother has said that the food is different there. I know he's miserable, underneath his smiles and politeness. I'm developing a knack for this, I can sniff out hidden misery in others now with hardly any effort at all.

My father sits at the head of the table, beaming like the Jolly Green Giant. He lifts his glass, his gnome's eyes twinkling. "Mr. Banerji, sir," he says. He always calls his students Mr. and Miss. "You can't fly on one wing."

Mr. Banerji giggles and says, "Very true, sir," in his voice that sounds like the BBC News. He lifts his own glass and sips. What is in the glass is wine. My brother and I have cranberry juice in our wineglasses. Last year or the year before we might have tied our shoelaces together, under the table, so we could signal each other with secret jerks and tugs, but we're both beyond this now for different reasons.

My father ladles out the stuffing, deals the slices of dark and light; my mother adds the mashed potatoes and cranberry sauce, and asks Mr. Banerji, enunciating carefully, whether they have turkeys in his country. He says he doesn't believe so, although the stupidity of the bird is legendary. He says that the wild turkey, once abundant in the deciduous forests in these regions, is far more intelligent and can elude even practiced hunters. Also it can fly.

I sit picking at my Christmas dinner, as Mr. Banerji is picking at his. Both of us have messed the mashed potatoes

his over-large cuffs, his hands are long and thin, ragged around the nails, like mine. I think he is very beautiful, with his brown skin and brilliant white teeth and his dark appalled eyes. There's a child these colors in the ring of children on the front of the Sunday school missionary paper, yellow children, brown children, all in different costumes, dancing around Jesus. Mr. Banerji doesn't have a costume, only a jacket and tie like other men. Nevertheless I can believe he's a man, he seems so unlike one. He's a creature more like myself: alien and apprehensive. He's afraid of us. He has no idea what we will do next, what impossibilities we will expect of him, what we will make him eat. No wonder he bites his fingers.

"A little off the sternum, sir?" my father asks him, and Mr. Banerji brightens at the word.

"Ah, the sternum," he says, and I know they have entered together the shared world of biology, which offers refuge from the real, awkward world of manners and silences we're sitting in at the moment. As he slices away with the carving knife my father indicates to all of us, but especially to Mr. Banerji, the areas where the flight muscles attach, using the carving fork as a pointer. Of course, he says, the domestic turkey has lost the ability to fly.

"*Meleagris gallopavo*," he says, and Mr. Banerji leans forward; he says, and Mr. Banerji leans forward; "Meleagris gallopavo," he says, and Mr. Banerji leans forward; this is the right response. "A pea-brained animal, or bird-brained you might say, bred for its ability to put on weight, especially on the drumsticks"—he points these out—"certainly not for intelligence. It was originally domesticated by the Mayans." He tells a story of a turkey farm where the turkeys all died because they were too stupid to go into their shed during a thunderstorm. Instead they stood around outside, looking up at the sky with their beaks wide open and the rain ran down their throats and drowned them. He says this is a story told by farmers and probably not true, although the stupidity of the bird is legendary. He says that the wild turkey, once abundant in the deciduous forests in these regions, is far more intelligent and can elude even practiced hunters. Also it can fly.

I sit picking at my Christmas dinner, as Mr. Banerji is picking at his. Both of us have messed the mashed potatoes

around on our plates without actually eating much. Wild things are smarter than tame ones, that much is clear. Wild things are elusive and wily and look out for themselves. I divide the people I know into tame and wild. My mother, wild. My father and brother, also wild; Mr. Banerji, wild also, but in a more skittish way. Carol, tame. Grace, tame as well, though with sneaky vestiges of wild. Cordelia, wild, pure and simple.

"There are no limits to human greed," says my father.

"Indeed, sir?" says Mr. Banerji, as my father goes on to say that he's heard some son of a gun is working on an experiment to breed a turkey with four drumsticks, instead of two drumsticks and two wings, because there's more meat on a drumstick.

"How would such a creature walk, sir?" asks Mr. Banerji, and my father, approving, says, "Well may you ask." He tells Mr. Banerji that some darn fool scientists are working on a square tomato, which will supposedly pack more easily into crates than the round variety.

"All the flavor will be sacrificed, of course," he says. "They care nothing for flavor. They breed a naked chicken, thinking they'd get more eggs by utilizing the energy saved from feather production, but the thing shivered so much they had to double-heat the coop, so it cost more in the end."

"Fooling with Nature, sir," says Mr. Banerji. I know already that this is the right response. Investigating Nature is one thing and so is defending yourself against it, within limits, but fooling with it is quite another.

Mr. Banerji says he hears there is now a naked cat available, he's read about it in a magazine, though he himself does not see the point of it at all. This is the most he has said so far.

My brother asks if there are any poisonous snakes in India, and Mr. Banerji, now much more at ease, begins to enumerate them. My mother smiles, because this is going better than she thought it would. Poisonous snakes are fine with her, even at the dinner table, as long as they make people happy.

My father has eaten everything on his plate and is digging for more stuffing in the cavity of the turkey, which resembles a trussed, headless baby. It has thrown off its disguise as a meal and has revealed itself to me for what it is, a large dead bird. I'm eating a wing. It's the wing of a tame turkey, the stupider bird in the world, so stupid it can't even fly any more. I am eating lost flight.

Kismas

Before the birth of Mrs. White Hat's baby, more frequently while the wind blew in October and without ceasing, after that dance Polly and I attended, the heathen asked, "How long 'till Kismas?"

Christmas to us meant warm fires, red berries, gifts in tissue paper. We found that the Navajo "Kismas" included the warm fires, but everything else was novel enough to make history.

We planned to watch the benighted Navajo cook dinner; we had even declared we would eat with them; we would spend the day watching their games. For our treat we prepared a hundred small bags each containing candy, cookies and a red apple.

Christmas Eve the heathen began to arrive over these hills. There were wagonloads of women and children and scores of men and young people on horses. Everybody was dressed in his best: beads, bracelets and silver belts glistened against the bright-colored velvet shirts and glossy sateen skirts, with miles and miles of flounces. I had made several of the skirts and I knew how many miles long a flounce was.

By dark some two hundred Navajos were present. The Utcitys were there: the head of the house in all his dignity, the Little Bidoni and his three wives, softspoken and sweet, and all the other sons and daughters and husbands and wives; the Little Cranks, living up to their name; the Old Lady and Old Man, with their children and grandchildren; Robert, greeting old friends, and White Hat and Mrs. White Hat and the children; Japon and his wife and their progeny, Mrs. Japon and the Old Lady giving each other a wide berth. Cla was present with his brothers and the Old Buzzard. Everybody's friends were present and all their relatives.

Apparently they expected "Kismas" to begin at once. Expecting to supply meat for the Christmas dinner, Ken had killed a beef, but now he took down a hind quarter and cut steaks and more steaks until there was enough to go around. The adults came and cook what they needed for their families for supper and for breakfast on Christmas morning. What they did not eat at once they were afraid to put down because some one would steal it, so all the evening they strolled about with great raw beefsteaks in their hands. Mrs. Japon and the Old Buzzard each had two.

We had provided several loads of wood so they could help themselves; and the Christmas fires, big and little, were all over the place. They were so all over the place, we were uneasy. One family settled down and built their fire within two feet of the walls of that frame shack of a store building. Ken had to go out and insist that they move elsewhere. They were indignant and thought it quite fussy in me to go out and shovel dirt over the bed of live coals they left.

Big fires were built on the level space, where the dancing was to be, and these, added to the light of a full moon, made the night so bright we could see the whole landscape around. The dancing was just for the Indians' amusement and ours and was in no sense ceremonial.

Now and then some of them danced a figure from a ceremonial dance but without the costumes and other accessories. The music was made on a clay water jar with water in it and a rawhide stretched over the top. One fellow played this, or beat it, and others shook rattles made of paper bags with beans in them.

The best dance of the lot was one performed by some of the older men. They had to dance and sing because the younger men knew neither the proper songs nor the dance; and Utcity, the Singer, and the other six who made up the figures sang, laughed and kept up the most violent sort of exercises until they dropped panting to the ground. They all assured us that when they were young men they could keep it up all night, but now they were old and full of meat beside, and they couldn't do what they used to do.

With that dance and others, and wrestling and racing about the fires, there was plenty of activity. There was nothing cold or solemn about the gathering; every one was laughing and happy. They were a most fun-loving people and laughed at the same things we thought funny.

All the evening I was trying to bake two loaves of fruit cake. It was done when we finally went to bed at midnight — done with a thick crust an inch deep all over it and a core of good cake in the middle. Keeping an oven fire of pitch wood and watching the dancing outside had been too much for the success of the cake. The wood-burning stove was temperamental at its best.

All night we smelled the piñon smoke from the camp fires, and when a different smoke drifted into our window, we got up and followed it to find that some one had put box boards on his fire. Lady Betty was nervous and growled every time we or any one else moved. When we got back in bed, after tracing the source of non-piñon smoke, she came to the side of the bed and put her cold nose in my hand. After a little she lay down with a loud sigh, but got up at once if she could not feel my hand. My arm was numb from keeping the hand where she could reach it. Poor Betty! She didn't get much sleep that night and a hard day she had ahead of her, too. Wild reservation life was no joy to a blooded bulldog like Betty.

What with our uneasiness about the Indian fires and their early rising habits, we were up early Christmas morning. While the men and boys went out to the flat mesa to race their horses, we women folk thought about dinner for the crowd. By eleven o'clock Mrs. White Hat and Mrs. Japon began making bread and the efficient way they went about it was a lesson to me.

A twenty-five-pound sack of flour, a frying pan or Dutch oven, a can of baking powder and a bucket of well water was the total of their equipment. They rolled back the top of the sack, put in a pinch of baking powder and mixed in enough water with their hands to make a dough stiff enough to handle easily. This was pulled and patted into a cake that covered the bottom of the cooking pan and fried in an inch or two of fat. The finished cakes were stacked in piles. It was an interesting performance; but after I had watched for a time, I realized they could not bake enough bread for the crowd that way, so I started to make biscuits in the oven. That was a full-time job. I learned then that one sack of flour just fills a washtub with biscuits.

While we women were preparing the bread, Ken had cut up the meat. Some women built up stones about the cooking fires to set rubs on, and soon we had three tubs of the meat simmering, each with an attendant stirring it with a long splinter of wood from the woodpile. The wash boiler did duty as a coffeepot. There was a forked cedar in it to hold the bag of coffee down. I was sure the whole dinner would be flavored with cedar, but it wasn't.

Other women I set to peeling onions and potatoes, and very handy they were at it too. These we added to the meat tubs. When everything was all well cooked, I mixed a pail of flour and water for thickening and added that, with salt, pepper and chili. The cooks tasted it often and said it was very good.

One of the children was sent out to the mesa edge to call the men; and in a few minutes they charged in, the ponies running pell-mell between the camp fires and jumping over the clutter of camp stuff, the Indians yelling like pirates and quirting on both sides. I never had heard a pirate yell, but I was sure a Navajo must be as good a yeller as a Comanche, and nothing else could make so much noise, unless it was a pirate.

The dripping ponies were left at one side and the Indians came to the fires. I dipped the stew into pans, all we had in the store; and then we passed tin cups of coffee and spoons for the stew. The family groups sat together and everybody ate and ate. Some of the heathen, I know, had not had a square meal for a month.

After the meal was over, the women cleaned the soot from the tubs and boiler with sand, while I scalded the spoons and pans. They were willing enough to do it, though they would have gone away and left everything dirty, if I had not suggested the dishwashing. I thought it best they do some little thing for their meal.

When that was done, the children lined up to get the bags of candy. I passed them out and soon became suspicious about the length of the line. Investigation revealed Mrs. Little Crank and a score of other mothers standing around the corner of the store, putting bags of candy into their blankets and sending the children back to stand in line for another. There was a sort of appreciation in the Navajo, but it was the sort that wanted all they could get from any one who wasn't looking.

By the middle of the afternoon they were all gone and we were allowed to eat something ourselves. Tired! But we agreed we had never seen such a Christmas and would not see another in a lifetime.

Among the last to go was Robert, who came to me and spoke in English, a thing he did not often do, as I had learned Navajo. "I wish you a Merry Christmas, San Chee (my name)," he said.

All day I had been too busy and excited to think, but that little attention made me homesick for something not Indian; and I stumbled into the store and hurried through to the living room, so Ken would not see the tears in my eyes.

He locked the store, polished the lamp chimney which I had not had time to touch and followed me. He set the lamp on the table and handed me an envelope. "Merry Christmas," he said. He turned at once to undress and I knew he knew I did not want him to see me cry.

In the envelope was the receipt for the second payment on the farm.

"Ken," I gasped.

"Better get to bed. It's been a long day," he answered sleepily.

Half undressed, I sat on the edge of the bed. Outside a cold moon climbed to where I could see it through the window. We had been at Covered Water more than a year. Did Ken want to own a farm or would he rather stay on the reservation?

The moon climbed higher, and the shell of a house snapped and cracked in the cold. The air was freezing; I could see my breath in the moonlight, but still I sat. I thought Ken asleep but suddenly he rolled over and spoke to me. When I faced him, he grinned at me in the moonlight.

With a gesture, I finished undressing and pulled the warm covers over me. My teeth were chattering and I blew out my breath sharply, to see the wraith of it in the moonlight. What difference whether we worked here or there, so we worked together?

170   Index

cultural sensitivity 23, 78, 126
cultural understanding 26, 29, 31–2, 49, 90, 141, 156; and the context of reading 157–8; emotion in 76–79; imagination in 135–6; insider perspective 23–5, 43, 46–8; Kramsch's model of 19; Model of Intercultural Competence 20; outsider perspective 24–6, 43–6, 48–9; and perception 19–20; six-level model of 20–1; and textual intervention 85
cultural visibility 2, 22–3
the cultural 21; see also culture
culture: conceptualisation of 2; divergent views of 3–4, 19–21; and education 10–11; and identity 155; as independent variable 4–5; and language 19; in reading comprehension studies 5–8; in reading research 21; see also cultural understanding; schema/schemata, culture-specific

decentring 103–9, 125–7, 136; see also distancing
Desert Wife (Hilda Faunce), analysis of fragments from 36–7, 40–9; used for assessment 160; comprehension and cultural understanding 135–7
dichotomies 85, 128–31, 133, 135; available vs. unavailable schemata 3, 7; present vs. absent schemata 3; product vs. process 7–8, 156; standard culture vs. minority group 109
difference 2, 53
distancing 55–6, 103, 115, 132, 157; critical 26, 29, 32, 47–8, 136, 157; see also decentring

education: bilingual 11; role of culture in 10–11
egocentricity, cultural 142
emotion: and affect 86–8; in comprehension 115–16; foregrounding of 87; schema 32, 85, 127, 156
emotion schemata 32; see also schema/ schemata
English: demonisation of 12–13; functions of in Argentina 11–12; literacy in 9; nativisation of 11
English as a foreign language (EFL) 10–12
English as a second/foreign language (ESL) 4

English Language Teaching (ELT) 10–12
English translators 12
essentialist views 8
ethnicity 1, 6, 8, 124, 155
ethnocentricity 23, 78, 85, 136, 142
ethnography 47, 53
Europeanisation 12

Falklands (Malvinas) War 13
Faunce, Hilda 36–7
Federal Law of Education (Argentina) 11
foci of attention 98–9
folk experience 9
follow-up interviews 4, 29, 53, 63, 85, 115, 117, 133, 156, 158–61; Beryl 63–6, 95–100, 115; Enrique Alejandro 129–36; Luz 76; Miranda Dana 76–8; Scarlet Rose 29–31; and self-assessment 138–9; Tacuara 58–63, 69–70; Tess 55, 120–7, 139–40; Victoria 104–8, 112–13, 142–7, 149–53
foreign language learning 10–11, 20, 31, 56–7, 87, 127
free recall protocol 80

García Canclini, N. 21
generalisations 56, 98, 106, 108, 120, 124, 128, 131, 133
Genetsch 2
group discussion 159–60
group phenomenon 53
Guerra de las Malvinas 13

hegemony 105; linguistic 9, 12
homogenisation, in Argentina 10

identity: construction of 1–2; culture and 155; diverging views of 3–4; formation of 24; national 12; in reading comprehension studies 8
images: and affect 87; visual 32; see also visual representation
image schemata 32, 85, 127, 156; see also schema/schemata; stereotypes/stereotyping
imagery, foregrounding of 87
imagination, in reading 86–7
immigrants, in Argentina 10
imperialism 10, 12, 13
inference questions 89
intercultural competence 160; see also cultural competence

Index

abstract knowledge structures 156
affect, in reading 86–8
Americanisation 12
Argentina: English literacy in 9; and the periphery 10–13; population demographics 10
Aristotle 3
artefacts, cultural 4
artificial intelligence 3–4
Asociación Argentina de Cultura Inglesa (Argentine Association of British Culture) 11
assessment: alternative forms of 89–90; reading response and visual representation in 89–90
Atwood, Margaret 36

Bartlett, Frederic 3
British Council 11
Butler, Judith 1

Cat's Eye (Margaret Atwood): analysis of fragments from 36, 40, 42–4, 46–8; used for assessment 160; clash of cultures in 117; cultural understanding in 118; elements of interest in 117; identification of emotions in 26–32; reading awareness with criticality and reflexivity 109–14; reading responses with critical cultural awareness 102–3; reading responses using emotions in comprehension 115–16; reading responses drawing on familiar knowledge 93–8; reading responses using foci of attention and schema processes 98–9; reading responses drawing on literary knowledge 99–102; reading responses with perspective-taking and decentring 103–4; self-assessment based on responses to (by Tess) 138–43; self-assessment based on responses to (by Victoria) 143–53
Catholic traditions 37, 75; *see also* Christianity
Christianity, textual references to 52, 93–5; *see also* Catholic traditions
cloze tests 80, 89
cognitive science 3–4
colonisation, ideological and cultural 12
comparison and contrast 53, 55
constructivism 6, 8, 80, 81
context: cultural 53, 132; of reading 157–8; as social construct 19; sociocultural 38, 53, 85, 155
critical cultural awareness 102–3, 125–7
criticality 58, 63, 65, 68–9, 109–14
cross-cultural research 4–6
cultural anthropology 2, 22
cultural aspects: erratic perception or omission of 21–2; identification of own values and ideas 23–4; insider perspective 23–5; outsider perspective 24–6; perception of C1 from C2 perspective 25–6; perception of C2 from C1 frame of reference 24; perception of C2 from C2 frame of reference 24–5; perception/identification of cultural differences 22–3
cultural awareness, critical 9
cultural competence; *see also* intercultural competence
cultural knowledge 84, 159
cultural reality, language and 19, 23, 24, 26, 28, 41, 42, 43, 46, 52

intertextuality 88
interviews, complementary role of 131–3

Kant, Immanuel 3
knowledge: cultural 84, 159; different kinds of 90; existing 56; familiar 93–8; five dimensions of 20; literary 99–102
knowledge in action 84, 158–9

language: and culture 6, 10, 12–13, 19, 25, 40, 49, 86, 120–1, 123; foreign 1, 4, 11, 20, 26, 93; and identity 24; of immigrants 10; instruction 10–11, 20, 31, 86–7, 127; native 52–3, 79, 117, 139; participants' use of 109, 129, 147–8, 155; and reading 1, 86; research on 4; written 84
local, in the 'periphery' 8

Malvinas/Falklands War 13
materialism 63–4
McDonaldisation 12
mestizo minority 10
Mi planta de naranja-lima (José Mauro de Vasconcelos): analysis of fragments from 36, 38–9, 41–4, 52; used for assessment 160; contrasts in 117; elements of interest in 117; reading responses comparing to *Cat's Eye* 100–1; student reflections on 54–5, 57, 60–8, 70–8
Model of Cultural Understanding 155–7; level 0 (perception or omission of cultural aspects) 21–2, 38; level 1 (perception/identification of cultural differences) 22–3, 38–42; level 2 (identification of values and ideas; insider perspective) 23–4, 43; level 3 (perception of C2 from C1 reference; outsider perspective) 24, 43–6; level 4 (perception of C2 from C2 frame of reference; insider perspective) 24–5, 46–8; level 5 (perception of C1 from C2 perspective; outsider perspective) 25–6, 48–9; perspectives on 49–50; in text selection and analysis 35–7; using the model to analyse comprehension of texts in a foreign language 26, 31, 37–49
Model of Intercultural Competence 20
multiple choice tests 80, 81, 89

narrative interventions 88
narrator, voice of 87

objectivism, truth of 8
open-ended questions 89
Other, interpreting 84

parody 88
performativity 1
periphery 8–9; Argentinean 10–13; readers from 53
personal themes 117–20
perspectives, multiple 20
perspective-taking 103–9, 125–7
Piaget, Jean 3
Plato 3
power inequality 9
product vs. process dichotomy 7–8, 156

readers: cultural experience of 158; identity of 1; local 53
reading: critical 157; cultural dimension of 88–9; and cultural understanding 157–8; diverging views of 3–4; EFL 13; imagination and affect in 86–7; sociocultural view of 1
reading comprehension: analysis in readers' first language 52–3; assessment of 89; based on layers of understanding 8; constructivist view of 80; influence of culture-specific schemata on 5–7; influence of religious affiliation on 6; influence of rhetorical schemata on 6; product-process dichotomy in 7–8; selection of texts 160
reading comprehension studies: comparing and contrasting, within familiar knowledge and experiences 53–5; essentialist views 8; interpretation of the texts by students 52–4; reading comprehension study, using texts about American Christmas celebrations 35–50; static views 8
reading research: need for consistency in 80; use of multiple measures 80
reading response: in assessment 89–90; critical cultural awareness 102–3; using different foci of attention and schema processes 98–9; drawing on familiar knowledge 93–8; drawing on literary knowledge 99–102; emotions in comprehension 115–16; pedagogic adaptations of 87–90; pedagogic value 87; perspective-taking and decentring 103–9; reading

response, criticality and reflexivity 109–14; as research instrument 82–6; tasks 82, 159–60
recall tasks 80, 89
reflections 120–5; meta-cultural 69
reflexivity 58, 65, 109–14
religious motifs 37, 67, 117
re-registration 84
research instruments, reading response and visual representation 82–6
research: using *Cat's Eye* 26–32; using Catholic and Jewish children 6; classroom-based 8–9; community-based 9; cross-cultural 4–6; on culture and reading comprehension 4–7; using English-speaking students and rhetorical schemata 6; methodological perspectives 158–9; model for 159–61; using natives of India living in the United States 5–6; and the power of writing and speaking 159; subcultural 5; using two versions of Eskimo stories 6–7
re-writing 83

schema/schemata 2–3, 155; cultural 4; culture-specific 5–7; dimensions of 156; diverging views of 3–4; emotion 32, 85, 127, 156; image 32, 85, 127, 156; in reading comprehension studies 8; rhetorical 6; as sociocultural and historical constructions 8; sociocultural perspective on 3; three types of 7
schema processes 98–9
schema theories 4, 85
self-assessment 138–9; excerpt 1 (self-assessment by Tess) 138–43; excerpt 2 (self-assessment by Victoria 143–53
semiotic systems 160
sentence completions 80, 89
speaking, power of 159

static views 8
stereotypes/stereotyping 9, 23, 24, 44, 55–6, 58, 63, 120–5, 139
subcultural research 5
summaries 80, 89
symbolic competence 19

text, combining with images *see* visual representation
textual intervention 83–4, 88
textual transformation 83–4, 87, 159–60
transcultural flows 9
transformation 84
translanguaging practices 9
true/false questions 80, 89
truth of objectivism 8

understanding, layers of 157

variability, in reader response 81
Vasconcelos, José Mauro de 36
vision, double 20
visual representation 87–9, 158–60; alternative and simultaneous interpretations 133–5; in assessment 89–90; and the complementary role of the interviews 131–3; focus on dichotomies 128–31; imagination in cultural understanding 135–6; personal themes in 117–20; pedagogic adaptations of 87–90; perspective-taking, decentring and critical cultural awareness 125–7; as research instrument 82–5; stereotypes, generalisations and reflections 120–5
voice 87, 90

Wattles, Ruth 37
webs of meaning 53
writing, power of 159